Bringing the Common Core Math Standards to Life

As middle school math teachers shift to the Common Core State Standards, the question remains: What do the standards actually look like in the classroom? This book answers that question by taking you inside real Common Core classrooms across the country. You'll see how exemplary teachers are meeting the new requirements and engaging students in math. Through these detailed examples of effective instruction, you will uncover how to bring the standards to life in your own classroom.

Special features:

- A clear explanation of the big shifts happening in the classroom as a result of the Common Core State Standards.
- Real examples of how exemplary teachers are meeting the CCSS by teaching problem solving for different learning styles, proportional reasoning, the Pythagorean theorem, measurements, and more.
- A detailed analysis of each example to help you understand why it is effective and how you can try it with your own students.
- Practical, ready-to-use tools you can take back to your classroom, including unit plans and classroom handouts.

Yvelyne Germain-McCarthy is Professor Emerita of Mathematics Education at the University of New Orleans. She is a frequent speaker at conferences and a consultant to school districts.

Other Eye On Education Books, Available from Routledge

(www.routledge.com/eyeoneducation)

Strategies for Common Core Mathematics:
Implementing the Standards for Mathematical Practice, 6–8
Leslie Texas and Tammy Jones

Guided Math in Action:
Building Each Student's Mathematical Proficiency with Small-Group Instruction
Nicki Newton

Using Formative Assessment to Drive Math Instruction in Grades 3–5
Jennifer Taylor-Cox and Christine Oberdorf

Math in Plain English:
Literacy Strategies for the Mathematics Classroom
Amy Benjamin

Using Children's Literature to Teach Problem Solving in Math:
Addressing the Common Core in K-2
Jeanne White

Bringing the CCSSM Standards to Life:
Exemplary Practices from High School
Yvelyne Germain-McCarthy

Authentic Learning Experiences:
A Real-World Approach to Project-Based Learning
Dayna Laur

Teaching Students to Dig Deeper:
The Common Core in Action
Ben Johnson

Common Core Literacy Lesson Plans:
Ready-to-Use Resources, 6–8
Edited by Lauren Davis

Big Skills for the Common Core:
Literacy Strategies for the 6–12 Classroom
Amy Benjamin and Michael Hugelmeyer

Assessing Critical Thinking in Middle and High Schools:
Meeting the Common Core
Rebecca Stobaugh

Bringing the Common Core Math Standards to Life

Exemplary Practices from Middle Schools

Yvelyne Germain-McCarthy

Routledge
Taylor & Francis Group

NEW YORK AND LONDON

This edition published 2014
by Routledge
711 Third Avenue, New York, NY 10017

and by Routledge
2 Park Square, Milton Park, Abingdon, Oxon OX14 4RN

Routledge is an imprint of the Taylor & Francis Group, an informa business

First edition (as *Bringing the NCTM standards to Life: Exemplary Practices for Middle Schools*) © Eye On Education 2001

© 2014 Taylor & Francis

Library of Congress Cataloging in Publication Data
Germain-McCarthy, Yvelyne, 1948- author.
[Bringing the NCTM standards to life]
Bringing the common core math standards to life : exemplary practices from middle schools / Yvelyne Germain-McCarthy.
    pages cm
Includes bibliographical references and index.
1. Mathematics—Study and teaching (Middle school)
—United States.   2. Mathematics—Study and teaching
(Secondary)—United States.   I. Title.
QA13.G47 2014
510.71'273—dc23
                           2013042309

ISBN: 978–0–415–73473–8 (hbk)
ISBN: 978–0–415–73341–0 (pbk)
ISBN: 978–1–315–81977–8 (ebk)

Typeset in Palatino
by RefineCatch Limited, Bungay, Suffolk, UK

Printed and bound in the United States of America by Publishers Graphics, LLC on sustainably sourced paper.

Contents

Acknowledgements viii
Foreword ix
About the Author x
Preface xi

1   **Trends and Issues Leading to the Common Core**
    State Standards 1
    Curriculum and Evaluation Standards 2
    Professional Standards for Teaching Mathematics. 2
    The Assessment Standards. 3
    The Third International Mathematics Study 5
        Trends in International Mathematics and Science Study 6
    Constructivism. 7
    Skills for Citizens of the Twenty-first Century .8
    Principles and Standards for School Mathematics. 10
        Principles for School Mathematics. 11
        Standards and Process for School Mathematics. 11
        NCTM's Quest for a Coherent Curricula .12
    The NCTM Standards and Citizens' Attributes for the
        Twenty-first Century: The New Basics 12
    The Common Core State Standards 14
        The Common Core State Standards for Mathematics (CCSSM) 14
    CCSSM Assessment. 21

2   **Exemplary Practice: What Does it Look Like?** 30
    Envisioning Reform-based Classroom Environment. 32
    Exemplary Practices 38

3   **Gail Englert: Conceptual Foundation for Proportional**
    Reasoning. 43
        Mathematical Practices: 44
        Activity 2: Absolute and Relative Thinking 47
        Activity 3: Index Card Ratios and Proportions Activity 51
    Discussion Between Colleagues 61
    Commentary. 62
    Unit Overview 64

4   Laura Mullen: Learning Styles and Problem Solving 72
 Preparatory Activities 73
 Engaging Students 74
  Example 1 79
  Example 2 79
  Example 3 81
 Discussion Between Colleagues 82
 Commentary 86
 Unit Overview 88

5   Thomas Wright: Making Sense of the Pythagorean Theorem 90
 Launch 92
 Explore 97
 Data Sharing 97
 Discussion Between Colleagues 104
 Commentary 107
 Unit Overview 108

**6   Madeline Landrum: Modeling Real World Problems with
     Multi-Step Inequalities** 111
 Discussion Between Colleagues 115
 Commentary 116
 Unit Overview 118

7   Merrie Schroeder: Statistics with Snack Food 120
 Discussion Between Colleagues 130
 Commentary 133
 Unit Overview 135

8   Teachers Adapting Tasks to Closely Align to CCSSM 137
 Teachers' Adaptation of Tasks 140
  Delores Espinoza 141
  Kristin Mullins 143
  Cynthia Trotman 146
  Stacy Remphrey 148
  Megan Farrelly 152

9   Jim Specht: The Last Great Race 156
 Engaging Students 157
 Discussion Between Colleagues 168

Commentary. 170
Unit Overview 172

10 Ivan Gill: What is a Gill? Meaningful Connections Between
    Measurement and Graphing 174
    The Launch. 175
    Explore 176
        Unit Measure of the Gill. 176
    Collecting Data. 178
    Mass Versus Weight, and the Search for Volume if Given Mass 182
    A Dense Discussion. 187
    Discussion Between Colleagues 194
    Commentary. 196
    Unit Overview 198

11 Paterson School 2: Journey Beyond TIMSS 200
    Top Ten Reasons Why Lesson Study Could Fail in the
        United States 203
    Six Reasons Why Lesson Study Worked at School 2 205
    A Profile of Japanese-style Teaching at School 2. 207
    Colloquium. 216
    Discussion Between Colleagues 221
    Commentary. 223
    Update on Lesson Study at P.S.2 225

    References. 226

Acknowledgements

I would like to express sincere appreciation to the teachers profiled in this book for their hard work and commitment to improving the teaching and learning of our children. In particular, I wish to thank them for sharing their ideas and responding to my many communications. Too numerous to mention by name, I also wish to express gratitude to the countless teachers with whom I have worked for sharing their passion for learning, their expertise in teaching, and their belief in their students' success.

Acknowledgement is due to Robert Sickles and Lauren Davis for suggestions that sparked improvements in this second edition of the book. I also want to thank Kerry Davidson, Bryan Jones and Noreen Lackett for their expert leadership of the Louisiana State Systemic Initiative Program; co-directing grants from this program have challenged me to grow in the areas of developing effective professional development experiences for teachers. I thank too, Craig Jensen, Dongming Wei, Kenneth Holladay, Ivan Gil and Norma Felton who worked with me on the grants and helped to form the University of New Orleans Mathematics and Science Collaborative for Teaching and Learning that sparked collaborative enterprises between local schools and the mathematics and education departments.

I offer special appreciation to my family: my loving heavenly Father, my parents, Georges and Eugenie Germain; my brothers, Gerard Germain, Serge Germain and Claude Germain for their love and unfailing support. Most importantly, I extend loving gratitude to my husband, Henry McCarthy, my sons Julian McCarthy and Germain McCarthy, and my nephew Carlos Germain for their love, patience and encouragement.

Finally, I wish to dedicate this book to children in impoverished sections of the world where freedom, or the means to participate in the types of learning environments described in this book, are but a dream. I donate my proceeds from this book to promoting the best education available to children from Rivière Froide, a small town in my homeland, Haiti.

Foreword

The *Principles and Standards for School Mathematics* by the National Council of Teachers of Mathematics (NCTM) and The Common Core State Standards for Mathematics (CCSSM) propose that all students be given opportunities to learn mathematics from competent teachers who can engage students in rich and relevant mathematics. These documents recommend that teachers not "dispense knowledge" but be "facilitators of active learning." The terms in quotes, while easy to understand at one level, are not easily translated to the classroom teaching and learning environment expected by the documents.

The book, *Bringing the Common Core Math Standards to Life: Exemplary Practices for Middle Schools* by Yvelyne Germain-McCarthy, vividly shows readers how classroom teachers may successfully implement the terms in quotes. It profiles teachers who daily strive to approach more closely the NCTM vision through their individual efforts or through collaboration with others. Readers are invited into the teachers' classrooms to view a dynamic environment where students are engaged in the process of thinking and challenging each other as mathematicians. Readers "see" how collaborators, both in and outside of the teachers' schools, are welcomed to enrich that environment. They "listen" to teachers' dialogues after the classroom episode to get a clearer idea of the nuts and bolts of making the vision happen. Noteworthy, too, is the book's success in addressing issues of concern related to teaching mainstreamed students, students in special education, or students in a school labeled "low performing" due to low standardized test scores. Lesson overviews that summarize key ideas from each profile facilitate readers' application or adaptation of the lessons. Finally, the author's commentary section directly connects the lessons to broader issues in the areas of research. This book provides a variety of reform ideas through realistic examples of what it means for teachers to apply the Standards.

Lee V. Stiff
Past President, National Council of Teachers of Mathematics

About the Author

Yvelyne Germain-McCarthy is Professor Emerita of Mathematics Education at the University of New Orleans, where she has directed and taught the elementary and secondary mathematics methods courses for graduate and undergraduate students. She received her B.S. in mathematics and M.Ed. in mathematics education from Brooklyn College. She earned her Ph.D. in mathematics education from Teachers College at Columbia University. She taught high school and middle grades mathematics for 17 years.

As project co-director of systemic initiative grants in Louisiana, she continues to lead efforts to implement reformed-based instruction in classes of inservice mathematics and science teachers. These have provided many opportunities for her to work with teachers and students to support student learning. She has written books, is a frequent speaker at professional conferences and has also written articles for NCTM and other professional organizations.

Her work in education and the community has earned her recognitions that include: the Brooklyn College School of Education's Dorothy Geddes Mathematics Education Award for dedication and excellence as a teacher of mathematics and teacher educator; Milton Ferguson Faculty Award from the University of New Orleans' College of Education and Human Development for her contributions and commitment to education; *New Orleans City Business* Woman of the Year Honoree as one of 50 women making notable contributions to both the local business community and society at large. One of her articles was selected by NCTM for CD and online reproduction because of its significant contribution to particular areas of mathematics education.

Currently serving as consultant to school districts, her teaching and research interests continue to focus on helping teachers and students develop a solid conceptual understanding of mathematics as well as an appreciation for engaging in a collaborative and reflective process for teaching and learning.

Preface

This book is a revision of the book, *Bringing the NCTM Standards to Life: Exemplary Practices for Middle Schools*. In this revised version, some profiles of teachers and their lessons were deleted, others were updated to integrate the Common Core State Standards for Mathematics (CCSSM), and four new profiles were added. The audience for this book is anyone interested in gaining insight into how the reform movement in mathematics as advocated by NCTM and CCSSM is being implemented by teachers in the United States.

Teachers and teacher educators will find the book useful for its examples of reformed-based strategies that pose challenges for teachers as they strive to teach and assess more rigorous content with the mathematical practices. Given the vast amount of information available on the web for integrating the CCSSM, the book may lessen anxieties teachers have in trying to make sense of and integrating the materials through its demonstrations of how exemplary educators make decisions on which resources to use, how, and when. For administrators in schools and districts, it will help bring to the forefront the necessary support teachers need to implement the CCSSM. The companion book, *Bringing the Common Core State Standards to Life: Exemplary Practices from High School*, provides similar insights.

The teacher profiles are descriptions constructed from classroom visits, written statements, interviews, and videos of how the teachers implement standards-based lessons in their classrooms. These profiles of educators across the nation who have gone beyond mere awareness of the CCSSM to conceptualizing and implementing them with students in grades 6–8 are brought to life through classroom scenarios and discussions with each teacher.

Chapter 1 presents overviews of the NCTM and CCSSM documents and some of the research providing the rationale for their development. Chapter 2 describes key elements of exemplary practices and a description of NCTM's vision for the implementation of the standards. Chapters 3–9 are profiles of teachers who are successfully implementing CCSSM with students at varying points along the achievement spectrum or with students having limited English proficiency. Chapter 10 shows how university mathematics and education professors, collaborating with teachers, can be powerful forces in creating engaging activities for teachers to incorporate into their own teaching to increase student learning. Chapter 11 is a report of the first lesson study open house conducted in the United States. It profiles a school–university–community effort to implement this Japanese approach to curriculum and teaching that was implemented to improve students' learning in a school that was taken over by the State due to low performance on high-stakes tests. The chapter documents the first lesson study process in the U.S. and discusses the challenges for its implementation in the United States.

In most chapters, there is a Discussion Between Colleagues section that clarifies or expands ideas from the profile. A Unit Overview summarizes key ideas to help teachers implement or modify the lessons, and a final Commentary highlights the specific standards, issues, or research that informed the strategies used by the teachers. Although the Unit Overviews list specific grade levels, readers will find that the lessons can be readily modified; ideas for extensions of the curricula will emerge not only because of the richness of the activities but also because the lessons move from concrete activities to higher-level abstract concepts. Thus, this reform-based approach provides ways to vary the emphasis of the concepts presented and the connections across grade levels.

While the profiles incorporate a number of different content standards, they *all* reflect the NCTM principles for equity, curriculum, teaching, learning, and assessment. All profiles demonstrate many classroom applications of the NCTM process standards now embodied in the CCSSM Mathematical Practices. The profiles will give readers ideas on how to implement CCSSM as well as an opportunity to learn a different way for presenting or using a mathematical concept or tool.

Figure 0.1 summarizes the content, standards, and math practices addressed in each profile. A specific practice or principle is listed for those profiles that have such a focus.

Figure 0.1 Principles, Standards, and Practices in the Profiles

Chapter: Teacher(s)	NCTM Principles	Grades/ Content	NCTM/CCSSM Math Practices
3: Gail Englert	1–5 Teaching	6th Grade Ratio and Proportions, Equations and Expressions	Problem Solving Communication Repeated Reasoning
4: Laura Mullen	1–5 Assessment	6th/7th Grade Numbers, Geometry, Expressions and Equations	Problem Solving Reasoning Representation
5: Thomas Wright	1–5 Curriculum	7th grade Numbers, Geometry, Algebra	Communication Use of Tools Connection
6: Madeline Landrum	1–6	6th Grade Equations and Expressions	Communication Representation Connection
7: Merrie Schroeder	1–6	6th/7th Grade Numbers, Geometry, Data Analysis Measurement,	Communication Representation Connection
8: Adapted Tasks	1–6	Algebra, Geometry Measurement Equations and Expressions Functions	Problem Solving Connection Representation Use of Tools Model with Math Attend to Precision
9: Jim Specht	1–6 Technology	Numbers, Geometry Measurement, Algebra, Statistics	Problem Solving Connection Representation Use of Tools Model with Math Attend to Precision Look for Structure
10: Ivan Gill	1–5 Learning	Algebra, Geometry Measurement	Problem Solving Connection Representation Use of Tools Model with Math Attend to Precision
11: P.S. 2	1–5 Curriculum	Numbers, Geometry Measurement	Problem Solving Communication Representation Model with Math

1

Trends and Issues Leading to the Common Core State Standards

In April 2000, NCTM unveiled a political document, *Principles and Standards for School Mathematics*.... Most in attendance came to hear about the mathematics content and professional development updates of *Curriculum and Evaluation Standards for School Mathematics*, released in 1989. Few regarded *Principles and Standards for School Mathematics* as a political statement about school mathematics and school change. Few recognized the need for NCTM to deepen its political initiatives to better promote the ideals of the *Standards*.

The original 1989 *Standards* document was a political document. It talked about the content of mathematics, the pedagogy of mathematics classrooms, and the evaluation of mathematics curricula. The *Standards* suggested ways to improve the status of countless underserved students and changed the status quo in all classrooms across the United States and Canada. Because of this *Standards* document, we continue to question what we believe about ourselves and about others. It has forced us to make educational and political decisions about what we are willing to do to turn the vision of a high quality mathematics education for every child into a practical set of behaviors. It has reached far beyond the schools into the universities, industry and business, and political institutions.

(Lee V. Stiff, Past President, National Council of Teachers of Mathematics, NCTM, 2001, p. 3)

As Stiff predicted, the *NCTM Standards* continue to impact education decision makers and its political influence has now extended to recommendations for the statewide adoption of its basic tenets. The Common Core State Standards for Mathematics (CCSSM) can be considered an updated version of the *NCTM Standards* that has very strong political support since CCSSM is a state-led effort. A review of the major standards documents produced or motivated by NCTM will support an understanding of the CCSSM.

Curriculum and Evaluation Standards

In the above quote from the "President's Message" column of the December, 2001 *News Bulletin* of NCTM, Stiff summarizes the major thrust of NCTM's reform efforts as that of making mathematics accessible to all students. Past NCTM President Glenda Lappan further highlights the key components:

> What is the reform of mathematics teaching and learning guided by NCTM's Standards all about? My answer is that we are about the following three things: upgrading the curriculum, improving classroom instruction, and assessing students' progress to support the ongoing mathematics learning of each student. (NCTM, May/June, 1999)

In 1989, NCTM's *Curriculum and Evaluation Standards for School Mathematics* recommended that we teach and assess students in very non-traditional ways. It called for less attention to procedural manipulation without understanding and more of a focus on conceptual understanding and connecting mathematics across its content areas and to other disciplines. Noting that mathematics education needs to continually address societal needs, it also included recommendations to add certain topics such as probability and statistics and technology when appropriate.

Professional Standards for Teaching Mathematics

In addition to the shift in curriculum, NCTM supports four other major shifts in learning, teaching, and assessment. In learning, the shift supports actively involving students in problems that are authentic and giving students access to a variety of mathematical tools to support mathematical reasoning; in teaching, the shift supports a variety of approaches to reach all students; in assessment practices, the shift supports integrating teaching with multiple types of assessments.

What are some strategies for preparing teachers to reach all students? NCTM's *Professional Standards for Teaching Mathematics* document (1991) (*Teaching Standards*) suggests principles for the professional development of mathematics teachers and for the evaluation of mathematics teaching. It also provides guidelines for helping teachers create a rich mathematical environment in which all students are engaged in the challenging mathematics to make them *mathematically powerful*. Students with such power can demonstrate application of the standards by their ability to explore, conjecture, reason logically, and successfully apply a number of different strategies to solve non-routine problems. The *Teaching Standards* describe the elements necessary to prepare such teachers:

> If we are to reach the goal of developing mathematical power for all students then we must create a curriculum and an environment in which teaching and learning are to occur that are very different from the curricula and teaching environments of today's schools. The image of mathematics teaching we need includes elementary and secondary teachers who are proficient in the following skills:
>
> 1. Selecting mathematical tasks to engage the interest and intellect of students;
> 2. Orchestrating classroom discourse in ways that promote the investigation and growth of mathematical ideas;
> 3. Using, and helping students use, technology and other tools to pursue mathematical investigations;
> 4. Seeking, and helping students seek, connections to previous and developing knowledge;
> 5. Guiding individual, small group, and whole class work. (NCTM, 1991, 1)

Assessing students' acquisition of these skills requires tools that must extend beyond the traditional paper-and-pencil tests to include alternative means of assessments. These are highlighted in the *Assessment Standards*.

The Assessment Standards

The *Assessment Standards* (1991) address the principles educators should use to build assessments that support the development of mathematical power for all students. It recommends that teachers derive information from multiple sources during instruction and that, in addition to pencil-paper tests, evidence to support student learning be collected from sources that include close observation, one-on-one discussions, projects, homework, and classroom discourse. The five standards state that assessments should:

1. define the mathematics that all students need to know and be able to do;
2. enhance mathematical learning so that students' mathematical understanding is enriched as a result of the assessment;
3. promote equity so that teachers have high expectations for all students;
4. be an open process so that students have a clear understanding of the assessment's goals;
5. promote valid inferences about mathematics learning so that each student is given support when necessary to improve his or her performance.

A key change in the *NCTM Standards* from traditional methods is the use of assessment tools as a process for stimulating growth and interest in mathematics rather than as a way for separating and ranking students.

Recognizing that information is changing and increasing at a rapid pace, the writing group for the *Curriculum Standards* wisely planned to revisit and revise the *Curriculum Standards* in the future. NCTM past president Gail Burrill posed the following questions to illustrate the need for a future edition:

> Do history textbooks stop at the end of World War I? How does a map of Africa today compare to one from 20 years ago? What happened to science textbooks when DNA was discovered? Mathematics is no different—changes around us make changes in how we think about mathematics. Changes in what we know about how students learn affect the way we think about teaching. (NCTM, 1996, 3)

To alleviate concerns about yet another set of major changes, she clarifies that the *Principles and Standards for School Mathematics* will build on and extend the foundations of the original standards publications. Thus, teachers should continue aligning teaching with the *Curriculum Standards*, and should also:

> Think seriously about the meaning of the present standards and their implications for your classroom. Developing an understanding of what the *Curriculum Standards* are about is a continuous process

whose growth should be consonant with the *Curriculum Standards*, both old and new. (3)

If we substitute CCSSM for the *NCTM Standards* listed above, we find words of wisdom for the implementation of the CCSSM today.

The Third International Mathematics Study

Ironically, the findings of international tests that included Third International Mathematics and Science Study (1995) showed that, while Japanese teaching and learning adhered to NCTM recommendations, they were not prevalent in the United States. In 1995, TIMSS (Third International Mathematics Study) gathered data on half a million students from 41 countries, focusing on student achievement, curricula, and teaching. The fact that Japan's students scored highest while U.S. students scored below the international average, meant that a huge call to look carefully at the U.S. education system to determine where improvements could be implemented was made. In the report, *A Splintered Vision* (Schmidt, McKnight and Raizen, 1997), an examination of the curriculum and teacher data of TIMSS revealed that the U.S. curriculum was redundant and less challenging than those of many other countries. This report was a major catalyst for generating interest in developing a coherent and *national* vision on curriculum. The report adds, "Splintered visions produce unfocused curricula and textbooks that fail to define clearly what is intended to be taught, " and that U.S. curricula, textbooks, and teaching are "a mile wide and an inch deep" (http://lsc-net.terc.edu/do/conference_material/6783/show/use_set-oth_pres.html). Soon after the TIMSS report, the National Research Council published a book, *Adding It Up: Helping Children Learn Mathematics*(2001), which included recommendations supporting NCTM's recommendations for improving teaching, curricula, and teacher education during grades PreK-8. The committee identified five interdependent components of mathematical proficiency:

1. *Conceptual understanding* refers to the "integrated and functional grasp of mathematical ideas," which "enables them [students] to learn new ideas by connecting those ideas to what they already know."
2. *Procedural fluency* is defined as the skill in carrying out procedures flexibly, accurately, efficiently, and appropriately.
3. *Strategic competence* is the ability to formulate, represent, and solve mathematical problems.
4. *Adaptive reasoning* is the capacity for logical thought, reflection, explanation, and justification.

5. *Productive disposition* is the inclination to see mathematics as sensible, useful, and worthwhile, coupled with a belief in diligence and one's own efficacy. (NRC, 2001, 116)

Trends in International Mathematics and Science Study

TIMSS, administered every four years, is now called *Trends in International Mathematics and Science Study*. It continues to compare the mathematics and science knowledge and skills of fourth- and eighth-graders and its reports have the goal of helping countries make informed decisions about how to improve teaching and learning in mathematics. The reports includes trends in mathematics achievement over time for participants in previous TIMSS assessments in 1995, 1999, 2003, and 2007 as well as student performance at the TIMSS International Benchmarks. Since TIMSS 1999, U.S. students have exceeded the international average. TIMSS 2011 had 63 participating countries and 14 regional benchmarking jurisdictions (http://timss. bc.edu). While the United States exceeded the international average, a significant margin existed in just fourth grade math and students still are lagging behind the Asian countries. Ina V.S. Mullis, the co-executive director of the TIMSS International Study Center at Boston College raised this concern when she said, "This is a gap that has its roots in 1995 . . . and the gap has not narrowed over the years. And in some cases, such as [South] Korea, it's even widening" (Robelen, 2012). Of concern is the eighth grade, where nearly half of all students tested reached the advanced level in math in South Korea, Singapore, and Chinese Taipei (Taiwan) compared with only 7 percent of U.S. test-takers (http://timss.bc.edu). However, the United States should be proud of its nine states that opted to be compared with participating nations on some of the TIMSS 2011 assessments (Alabama, California, Colorado, Connecticut, Florida, Indiana, Minnesota, North Carolina, Massachusetts). All of the states performed above the TIMSS scale average in math except for one. Results for Massachusetts were particular strong in science because Singapore was the only nation to score higher and, 26 percent of Massachusetts's students reached the advanced level. In addition, Minnesota's eighth grade science was outperformed only by Singapore and Taiwan. Since TIMSS 1999, the United States has been looking closely at the Singapore and Japanese curriculum and textbooks (visit www.globaledresources.com/ resources.html for examples) for research on why they always score above the United States but based on the nine states performances, Jack Buckley, the commissioner of the National Center for Education Statistics, commented that "U.S. policymakers looking around the world for lessons on creating a strong education system may want to take a look closer to home first" (Robelen, 2012).

While much has been written above about the content results, it is important to note that TIMSS 1999 also videotaped classrooms. The analysis of the videotapes of eighth grade mathematics teaching interaction in typical classrooms of six countries that included Japan and the United States, show that while 54 percent of the mathematics lessons in Japanese classrooms challenged students to work on non-routine problems, 0 to 52 percent in the U.S. eighth grade mathematics lessons did so (Hiebert et al., 2003). These videos can be viewed at http://timssvideo.com/videos/Mathematics.

TIMSS 2011 added instruments to get better indicators of what goes on in classrooms. Its report on the extent of students' engagement in math and science lessons shows U.S. students losing some enthusiasm for math as they move from fourth to eighth grade: while 48 percent of fourth graders said they "like learning mathematics," only 26 percent said so by the eighth grade. Not surprisingly, the test score reflected that the less students like math, the lower their achievement, on average (http://timss.bc.edu). Internationally, there is also a drop in students' engagement with math lessons from fourth to eighth grade. While 69 percent of fourth graders around the world had math teachers reporting making efforts to use instructional practices intended to interest students and reinforce learning, only 39 percent reported doing so at the eighth grade (http://timss.bc.edu). Thus, keeping students' interest and positive engagement in mathematics are the major challenges that the education community must continue to strive to achieve by providing resources to address teaching, learning, assessment and the challenges of poverty in our society.

Constructivism

Because constructivism is applied or experienced in an environment where learners are trying to make sense of a problematic situation by constructing their own knowledge about the world around them, it is a framework for the CCSSM. Jean Piaget (1973), stated:

> To understand is to discover [that] . . . a student who achieves a certain knowledge through free investigation and spontaneous effort will later be able to retain it: he will have acquired a methodology that can serve him for the rest of his life, which will stimulate his curiosity without the risk of exhausting it. At the very least, instead of his having his memory take priority over his reasoning power . . . he will learn to make his reason function by himself and will build his ideas

freely . . . The goal of intellectual education is not to know how to repeat or retain ready-made truths. It is in learning to master the truth by oneself at the risk of losing a lot of time and of going through all the roundabout ways that are inherent in real activity. (106)

Thus, learning is not simply the acquisition of information and skills; it also includes the acquisition of a deep understanding that requires time but that enables the learner to better construct meaning from a problem. Learning occurs when a novel situation contradicts the learner's beliefs and therefore requires new constructs to make sense of and interpret the situation (Confrey, 1990).

Simon (1995) notes that constructivism does not define a specific way to teach mathematics. Rather, it "describes knowledge development whether or not there is a teacher present or teaching is going on" (117). Attention to the misconceptions of students provides teachers with a rich source of information that allows them to detect and understand in which areas students need guidance. The teacher's task is to help students learn to find tools that are useful for solving problems—ideally, problems that students have identified from their own work.

Some constructivists view the small group process by which students work together on mathematical tasks that require a high level of communication about a problem, a crucial component of the development of conceptual understanding. Social interaction as an essential factor in a learner's organization of experiences underlies the theory of social constructivism. According to Vygotsky (1978), "Any function in the child's cultural development appears twice on two planes. First it appears on the social plane, and then on the psychological plane" (57). A focus on the processes by which a learner constructs meaning from social interactions opens a window for researchers to examine those processes because it "constitutes a crucial source of opportunities to learn mathematics in that the process of constructing mathematical knowledge involves cognitive conflict, reflection, and active cognitive organization . . . As such, mathematical learning is . . . an interactive as well as [a] constructive activity" (Cobb, Wood, and Yackel, 1990, 127). Thus, the constructivist approach begins with what the students' already think and believe regarding a particular idea. Students' attempts to verify these ideas then serve as catalyst for the learning process.

Skills for Citizens of the Twenty-first Century

Rather than a classroom based on constructivist application of teaching and learning, some teachers still practice a traditional approach based on giving students the rules to memorize without understanding of why they make sense. This is contrary to brain-based researchers who view the mind's design as that of a "pattern detector." Learners continually search for meaning by creating patterns. Lectures or rote memorization produce a type of learning that is classified as *surface knowledge*. Although this is important, success in the twenty-first century will require *meaningful knowledge*, or knowledge that makes sense to the learner. Teaching that strives to maximize the way that the brain processes information not only enhances and increases the likelihood of meaningful knowledge but also helps citizens develop the attributes they need to thrive in the twenty-first century. In 1997, Caine and Caine described the attributes still relevant today (97–98, adapted slightly):

1. An inner appreciation of interconnectedness.
   In a world where everything is relationship, more is needed than to intellectually understand the concept of relationship. People need to have . . . an inner sense of connectedness that culminates in insight.
2. A strong identity and sense of being.
   In a fluid and turbulent world, it is very easy to become confused and disoriented. People need a coherent set of purposes, values, and beliefs. Moreover, those values should include an appreciation of life, opportunity, and respect for individual and cultural differences.
3. The capacity to flow and deal with paradox and uncertainty.
   We need to have ways of thinking and interpreting that help us see patterns in paradox. At the same time, we need to appreciate the constant mystery and to understand that at some levels, no fixed answers are possible.
4. A sufficiently large vision and imagination to see how specifics relate to each other.
   There is always more than we can know, and the extent of our ignorance is increasing. People frequently, naturally, and inevitably come face-to-face with the unfamiliar, the unexpected and the unknown. People therefore need an internal frame of reference that enables them to . . . see patterns in chaos, and to perceive commonalities.
5. A capacity to build community and live in a relationship with others.
   We have to be able to function both as individuals and as parts of greater social wholes.

If we accept these as desirable attributes, then schools need to develop or enhance curriculum to support the ability of students to attain these attributes in *every* subject. Describing the kind of environment and curriculum that is conducive to generating such self-directed learners has been the current focus of movements and studies that advocate reforms in the content and teaching of K-12 inservice and preservice teachers.

NCTM has advocated changes toward a more focused, rigorous curriculum as well as an integrated approach to teaching and assessment practices for helping students develop the understanding and habits of mind necessary to address the challenges of the twenty-first century. The habits of mind are reflected in what Dewey (1929) calls a "disciplined mind": "A disciplined mind takes delight in the problematic . . . The scientific attitude may almost be defined as that which is capable of enjoying the doubtful" (228).

Qualities of people who have such a mind include "a willingness to play with ideas, to explore alternative paths or procedures, to approach situations inquisitively, to persevere, to emphasize sense making and reasoning, and to find excitement in learning" (Chapin, 1997, 6). Such thinking includes the processes of science: making comparisons, generalizing, recording observations, and revising one's views because of new information.

Most students today shy away from a situation that is "doubtful." Indeed, they too often become frustrated and are quick to abandon problems for which they have no clear method of approach. According to Wheatley (1991),

> If you look at any of the work on creativity and learning, or if you look at your own creative process, it is not a nice orderly step-by-step process that moves you towards a great idea. You get incredibly frustrated, you feel you'll never solve it, you walk away from it, and then Eureka!—an idea comes forth. You can't get truly transforming ideas anywhere in life unless you walk through that period of chaos. (3)

It is likely that most students who are not encouraged or allowed to pursue such experiences or, "productive struggle," will have little desire to continue the study of mathematics and may be incorrectly perceived by some parents or teachers to not have a "math brain." What students need is a balanced curriculum in which mathematical content is learned and applied in a problem-solving environment that allows them to process and practice these attributes.

Principles and Standards for School Mathematics

In 2000, NCTM integrated its recommendations about curriculum, teaching, and assessment into one document called the *Principles and Standards For School Mathematics* (hereforth called *Principles and Standards*). *Principles and*

Standards consists of six principles, five processes and 10 standards that describe characteristics of quality instructional programs and goals for students' mathematical knowledge. Together they form the basis for developing effective mathematics instruction within four grade band chapters: pre-kindergarten through grade 2, grades 3–5, grades 6–8, and grades 9–12. At the high school level, "All students are expected to study mathematics each of the four years that they are enrolled in high school, whether they plan to pursue the further study of mathematics, to enter the work force, or to pursue other postsecondary education" (288).

Principles for School Mathematics

The *Principles and Standards* build on the solid foundation provided in the *NCTM Standards* documents through a set of six principles that address the question: What are the characteristics of mathematics instructional programs that will provide all students with high-quality mathematics education experiences across the grades? They focus on:

- ◆ *Equity:* "Excellence in mathematics education requires equity—high expectations and strong support for *all* students" (12).
- ◆ *Curriculum:* "A curriculum is more than a collection of activities: it must be coherent, focused on important mathematics, and well articulated across the grades" (14).
- ◆ *Teaching:* "Effective mathematics teaching requires understanding what students know and need to learn and then challenging and supporting them to learn" (16).
- ◆ *Learning:* "Students must learn mathematics with understanding, actively building new knowledge from experience and prior knowledge" (20).
- ◆ *Assessment:* "Assessment should support the learning of important mathematics and furnish useful information to both teachers and students" (22).
- ◆ *Technology:* "Technology is essential in teaching and learning mathematics; it influences the mathematics that is taught and enhances students' learning" (24).

Standards and Process for School Mathematics

Ten standards address the question: What mathematical content and processes should students know and be able to do as they progress through school? Of the ten, five are mathematical content standards that describe what students should know and be able to do within the areas of number and operations, algebra, geometry, measurement, data analysis, probability, and statistics.

Five process standards address students' acquisition, growth in, and use of mathematical knowledge in the areas of problem solving, reasoning, connections, communication, and representation.

NCTM's Quest for a Coherent Curricula

In response to TIMSS 1999 reports that the U.S. curriculum is unfocused and covers too many topics, NCTM released the *Curriculum Focal Points for Prekindergarten through Grade 8 Mathematics: A Quest for Coherence* to identify the most important mathematical topics for each grade level K-8 to guide the development of mathematics curriculum and instruction (2006, henceforth called *Focal Points*). *Focal Points* specifies the mathematical content that a student needs to not just know, but understand, deeply. It assumes that the principles and processes described by *Principles and Standards* will guide the teaching of the areas. At each grade level for PreK-8, it clusters the most important concepts and skills and adds a focus on reasoning and skill to arithmetic, geometry, and algebra which are a foundation for the further study of math and science. To clarify that a balance between skill and concept is necessary, the need for good understanding of basic facts is stated explicitly. Why is there a need for focal points? According to NCTM,

> Many factors have contributed to the need for a common mathematical focus for each grade level, pre-K–8. These include the increased emphasis on accountability testing, high levels of mobility of both students and teachers, and greater costs of curriculum development. A focused, coherent mathematics curriculum with a national scope has the potential to ease the impact of widely varying learning and assessment expectations on both students and teachers who relocate. In addition, a focused curriculum would allow teachers to commit more time each year to topics receiving special emphasis. At the same time, students would have opportunities to explore these topics in depth, in the context of related content and connected applications, thus developing more robust mathematical understandings. (NCTM, 2006, 4)

The NCTM Standards and Citizens' Attributes for the Twenty-first Century: The New Basics

A review of Caine and Caine's essential attributes for citizens of the twenty-first century shows they closely correspond to *Principles and Standards for School Mathematics* as described by the *Standards*:

- The "inner sense of connectedness" of the first attribute, which we translate as deep conceptual understanding, occurs from information that allows the brain to seek, extract, and make sense of patterns. It is through such a process that students, taught from a constructivist perspective, are encouraged to make sense of new information.
- The "strong identity" of the second attribute equates to students' confidence in working with mathematics when their ideas have been respected and valued in a classroom where equity is applied. Students' appreciation for, as well as confidence in, mathematics is increased when the contributions of various cultures in the development of mathematics are discussed and valued.
- "The capacity to . . . deal with . . . uncertainty" of attribute 3 is fostered through instruction that has students solving rich problems for which there may be no answer, one answer or multiple answers. Using technological tools and varying representations facilitate students' search for patterns to make sense of non-routine problems.
- The view of "how specifics relate to each other" of attribute 4 results from experiences requiring students' application of reasoning and logical thinking processes to make connections among ideas that may appear disparate.
- The "capacity to build community" is fostered, again, in classrooms where equity issues are positively addressed, cultures are valued, and students are encouraged to solve problems in cooperative groups.

In his first address as NCTM President, Lee Stiff's (2000) message, in effect, strongly supported these attributes. He said:

NCTM has always argued for a strong foundation on learning the basics. Our vision of basics, however, goes beyond mere number-crunching skills. We hope *Principles and Standards* will help educators, school boards, parents, and business leaders recognize that the new economy demands greater and more sophisticated mathematical knowledge. "Shopkeeper's math" alone is not enough in a high tech environment. NCTM's vision of school mathematics prepares students to meet the challenges that lie ahead in a future they can't imagine. (3)

An article entitled, "Why the word career has become obsolete" by May (2012) echoes Stiff's views. He writes,

The iconic "gold watch" career path, in which people stay with the same employer for their entire working lives, has become anachronistic

... But what does career mean in a world where the people at the top don't know what must be known? What does career mean when the rules of the game change daily? We live in an age when the most important skill is the ability to acquire new skills ... Your career success is a function of how successfully you keep yourself upgraded. http://www.computerworld.com/s/article/9234728/Thornton_A._May_Why_the_word_career_has_become_obsolete

Hereafter, I refer to reformed mathematical content that is taught from the perspectives of these attributes or process standards, as the "new basics."

The Common Core State Standards

The *Common Core State Standards* (CCSS) for mathematic, English-language arts and science arose from state-led efforts to better prepare U.S. students for the future for college and career by defining the knowledge and skills students should have within their K-12 education no matter where they lived in the United States. The Council of Chief State School Officers (CCSSO) and the National Governors Association Center which are the leading organizations for the standards development process, formed several working groups to insure that input was received from teachers, parents, administrators, community organizers and national education experts so that the standards would be clear and realistic, while building upon strengths and lessons of current state standards and standards of top-performing nations.

Through a CCSS Initiative, adopting states and territories collaborate to create and share tools for common assessments, curricula and instructional materials. Because this is a state-led initiative, the federal government is not involved in the development of the standards. Thus, the role of local education leaders is to decide how the standards are to be implemented and to make decisions about the curriculum. Across the three subject areas, there is an intersection of processes and tools that support interdisciplinary activities to engage students in real-world problems (www.corestandards.org/assets/CoreFAQ.pdf).

The Common Core State Standards for Mathematics (CCSSM)
Just before the release of the *Principles and Standards*, past president Gail Burrell, feeling the need to alleviate concerns about yet another set of major changes, clarified that the *Principles and Standards* would build on and extend the foundations of the original *Curriculum Standards* publications. Thus, teachers should continue aligning teaching with the *Curriculum Standards*, and should also

"think seriously about the meaning of the present standards and their implications for your classroom. Developing an understanding of what the *Curriculum Standards* are about is a continuous process whose growth should be consonant with the *Curriculum Standards*, both old and new" (NCTM, 1996, 3).

We need to heed those thoughts today as we implement the CCSSM: Those teachers proficient in applying the *Principles and Standards* are already teaching to the CCSSM and should continue doing so as they integrate the updates from the CCSSM. Other teachers should be mindful that CCSSM is not just another set of standards but rigorous and critical standards for teaching and assessing competencies needed by our students to pursue post-secondary education and a successful career. The CCSSM consists of the content standards that delineate which content areas are to be taught, and the mathematical practices that provide the "how" to teach the content.

Content Standards

The K-8 standards have a balanced combination of procedural and conceptual understanding that are organized within six domains that define what students should know and should be able to do at each grade level. The domains are groups of related standards that are clustered as: ratios and proportional relationships, the number system, expressions and equations, functions, geometry, and statistics and probability. There is overlap of the standards within and across grade levels because of the connections existing within mathematics itself. Figure 1.1 shows the overlaps of the standards that may lead one to question how the problem of repetitive content across grades has been reduced or eliminated.

The answer to the question is based on the level of depth to be acquired at each grade level. The Progressions Documents for the CCSSM is a useful

Figure 1.1 Content Overlap Across Grade Levels

GRADES		
6	7	8
Ratio and Proportional Relationships		Functions
Expressions and Equations		
The Number System		
Geometry		
Statistics and Probability		

tool to show how the domains progress across the grades by describing a sequence of increasing depth in understanding, skill or sophistication (http://ime.math.arizona.edu/progressions).

Instructional Shifts

Three major shifts from traditional teaching to the common core are: a greater *focus* in mathematics to learn the important mathematics and engage in discussions that reflect the mathematical practices; *coherence* to make connections within and across grade levels so that math is viewed as a discipline where connections at one level provide deeper understanding for another; and *rigor* in major topics to provide for a balance between concept understanding, procedural skill and fluency, and application. Figure 1.2 shows the fluency expectations for the grade levels (adapted from http://tncore.org/sites/www/Uploads/2.25.13Additions/fluency%20documents%20final.pdf).

The Standards for Mathematical Practice

The Standards for Mathematical Practice describe the attributes of mathematically proficient students and are the same from elementary school through high school. What differs is the task used to increase the depth of understanding as students engage with and master new and more advanced

Figure 1.2 Fluency by Grade Levels

Grade	Required Fluency
K	Add and subtract within 5
1	Add and subtract within 10
2	Add/subtract within 20 Add/subtract within 100 (pencil and paper)
3	Multiply/divide within 100 Add/subtract within 1,000
4	Add/subtract within 1,000,000
5	Multi-digit multiplication
6	Multi-digit division Multi-digit decimal operations
7	Solve $px+q=r$, $p(x+q)=r$
8	Solve one-variable linear equations, problems involving volumes of cones, cylinders, and spheres, 2×2 systems of equations

mathematical ideas. The details below include the connection to the NCTM process standards in parentheses. The practices recommend that students be able to:

1. Make sense of problems and persevere in solving them. (NCTM's Problem Solving)
   Mathematically proficient students start by explaining to themselves the meaning of a problem and looking for entry points to its solution. They analyze givens, constraints, relationships, and goals. They make conjectures about the form and meaning of the solution and plan a solution pathway rather than simply jumping into a solution attempt. They consider analogous problems, and try special cases and simpler forms of the original problem in order to gain insight into its solution. They monitor and evaluate their progress and change course if necessary. —CCSSM

2. Reason abstractly and quantitatively. (NCTM's Reasoning and Proof)
   Mathematically proficient students make sense of quantities and their relationships in problem situations. They bring two complementary abilities to bear on problems involving quantitative relationships: the ability to decontextualize—to abstract a given situation and represent it symbolically and manipulate the representing symbols as if they have a life of their own, without necessarily attending to their referents—and the ability to contextualize, to pause as needed during the manipulation process in order to probe into the referents for the symbols involved. Quantitative reasoning entails habits of creating a coherent representation of the problem at hand; considering the units involved; attending to the meaning of quantities, not just how to compute them; and knowing and flexibly using different properties of operations and objects. —CCSSM

3. Construct viable arguments and critique the reasoning of others. (NCTM's Communication; Reasoning and Proof)
   Mathematically proficient students . . . justify their conclusions, communicate them to others, and respond to the arguments of others. They . . . distinguish correct logic or reasoning from that which is flawed, and—if there is a flaw in an argument—explain what it is . . . Elementary students can construct arguments using concrete referents such as objects, drawings, diagrams, and actions. Such arguments can make sense and be correct, even though they are not generalized or made formal until later grades. . . . Students at all grades can listen or read the arguments of others, decide whether

they make sense, and ask useful questions to clarify or improve the arguments. —CCSSM

4. Model with mathematics. (NCTM's Representation, Connection) Mathematically proficient students can apply the mathematics they know to solve problems arising in everyday life. . . . In early grades, this might be as simple as writing an addition equation to describe a situation. . . . Mathematically proficient students who can apply what they know are comfortable making assumptions and approximations to simplify a complicated situation. . . . They are able to identify important quantities in a practical situation and map their relationships using such tools as diagrams, two-way tables, graphs. . . . They . . . reflect on whether the results make sense. . . . —CCSSM

5. Use appropriate tools strategically. (NCTM's Problem Solving, Representation)
Mathematically proficient students consider the available tools when solving a mathematical problem. These tools might include pencil and paper, concrete models, a ruler, a protractor, a calculator, a spreadsheet. . . . Proficient students are sufficiently familiar with tools appropriate for their grade or course to make sound decisions about when each of these tools might be helpful, recognizing both the insight to be gained and their limitations. —CCSSM

6. Attend to precision. (NCTM's Communication)
Mathematically proficient students try to communicate precisely to others. They try to use clear definitions in discussion with others and in their own reasoning. They state the meaning of the symbols they choose, including using the equal sign consistently and appropriately. They are careful about specifying units of measure, and labeling axes to clarify the correspondence with quantities in a problem. They calculate accurately and efficiently. . . . In the elementary grades, students give carefully formulated explanations to each other. . . . —CCSSM

7. Look for and make use of structure. (NCTM's Connection)
Mathematically proficient students look closely to discern a pattern or structure. Young students, for example, might notice that three and seven more is the same amount as seven and three more, or they may sort a collection of shapes according to how many sides the shapes have. Later, students will see 7×8 equals the well-remembered $7 \times 5 + 7 \times 3$, in preparation for learning about the distributive property. . . . They also can step back for an overview and shift perspective. They can see complicated things, such as some algebraic expressions, as single objects or as being composed of several objects. . . . —CCSS

8. Look for and express regularity in repeated reasoning. (NCTM's Reasoning and Proof)
   Mathematically proficient students notice if calculations are repeated, and look both for general methods and for shortcuts. Upper elementary students might notice when dividing 25 by 11 that they are repeating the same calculations over and over again, and conclude they have a repeating decimal. . . . As they work to solve a problem, mathematically proficient students maintain oversight of the process, while attending to the details. They continually evaluate the reasonableness of their intermediate results. —CCSSM

A close look at the practices show that they are founded on the NCTM process standards (problem solving, reasoning and proof, communication, representation, and connections) and the strands for mathematical proficiency from National Research Council's report, *Adding It Up* (adaptive reasoning, strategic competence, conceptual understanding, procedural fluency and productive disposition). The practices are about students having the ability to engage in problems that are new to them and for which they have no immediate algorithm. This requires that they have a positive disposition towards mathematics and are willing to persist towards a solution by trying different strategies that require procedural fluency and/or conceptual pathways. Persistent students are willing to engage in challenging tasks because they accept false starts and struggles as a by-product of learning. They also take time to reflect on their process so that they can redirect their thinking, if necessary. They attend to precision in their computations and in communicating their understanding of the problem in writing and verbally. To attain these habits of mind, students must have had experiences developing the necessary strategies for working through difficult problems by engaging in what is called, productive struggle:

> The focus of the productive struggle is on the mathematical learning goals embedded in the problem or situation—it's not about guessing what the teacher wants to hear or about finding a particular answer. It is about the *process of thinking*, making sense, and persevering in the face of not knowing exactly how to proceed or whether a particular approach will work. Exploring, investigating one or multiple approaches, and articulating a chain of reasoning behind the approaches also characterize productive struggle (Silva and White, 2012).

Thus, productive struggle is an overarching habit of mind that students need to attain in order to be successful in applying the other practices. That they also attend to precision in their work not only requires solid foundation of the basic facts so that they get correct answer(s), but also have appropriate vocabulary and an understanding of symbols and units so that they clearly can communicate verbally and in writing. Problems that are based in real-life and engaging contexts are good resources for having students attain such skills and habits to become *proficient* as defined by CCSSM:

> Proficient students expect mathematics to make sense. They take an active stance in solving mathematical problems. When faced with a non-routine problem, they have the courage to plunge in and try something, and they have the procedural and conceptual tools to carry through. They are experimenters and inventors, and can adapt known strategies to new problems. They think strategically.

The practices for modeling and using tools strategically (4 and 5) focus on the ability to use tools to model situation in the world and/or mathematics using appropriate tools that include diagrams, tables, graphs, manipulatives and estimations. Of importance is that students also view mathematics as a problem-solving tool for making sense of problems. For students to use tools *strategically* requires that several tools be available and that the students, not the teacher, decide which to use for a given problem.

Bill McCallum, one of the lead writers of CCSSM, created a structural diagram (Figure 1.3) to cluster the practices and cautions us to use the practices strategically because, he writes,

> If you think about it long enough you can associate just about any practice standard with any content standard, but this sort of matrix thinking can lead to a dilution of the force of the practice standards— if you try to do everything all the time, you end up doing nothing. (http://commoncoretools.me/2011/03/10/structuring-the-mathematical-practices/, retrieved October 20, 2013)

Figure 1.3 shows how practices one and two are overarching practices if mathematics is to be taught within a problem-solving framework (http://commoncoretools.files.wordpress.com/2011/03/practices.pdf).

Content standards that set an expectation of *understanding* are areas for integrating the content standards and the practice standards—even across content areas: Students also engage in reading or writing logical arguments based on substantive claims, sound reasoning, and relevant evidence. In the

Figure 1.3

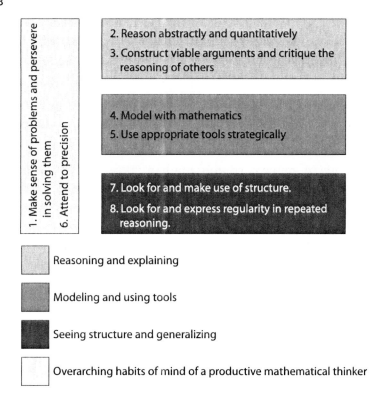

science standards, students ask questions and define problems, plan and carry out investigations, and engage in argument from evidence (Board on Science Education, 2012). In all three areas, if we launch the content with an engaging problem in a focused area that requires students to think deeply, and we allow them to do so, then we have a situation that meets the conditions for productive struggle, the math shifts, and some, if not all, of the mathematical practices. "The single most important principle for improving the teaching of mathematics is to allow the subject of mathematics to be problematic for students" (Hiebert et al., 1996). We should note that, in order for the problem to be problematic for the students, the student must be interested in solving it.

CCSSM Assessment

To achieve student mastery of the skills and concepts, both the practices and content must intertwine or interact in a way such that the practices guide probing class discourse for the acquisition of the skills and concepts, while the content is set within an engaging context that is best learned through the practices. Creating assessments to measure this complex inter-action is the work of two state-led consortiums charged with developing a system of valid and reliable CCSS assessments: Smarter Balanced Assessment Consortium (SBAC, see www.smarterbalanced.org) and the Partnership for Assessment of Readiness for College and Careers (PARCC, see www. parcconline.org). By 2014–2015, some states adopting the Common Core will administer new tests given on computers rather than on paper that will replace their current state math and English language arts tests. Types of questions targeted for such measures are selected-response items; technology-enhanced items to assess a deeper understanding of content and skills than would otherwise be possible with traditional item types; constructed-response items, and performance tasks. To view SBAC sample test items retrieved October 5, 2013, see http://sampleitems.smarterbalanced.org/itempreview/sbac/index.htm. For PARCC sample test items go to www.parcconline.org/samples/math.

To help teachers decide where to place emphasis when teaching the content, PARCC's Model Content Frameworks for Mathematics designates clusters as Major, Additional and Supporting for each grade and course:

◆ Major clusters will be a majority of the assessment.
◆ Supporting clusters will be assessed through their success at supporting the major clusters.
◆ Additional clusters will be assessed as well. (p. 14)

(www.parcconline.org/sites/parcc/files/PARCCMCFMathematicsNovember 2012V3_FINAL.pdf). However, it clarifies that the demarcation should not imply that some content in the standards should be excluded since that will leave students underprepared for later grades content caused by the resulting gaps in skills and understanding.

CCSS assessments that contribute to our understanding of the academic strengths and weaknesses of our students will serve as tools to help states allocate resources for improvements in professional development and student support. However, if they have to be high-stakes (i.e. based on poor results, students are held back from graduation or teachers fired), then time should be allotted for programs to be put in place to help with implementa-tion so that teachers and students have the support necessary to succeed. Otherwise, history shows the negative consequences contribute to fear, which, among other things, promotes cheating at multiple levels. It would be ideal, in my opinion, if the assessments were for formative purposes only.

Figure 1.4 Grade 6 Content Emphasis

Grade	Major Clusters	Supporting Clusters	Additional Clusters
6th	Ratios/Proportional Reasoning: Understand ratio concepts and use ratio reasoning to solve problems.		
	The Numbers System: – Apply and extend previous understandings of multiplication and division to divide fractions by fractions. – Apply and extend previous understandings of numbers to the system of rational numbers.		Compute fluently with multi-digit numbers and find common factors and multiples.
	Expression and Equations: – Apply and extend previous understandings of arithmetic to algebraic expressions. – Reason about and solve one-variable equations and inequalities. – Represent and analyze quantitative relationships between dependent and independent variables.		
	Geometry:	Solve real-world and mathematical problems involving area, surface area, and volume.	
	Statistics and Probability:		Develop understanding of statistical variability. Summarize and describe distributions.

Will teachers and students then not take them seriously? I think they will because most teachers and students with scores below the national average will be motivated to do better because they care and the negative pressures are still huge because the principals, teachers, parents and community all have access to the results *regardless* of whether or not the assessments are high-stakes.

Figure 1.5 Grade 7 Content Emphasis

Grade	Major Clusters	Supporting Clusters	Additional Clusters
7th	Ratios/Proportional Reasoning: Analyze proportional relationships and use them to solve real-world and mathematical problems.		
	The Numbers System: – Apply and extend previous understandings of operations with fractions to add, subtract, multiply, and divide rational numbers.		Compute fluently with multi-digit numbers and find common factors and multiples.
	Expression and Equations: – Use properties of operations to generate equivalent expressions. – Solve real-life and mathematical problems using numerical and algebraic expressions and equations.		
	Geometry:		– Draw, construct and describe geometrical figures and describe the relationships between them. – Solve real-life and mathematical problems involving angle measure, area, surface area, and volume.
	Statistics and Probability:	– Use random sampling to draw inferences about a population. – Investigate chance processes and develop, use, and evaluate probability models.	Draw informal comparative inferences about two populations.

Figure 1.6 Grade 8 Content Emphasis

Grade	Major Clusters	Supporting Clusters	Additional Clusters
8th	The Numbers System:		Know that there are numbers that are not rational, and approximate them by rational numbers.
	Expression/Equations: – Work with radicals and integer exponents. – Understand the connections between proportional relationships, lines, and linear equations. – Analyze and solve linear equations and pairs of simultaneous linear equations.		
	Functions: Define, evaluate, and compare functions.	Use functions to model relationships between quantities.	
	Geometry:	– Understand congruence and similarity using physical models, transparencies, or geometry software. – Understand and apply the Pythagorean Theorem.	Solve real-world and mathematical problems involving volume of cylinders, cones and spheres.
	Statistics and Probability:	Investigate patterns of association in bivariate data.	

NCTM president Linda Gojak (2013) reminds assessment-makers and teachers that:

> If we are to realize the potential of the Common Core, we must begin to think about assessment differently. We must assess students daily through the questions we ask and the tasks we present. We must use the information that we gather from listening to our students to decide our next instructional moves. We cannot wait for end-of-the-year

high-stakes assessments to determine whether students have learned the mathematics. We cannot spend hours of valuable instructional time on formal assessments. (NCTM, Summing Up, 4/13)

Finally, an NCTM publication providing recommendations and guidelines to help teachers teach important mathematics to students regardless of the state standards is *Principles to Actions: An Urgent Agenda for School Mathematics* (2014). Visit NCTM's website for more information (www. nctm.org).

A list of resources for implementing the CCSSM is in Figure 1.7.

Figure 1.7 Web-Based CCSS Resources

CCSS Documents for:

> **Math: www.corestandards.org/Math**

> **Special Ed: www.ode.state.or.us/search/page/?id=3741**

Informative Videos about the CCSS:

> **www.youtube.com/user/TheHuntInstitute#p/u/0/9IGD9oLofks**

NCTM www.nctm.org
Online NCTM provides information and publishes math events, books and journals. Its Illumination site (illumination.nctm.org) has free access to lesson plans, resources, and reflections that are provoked by classroom video vignettes of teaching and learning; NCTM also offers institutes for professional development on the CCSSM throughout the U.S.

The Charles A. Dana Center
The Charles A. Dana Center at The University of Texas at Austin and education company Agile Mind, Inc., with support from the Bill and Melinda Gates Foundation, are pleased to announce to launch of an **online CCSSM toolbox,** available at www.CCSSMtoolbox.org or www.CCSSMtoolbox.com. **The toolbox is freely available** to support educators and learners as they implement the mathematics standards.

CCSS Blogs: Dr. William McCallum, head of the mathematics department at the University of Arizona and one of the lead authors of the Common Core State Standards for Mathematics, maintains a blog about resources related to CCSSM implementation at http://commoncoretools.me.

Illustrative Mathematics http://illustrativemathematics.org
Illustrative Mathematics provides guidance and develops resources to support the implementation of the standards. The Illustrative Mathematics project has developed hundreds of tasks that illustrate the meaning of each standard and provide instructional best practices for teachers.

Inside Mathematics www.insidemathematics.org
This professional resource for educators features classroom examples of innovative teaching methods, insights into student learning, and tools for mathematics instruction which are being aligned to the Common Core.

PBS Learning Media http://lpb.pbslearningmedia.org/
Site has lessons and videos on important topics in most subjects and at all grade levels.

SUPPORTING ELLS IN MATHEMATICS http://ell.stanford.edu/

The goal of these materials is to illustrate how Common Core aligned math tasks can be used to support math instruction and language development for ELLs at three grade spans (elementary, middle, and high school) using adapted tasks from two publicly accessible curriculum projects, **Inside Mathematics** and **Mathematics Assessment Project**.

LearnZillion www.learnzillion.com/topics#topic- 0
Site has YouTube videos on important math topics. Lessons/Tasks/Tests are aligned to CCSS & Practices and grouped by level of difficulty.

North Carolina Common Core Instructional Support Tools — Unpacking the Standards — Math
www.ncpublicschools.org/acre/standards/common-core-tools/#unpacking
For each grade level and CCSS area, this document provides explanations and examples for each Standard for Math and ELA and what each looks like by grade level.

NY State Education Department www.p12.nysed.gov/apda/common-core-sample-questions
This site includes sample 3–8 math and ELA questions to help students, parents, and educators better understand the instructional shifts demanded by the Common Core and the rigor required to ensure that all students are on track to college and career readiness.

Engage New York http://engageny.org
This is another Common Core Site for New York State. You'll find videos, lessons and general resources here. New York will be posting curriculum units shortly to this site.

Ohio Department of Education
www.education.ohio.gov/GD/Templates/Pages/ODE/ODEDetail.aspx?page=3&
Each grade level document unpacks the standards and provides instructional strategies, sample items, common misconceptions, and connection to diverse learners and links to other resources aligning to the standard.

Progressions for the Common Core in Mathematics
http://ime.math.arizona.edu/progressions
The authors of the Common Core State Standards in Mathematics release draft papers that provide in-depth discussion of the domain progressions across grades, highlight connections across domains, elaborate on the learning expectations for students, and provide instructional suggestions.

Student Achievement Partners
www.achievethecore.org
Student Achievement Partners offer a variety of practical resources and examples for working with the Common Core Standards in both E/LA and Mathematics.

Teaching Channel https://www.teachingchannel.org/
This site includes videos of classroom vignettes with teacher voice-overs relating to CCSS. (most about 10 min.)

Think Math has ideas for lessons
http://thinkmath.edc.org

Hands-on: Online Resources for Mathematics

National Library of Virtual _Manipulatives_ www.nlvm.usu.edu/en/?
A digital library containing Java applets and activities for K-12 mathematics. Just download the free trial version and you can use as often as necessary.

Set the Manipulatives Free http://jimmiescollage.com/2009/08/set-the-manipulatives-free/
This site has many resources for using manipulatives. Below are samples from the site:

> ---Hand Made Manipulative Instructions
> http://mason.gmu.edu/~mmankus/Handson/manipulatives.htm

> ---Printable Manipulatives
> http://olc.spsd.sk.ca/de/math1-3/p-printables.html

> ---Activities for Manipulatives Grades 4–5
> http://mathcentral.uregina.ca/RR/database/RR.09.98/loewen2.html

> ---Printable Math Game Boards (pdf & doc)
> http://olc.spsd.sk.ca/de/math1-3/mathgameboards.html

The Kentucky Center for Mathematics—Math Manipulatives
www.kentuckymathematics.org/resources/mathmanipulatives.asp
Websites for games, printing _free manipulatives_, virtual manipulatives, finding _online manipulatives_ for fractions, decimals, functions and more

Electronic worksheets for grades K—High School Geometry
www.ixl.com/promo?partner=google&phrase=Search%20-%20math%20worksheets&gclid=CLDistTI mbgCFWRp7AodjBIATA

INTERACTIVE WHITE BOARDS

Promethean Planet for

> **Math: www.prometheanplanet.com/en-us/resources/subjects/math/**

SMART EXCHANGE: http://exchange.smarttech.com/#tab=0

Math Websites for Interactive Whiteboards—most, if not all, are free
www.theteachersguide.com/InteractiveSitesMathSmartBoard.htm

Free Interactive Whiteboard Teacher tools www.dreambox.com/teachertools

Mathematical Modeling Lesson Plans—Indiana University
www.indiana.edu/~iucme/**mathmodeling**/**lessons**.htm?
These lesson plans were developed by IMI mathematics teachers and tested in their classrooms. The lessons cover a wide range of topics and grade levels ranging from 7th grade through 12th grade. These are all Word document files that can be saved to your computer.

Assessments

Mathematics Assessment Project: Funded by the Gates Foundation this site provides, units, lessons, assessment and professional development on the common core for middle and high school grades. http://map.mathshell.org/materials/background.php

Partnership for Assessment of Readiness for College and Careers (PARCC) www.parcconline.org/ PARCC is a 23-state consortium working together to develop next-generation K-12 assessments in English and math.
You can view sample tasks for:
Elementary at www.ccsstoolbox.com/parcc/PARCCPrototype_main.html
Middle school at: www.ccsstoolbox.com/parcc/PARCCPrototype_main.html
High school at www.ccsstoolbox.com/parcc/PARCCPrototype_main.html

Smarter Balanced Assessment Consortium
www.smarterbalanced.org/
Smarter Balanced Assessment Consortium is a state-led consortium developing assessments for 25 states that are aligned to the Common Core State Standards in English language arts/literacy and mathematics that are designed to help prepare all students to graduate high school college- and career-ready. You can view their released sample items for math and ELA—all done on the computer—**must visit this site**.
Math items are at http://sampleitems.smarterbalanced.org/itempreview/sbac/index.htm
ELA items are at
http://sampleitems.smarterbalanced.org/itempreview/sbac/ELA.htm

National Assessment of Educational Progress—Released items

ADDITIONAL VIDEOS

Dan Meyer's Table of list of Three-Act Math Tasks
https://docs.google.com/spreadsheet/ccc?key=0AjIqyKM9d7ZYdEhtR3BJMmdBWnM2YWxWYVM1U WowTEE#gid=0

Dan Myer's GRAPHING STORIES in three acts http://graphingstories.com/
Andrew Stadel 3-Act Math Tasks list
https://docs.google.com/spreadsheet/ccc?key=0AkLk45wwjYBudG9LeXRad0lHM0E0VFRy OEtRckVvM1E#gid=0

More Video Links:
- ◆ Mental Math – Decomposing Two-digit numbers (Third Grade)
  www.teachingchannel.org/videos/third-grade-mental-math?fd=1
- ◆ Graphing Linear Equations – Full Body Style (Eighth Grade)
  www.teachingchannel.org/videos/graphing-linear-equations-full-body-style?fd=1
- ◆ Statistical Analysis to Rank Baseball Players (High School)
  www.teachingchannel.org/videos/statistical-analysis-to-rank-baseball-players

YUMMY MATH www.yummymath.com/
Provide real-life activities organized by content and grade levels.

Implementing the Mathematical Practice Standards
http://mathpractices.edc.org/
A site with illustrations of student dialogues to help explore how to connect the mathematical practices to the content standards.

2

Exemplary Practice: What Does it Look Like?

While I was helping my daughter Georgine with her math homework, I asked her to explain why she chose the operation she used to solve a problem. Not only did she not know, but also she did not care. She was more interested in getting the right answer by plugging in the proper formula. This is how she was taught math, and she doesn't seem to want to change the way she learned it. I can only generalize that this is how many students are responding to attempts by teachers to create conceptual understanding. This age group is where so many students lose interest in math—just when they should be finding the beauty of it. Perhaps I shouldn't worry too much; Georgine's passion lies in social studies and literature. She is not a "math-brained" child, I guess. Are these children born, and not made that way?

(Hermiaune, Preservice teacher)

We can surmise that Georgine has procedural fluency but because she lacks conceptual understanding, she is not able to apply the strategic and adaptive competencies necessary to solve real life problems, which in turn contributes to her unproductive disposition towards mathematics. Many students perceive mathematics to be a bunch of numbers that plug in to formulas to solve problems. More often than not, the problems they are asked to solve are not *their* problems, nor do the problems come close to something they are interested in pursuing. Georgine's experiences with mathematics are similar to those that I had as a mathematics student—the mathematics that I learned focused on finding the teacher's or the book's answer to a problem. But when I studied mathematics methods at Brooklyn College, my classmates and I explored a different kind of teaching and learning. Rather than lecture us about what we needed to know, Professor Dorothy Geddes invited us to experience mathematics as a dynamic discipline that sometimes required tools such as toothpicks, geoboards, or mirrors to resolve thought-provoking problems. Her definition of mathematical competence clearly went beyond numbers and computations; she included the ability to test a hypothesis, find patterns, and communicate understanding—all of which are recommended by CCSSM as essential elements for both teaching and learning mathematics.

In her reflection, pre-service teacher Hermiaune writes about her concern for getting Georgine to understand and appreciate mathematics. Unfortunately, Hermiaune's acceptance of Georgine's dislike of mathematics as a natural outcome contributes to the problem. Another is that of some teachers bypassing conceptual understanding to "fast forward" to rules. In her article on teaching to the CCSS, Crowley (2013) writes about what she learned from mathematics educator Ann Shannon who would describe this fast forwarding process as teachers' tendency to "GPS" students by giving them step-by-step directions for solving problems followed by worksheets to practice the steps. If those steps bypass concept understanding, then students will likely not be able to apply the concept to real-world situations or have the concept serve as a simpler problem whose process or solution helps to solve more difficult problems:

> What Ann Shannon would say is that in this particular situation, the students have been "GPS-ed" from problem to solution. Just as when I drive in a new city using my global positioning system, I can follow the directions and get to where I need to go. But I can't replicate the journey on my own. I don't have a real understanding of the layout of the city. If a road were blocked because of a parade, for example, I would be in trouble because I have no real understanding of the city's geography. (p. 1)

We need to shift away from GPS-ing students, which is the traditional way for teaching mathematics, and also away from believing that non-"math brained students" shouldn't be expected to understand math. What happens to Georgine's mathematics learning when her mom or her teacher believes that she does not have a "math brain"? The answer depends on their response. If they decide that it is acceptable for Georgine not to succeed in mathematics because she's smart in other areas—just not in mathematics—and that there is no reason to work to enhance her mathematical understanding, then Georgine may never change her own attitude about mathematics. On the other hand, if the belief that Georgine is not "math-brained" encourages her mother and her teacher to work toward connecting the mathematics that she is learning to her strong areas of interest by thinking about how math is integrated in literature, art, science, the movies, music, politics, sports, puzzles, or some other interest of Georgine's, then she has a chance to understand, appreciate, and maybe even like mathematics. The reality is that every student has a unique and complex brain and our classrooms are composed of many Georgine's with many varying interests and aptitudes but they can all learn to do and appreciate mathematics.

Envisioning Reform-based Classroom Environment

The information in Chapter 1 listing CCSSM recommendations for reforming curriculum, teaching, and assessment provides ideas on what a classroom influenced by reform principles should look like to reach students. Not surprisingly, creating coherent lessons that promote such reform is not easy, partly because acquiring a clear vision of the mathematical practices and how they interrelate and connect to the content requires different ways of thinking, as well as practice, guidance, and time to evolve.

Teachers or curriculum writers must exercise caution against a limited vision of the CCSSM that might lead to a superficial or misguided application. As an example, consider the following lesson in an eighth-grade algebra class and ask, "How different are the teaching, instructional activities, and student participation from those of a traditional classroom?"

> The bell rings and Nancy's students enter class. They quickly sit in their assigned groups of four and take out their calculators. Nancy's goal for the class is to have them model addition of integers with colored counters. She begins with a review of the properties of integers and their representations with the counters, then gives each student a package of counters and a work sheet on addition of integers. Students decide who will do which problem and the groups set to work. Nancy visits each group to monitor their progress.

This description includes many of the concepts that we associate with reform: The students are working in groups with manipulatives that include calculators and the teacher monitors progress. How could the lesson not be reform based? Let us take a closer look.

In her discussion of the colored counters, Nancy first defines the use of the counters: a black counter represents a positive number and a white is a negative number. Hence three black counters represent +3. Next she tells students how to add integers having the same signs and then models the example with the counters: "To add two integers with the same sign, just add the numbers and keep the sign. So, (+2) plus (+3) equals +5, and we can show this is true with the counters." She draws three black counters and adds two more blacks to show a total of five black counters or, +5. She next explains how to add when signs are different: "If the signs are different then subtract the two numbers and take the sign of the larger number. So, what do we get for (−3) + (+4)?" A student gives the correct answer of +1 and Nancy then draws three white counters and four black counters on the board to verify the answer. A student asks "Why do we have to use the counters if we can get the answer by using your rules?" Nancy responds that this is just another way to do such problems. As she hands each student a sheet with exercises on addition of integers, Nancy instructs students to use the counters to show the results of their actions. Students decide who will do which problem and begin working. Some use calculators with their worksheet; and when most are finished, they wait for other students to finish working. Nancy visits each group, correcting any students' errors. When the groups finish, she assigns different students to put problems on the board.

Our closer scrutiny shows that what looks like reformed teaching lacks key ingredients of reform. Consider Nancy's arrangement of students' seats in pairs versus in rows of desks that may not be conducive to small group processing of ideas. Note that the CCSS/NCTM recommend that students work in small groups since "This approach is often very effective with students in the middle grades because they can try out their ideas in the relative privacy of a small group before opening themselves up to the entire class" (NCTM, 2000, 272). However, in Nancy's groups, students worked individually applying her rules, therefore there was little motivation for group members to share ideas, even though the small group size would have made that easy to achieve. Furthermore, it was Nancy, not group members, who judged the correctness of answers and determined who would report answers on the board: She did not try to assess students' understanding, pose questions to provoke further thinking, or suggest to students that they enlist the help of other group members.

Whitely (1991) succinctly describes key elements for facilitating small groups. He writes that in preparing for classroom instruction,

...a teacher selects tasks which have a high probability of being problematical for students—tasks which may cause students to find a problem. Secondly, the students work on these tasks in small groups. During this time the teacher attempts to convey collaborative work as a goal. Finally, the class is convened as a whole for a time of sharing. Groups present their solutions to the class, not to the teacher, for discussion. The role of the teacher in these discussions is that of facilitator, and every effort is made to be nonjudgmental and encouraging. (15–16)

Next, consider Nancy's use of manipulatives. Properly used, manipulatives provide an alternative, concrete representation that is conducive to students' initial discovery or understanding of more abstract concepts or algorithms. They are valuable when they are introduced as an integral first step of a lesson to challenge students' thinking and to invite students at different levels of understanding to participate. Nancy's use of the colored counters does neither because she presents them from an algorithmic perspective. Yet colored counters are helpful to students' discovery of the rules for operations on integers through the application of mathematical practices MP4 (use of models), MP3 (construct and critique arguments), MP6 (Attend to precision) and MP8 (look for and express regularity). To help students reinvent the rules, Nancy should have students put calculators away and then discuss uses of integers as wells as their representations of opposite situations using an appropriate model. For example, using a win-lose model for playing the monopoly game translates "+3 dollars" to mean, "I won three dollars" and "−2 dollars" to mean, "I lost two dollars." The end results from adding them is, "I won 3, then lost 2, so I won only one dollar," which we represent as +1. The concept of opposite numbers follows easily since winning three dollars and then losing three dollars neutralize each other and yield zero: $(+3) + (-3) = 0$. Having explained this model to the class, she could then use it to develop the rules or she could at this point introduce colored counters as a visual approach to operations with signed numbers. She could say:

Let black counters represent positive numbers and white counters represent the negatives. How can we represent $(+3)$? (-2)? or 0? Consider this circle representing a set of colored counters where each black is matched with a white. What number does that represent? Let's define addition: to add two numbers is to place counters representing the numbers inside the circle and then to eliminate zeros. Let's go back now and use counters to find, $(+3) + (-2)$.

Once students eliminate zeros, they should see that only one black counter, or + 1 remains as the answer (see Figure 2.1). Nancy could then have students practice translating their own win-lose statements to operations with counters or using monopoly reasoning (MP4), explain their answers to group members (MP6), then justify and critique each others answers using one of the models (MP3).

After some practice, giving students (+234) + (−456) to add—still *without* a calculator—should either get a student to propose a rule which other students should test, or, will create the need for students to find a rule. From this point, students are ready to organize the work with the counters to seek patterns (MP8). Nancy could ask students for suggestions on how to proceed or have students complete a worksheet with a sequence of problems conducive to generating the rules (Figure 2.2). Once students have discovered a rule, they should test it with several examples, and if "Carlos" discovers the rule, then it becomes not the teacher's, but *Carlos's* rule for addition of

Figure 2.1 Using Colored Counters to Model Addition of Integers

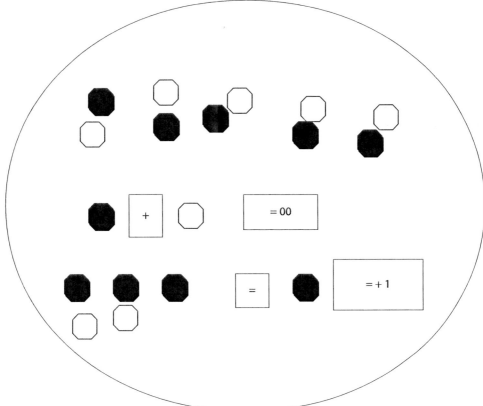

Figure 2.2 Structured Worksheet for Discovering Rules

For Addition of Integers

Directions: Work in groups. Complete the following problems with colored counters or use the win-lose story. Try to discover a pattern or rule that works for your group of problems and discuss with your group. Create three similar problems for each group using three digit integers. Apply your rule to find the sums. See any other patterns?

GROUP 1:	GROUP 2:	GROUP 3:	GROUP 4:
$(+4) + (+4) =$	$(-4) + (-4) =$	$(-4) + (+4) =$	$(+4) + (-4) =$
$(+6) + (+3) =$	$(-6) + (-3) =$	$(-6) + (+3) =$	$(+6) + (-3) =$
$(+3) + (+4) =$	$(-3) + (-4) =$	$(-3) + (+4) =$	$(+3) + (-4) =$
$(+6) + (+2) =$	$(-6) + (-2) =$	$(-6) + (+2) =$	$(+6) + (-2) =$
$(+1) + (0) =$	$(-1) + (0) =$	$(-5) + (+3) =$	$(+5) + (-3) =$
$(+2) + (+7) =$	$(-2) + (-7) =$	$(-2) + (+7) =$	$(+2) + (-7) =$
$(+4) + (+6) =$	$(-4) + (-6) =$	$(+4) + (-6) =$	$(-4) + (+6) =$
$(+6) + (+4) =$	$(-6) + (-4) =$	$(+6) + (-4) =$	$(-6) + (+4) =$

integers. Nancy must also attend to precision by using correct vocabulary and require that students do likewise. As an example, her rule for adding integers with different signs tells students to use the sign of the "larger number" rather than that with the "larger absolute value." Such careless use of vocabulary will pose problems for some students.

Second, what about Nancy's use of the calculator? Students who are using it as a quick way to merely get the answers to the problems are using it inappropriately. However, students using it to check their guesses for addition of large integers *after* they have thought of a rule, or to find new patterns, are engaging the full power of the calculator to promote higher thinking. Alternatively, the calculator could have been used as the manipulative for helping students *initially* get a rule. To do so, she could first do her introduction but then ask students to:

1. use the calculator to complete the worksheet;
2. look for a pattern to guess the calculator's rule;
3. create problems to verify your rule;
4. compute the answers to your problems using your rule;
5. use the calculator to check your rule;
6. if your rule fails, go back to step 2;
7. share and justify your rule;

8. think of real-life situations to model some of your problems and in your journal, explain how to get the answers.

In addition to the informal assessment Nancy gathers as she monitors the groups, she can collect the journal from step 8 for information on individual students' conceptual understanding of the lesson to decide who needs help and how to help them.

Was Nancy's approach bad? No, there might have been some educational gains for some students. Learners construct their own knowledge at all times and in all types of situations, but different instructional approaches may influence the quality and content accuracy of the construction. The fact that students faced each other in small groups rather than in rows looking at each others' backs surely promoted some worthwhile discussion among students, but the amount and quality of their interchange, in terms of learning the mathematics involved, would undoubtedly have been increased had Nancy designed the assignment to challenge students. Although the colored counters were not applied in the best way to enhance the students' ability to make connections between multiple representations, they still provided an alternative view of operations with integers terms, and they may have helped some students better understand the mathematics. Nancy also had students present their answers, thus opening an opportunity for students to share their thinking and summarize ideas.

I surmise that Nancy's perception of teaching mathematics is one that relies on teacher control or is conceptually rule driven. She probably has had little experience using various tools, such as manipulatives, to guide exploratory activities. However, the fact that she has elements that are conducive to reform activities in her class indicate that she is trying to embrace different approaches to teaching. What is lacking is implementation of the mathematical practices together with the mathematics content in her instruction. Her instruction and choice of activities are those of a teacher in transition to a reform-based teaching approach supported by CCSS. A clearer vision of what the Common Core Practices entails, is key to her success in moving forward with the transition.

Now let's consider a typical classroom of 30 students who are sitting in straight rows and busily working individually on a worksheet. Claudette, the teacher, stands at the front of the room or occasionally circulates about and looks over their shoulders. Is she teaching from a reform perspective? Maybe. It depends on what the worksheet requires and whether students have opportunities to learn in other ways on other days. Suppose Claudette's goal is for students to apply the heuristic "think of a simpler problem" to problems that are not routine. Below are the examples on the worksheet:

1. Find the last two digits of $11^{20} - 1$
2. Determine a rule for finding the following sum:

   $1^2 - 2^2 + 3^2 - 4^2 + 5^2 \ldots + 1999^2$

3. Be prepared to explain to the class your strategies for getting your answers.

The sheet is not of the "drill-and-kill" variety. It requires students to apply sound problem-solving heuristics to problems that are suitable for individual work. Further, the third question will promote the sharing of students' ideas and discourse. If she occasionally varies her teaching style, she may be teaching from a reform-based perspective.

The two examples above show that labeling an activity or class as reform-based or not requires close scrutiny of the work students do, how they do it, and whether a single teaching method is expected to be used exclusively. Let's consider the revisions made to Nancy's lesson and ask one final question: Is it now aligned to the CCSS? Some would say yes, somewhat, but ask: "What about a real-life challenging application out of which the need to compute signed numbers arises (MP1)? Why not have students do individual explorations first before going into groups?" My point is that probably many of us are teachers in transition with various levels of understanding what the CCSS imply. Further, we all come to the table with different experiences, expertise, and expectations but instrumental to helping us move closer to a common vision and philosophy for teaching and learning as supported by CCSS are, "opportunities to reflect on and refine instructional practice—during class and outside of class, alone and with others . . ." (NCTM, 2000, 19).

Exemplary Practices

There are exemplary practices that clearly demonstrate best practices for teaching and learning for understanding. For example, the teachers profiled in this book:

1. engage students in challenging, mathematically appropriate tasks that align with the CCSSM and make sense to students;
2. apply the mathematical practices to create a classroom atmosphere conducive to discourse that encourages students' alternative conjectures, approaches, and explanations;
3. use appropriate tools, cooperative group work, and individual instruction to accommodate students with different learning styles;

4. use alternative assessment methods to assess students and guide their instruction;

5. collaborate with colleagues and pursue other professional development activities to support or improve their practice.

Do any of the teachers lecture at times? Sure. Many of us learned from lectures (of course, how well we understood what we learned is subject to debate). Past NCTM President Gail Burrill (personal communication, April 1998) elaborates on perceptions to avoid when teachers attempt to implement reform:

We must avoid misinterpretations such as: everything must be done in cooperative groups; decreased emphasis means none at all; every answer to every problem has to be explained in writing; the teacher is only a guide; every problem has to involve the real world; computational algorithms are not allowed; students should never practice; and manipulatives are the basis for all learning. The challenge is to make choices about content and teaching based on what we can do to enable students to learn.

As mathematics leaders, we know very well to be wary of universal statements such as "For all x, y is true." We must be mindful that its negation, "There is an x for which y is false," is often true when x represents students in our class and y represents a statement about the effectiveness of a specific activity or method. Keeping our focus on all students' learning highlights the fact that our students are too diverse to be neatly served by instructional methods labeled "Use me all the time!" The key reflective question that should guide whatever approach we take is, "How can we best facilitate students' understanding of the mathematical content in a meaningful way that contributes to their success in the twenty-first century?" The following reflection from Mary, a pre-service teacher, summarizes some of these ideas:

Writing this final journal brings me back to last semester in my first math methods course. I was a wreck. I was not sure if I knew anything, learned anything, or was doing anything right. I am in a much better position at the end of this second and final math methods semester. I am confident that I know a great deal of math content, I know that I have learned a vast amount of information, and I am secure in my work and accomplishments. Having said that, I think that I am ready to concretely state my mathematical teaching philosophy, which I have yet to do solidly since last semester. I believe that every student is capable of learning and doing math. Some students come with an aptitude for math that allows them to absorb ideas and concepts relatively easily. Some students take time to figure things out. By tapping in to a student's interests, a link may be found to connect what they are most interested in to the math content. By doing so, the student will be able to find their interests within mathematical content and thrive. It is my job as their teacher to help them find that connection. I also believe that there are many types of learners. There are visual, kinesthetic, and auditory learners. Each of those students should be reached in every lesson that I create. It is my duty to allow students to learn the way they naturally do by fostering their needs in my lessons. I will not leave any student behind. Regardless of whatever hectic schedule I may be handling, there is always time to help a student that is struggling. I think that is it, for now. I am sure as I move along in my teaching career things will be added, changed, or revisited. For now, I am confident in my statement of my teaching philosophy.

Veteran teachers may read this reflection and think. . . "Good luck! She sure has a LOT to learn about the reality of teaching kids!" It is true that Mary has very high ideals (e.g., *every* lesson should include *all* learning styles) but, ideally, I believe that that is where teachers should start. She also has the teaching and learning philosophy our students need. Research from the American Association for Employment in Education (2014) report that, nationwide, the areas of greatest need in education-related disciplines include teachers and related service personnel in special education, mathematics and science. Since Mary is open to adjusting her thinking when necessary, the question is: what is needed to sustain Mary's enthusiasm for teaching mathematics so that she is still teaching after three years? On its website, the New York City of Department of Education provides research findings that may help to answer this question. Its research shows that a supportive environment that includes support and respect for teachers as well as an induction and mentoring programs for new teachers are key to retention. Note that while salary is not listed as a major factor, for some, it can be one of the factors for leaving:

> A special education, math or science teacher who encounters poor working conditions, including low pay and lack of support from school leaders is more likely to leave than one who finds a climate of collegiality and supports that are both material and financial.

Further, it states that:

> Retaining staff in special education, math and science, particularly in
> urban and rural areas and in the early years of their professional lives
> when they are most vulnerable to leaving the field, is a district's first
> step in developing high quality, hard-to-replace teachers who can in-
> crease achievement of all students. (www.p12.nysed.gov/specialed/
> publications/persprep/qualityteachers/retention.htm)

On one of Jerry Becker's list serve is a cartoon of a teacher being blamed
by "drive-by education experts" for the failure of her students. (What are you
doing Wrong? Posted: Mar 18, 2013 3:37 PM.) Poor teacher says nothing but
on the desk of her students are labels that read, homeless, teen mom, abused,
drugs, no books, no discipline, TV on 24/7 and . . . hungry. On her desk are a
pile of paperwork, test schedules, and a small box labeled "my own $ for
supplies." In her reflection, Mary writes, "I will not leave any student behind.
Regardless of whatever hectic schedule I may be handling, there is always
time to help a student that is struggling." If Mary teaches in a school having
students primarily from low socioeconomic backgrounds, can her determina-
tion help her students to perform well on the CCSS assessments? One would
expect that CCSS test scores of poor students will be much lower than those
of the rich because the latter can afford to go to schools that have better
resources and obtain extra support after school if needed. In his article
summarizing his research on the widening of the academic gap entitled, "No
rich child left behind," Reardon (2013) reports that, while differences in
quality between schools serving low- and high-income students are contrib-
uting factors, there is another having a larger impact. He writes,

> It may seem counterintuitive, but schools don't seem to produce much
> of the disparity in test scores between high- and low-income students.
> We know this because children from rich and poor families score very
> differently on school readiness tests when they enter kindergarten, and
> this gap grows by less than 10 percent between kindergarten and high
> school . . . That isn't to say that there aren't important differences in
> quality between schools serving low- and high-income students—there
> certainly are—but they appear to do less to reinforce the trends than
> conventional wisdom would have us believe. (http://opinionator.
> blogs.nytimes.com/2013/04/27/no-rich-child-left-behind)

A major factor he finds is that rich students are increasingly entering
kindergarten much better prepared to succeed in school than middle-class

students. His suggestions for breaking the link between educational success and family background include investing in developing high-quality child-care that is open to all students, and professional development for preschool teachers and childcare providers. But much more is needed, he writes,

> There is a lot of discussion these days about investing in teachers and improving teacher quality, but improving the quality of our parenting and of our children's earliest environments may be even more impor-tant. Let's invest in parents so they can better invest in their chil-dren. . . . These are not new ideas, but we have to stop talking about how expensive and difficult they are to implement and just get on with it.

He concludes with a statement that speaks to the success of the imple-mentation of CCSS:

> The more we do to ensure that all children have similar cognitively stimulating early childhood experiences, the less we will have to worry about failing schools. This in turn will enable us to let our schools focus on teaching the skills—how to solve complex problems, how to think critically and how to collaborate—essential to a growing economy and a lively democracy. (http://opinionator.blogs.nytimes.com/2013/04/27/no-rich-child-left-behind)

For implementation of CCSS to be successful, best practices suggest that it is crucial to provide teachers and students with the support they need to engage in the productive struggles necessary for transitioning to the demands of the new curriculum and assessment system. The support should include not only professional development for implementing the curriculum but a nurturing environment that blends theory with the day-to-day realities of teaching kids from different socio-economic backgrounds and cultures. While the CCSS is state-led, the help of the federal government is needed to address the societal needs cited above by Reardon (2013) so that the future will show students' performances on the CCSS assessments unaffected by their cultures or socio-economic level. Without this confluence of support, the CCSS may become another great reform movement that positively affects a select group of students.

The teachers in this book demonstrate how educators can try to move toward the CCSS goals by teaching the content through the mathematical practices and through collaborating with colleagues.

3

Gail Englert: Conceptual Foundation for Proportional Reasoning

My school is an urban school with a high percentage of students qualifying for free or reduced lunch. The teachers in my school expect a high level of engagement, and use the teamwork aspect of our instruction to teach students how to work together and to lead. Many of these students haven't been expected to act as leaders in the past, so at first this is difficult. But we are persistent, and they begin to see that, buried deep within them, is powerful number sense that can be used to solve problems. I have noticed that many students enter my middle school classroom with very little proportional sense. Some have learned to cross multiply, but are not sure why it works, or even when to use it—and when NOT to. Others have trouble understanding that there are multiple quantities to work with, and those that do recognize the different quantities don't always see the relationships that link them. In a way, I find this to be a lucky break, almost a clean slate upon which to help my students develop the reasoning they will use later in algebra, geometry and measurement.

(Gail Englert, James Blair Middle School in Norfolk, Virginia)

Gail's presentation at an NCTM conference as well as her sound advice to teachers as consultant to the Math Forum (http://mathforum.org/t2t/bios/gengler1.html) prompted me to invite her to submit a chapter for this book. She has been teaching for at least 30 years and has earned National Board Certification as well as Teacher of the Year for Norfolk Public Schools, in Norfolk, VA. When asked why she chose proportional reasoning as her topic, she said:

> It is an important topic with many facets of understanding that need to be taught before students can apply it fluently. It involves the ability to notice and use multiplicative relationships between related amounts; being able to predict what will happen to one amount; knowing what happens to another; and knowing if a change in amounts results in a proportional relationship. Being able to reason proportionally means much more than applying the cross-product algorithm and solving for an unknown amount. There is a need for algebraic reasoning and students who view the equal sign as an indication that a solution follows, rather than as a signal of equivalent values, will have difficulty progressing in their understanding of proportional reasoning, as well. It isn't just that one term of an equation is the same value as another term . . . there needs to be a multiplicative pattern involved that relates the two, so that as one changes, the other changes in response. It isn't just "doing the same thing to both sides." Students must be able to see the multiplicative relationships present in proportions and must understand the difference between absolute and relative change.

Gail also keeps up to date with articles and research for developing proportional reasoning. In this chapter, she applies suggestions of categories of informal activities for developing proportional reasoning from the book by Van de Walle, Karp and Bay-Williams (2013) that include providing opportunities for students experiences with the identification of multiplicative relationships before moving on to the selection of equivalent ratios, the comparison of ratios, scaling with ratio tables, and measurement activities. Problems involving percent and equivalent fractions are explored using problem solving rather than formal operations.

Activity 1: Concrete Examples of Proportionality

Gail starts the unit by distributing a copy of a worksheet (Figure 3.1) containing sets of pictures that are all the same, except that some have been oriented differently, rotated or flipped, or stretched or condensed disproportionately. She displays them on an overhead and asks students to work in small groups and to look carefully and jot down any observations they have while thinking about what they are seeing.

Figure 3.1

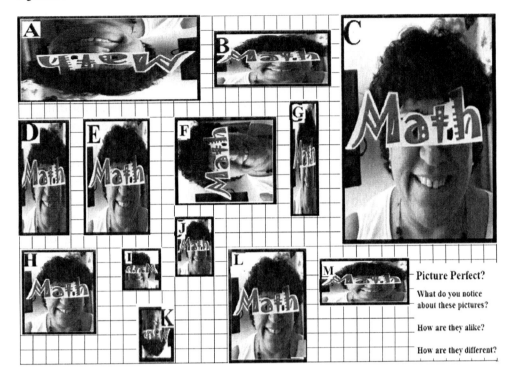

Group 1:

Katia: All the pictures are of the same person but they don't all look the same.

Gail: How are they different? What is different about the ones that are not exactly the same?

Alex: Well, if we use picture C as the regular picture, then H looks exactly like C, except it is smaller.

Myles: Picture I also looks like C and H, but is smaller and flipped around, facing in the other direction.

Zavier: Yeah, sort of like looking in a mirror.

At this point, Gail calls the class's attention and says, "Instead of using the word "regular" to describe picture C, let's agree to use the word "standard" or "normal" because the term "regular" has a special meaning in mathematics and we want to be careful and precise with our conversations. Also, Group 1 noticed that picture I looks flipped just like a reflection in a mirror. If you think it looks like a reflection in a mirror, then we can use the word reflect, in place of the word "flipped." She continues to circulate to find other opportunities to introduce vocabulary and deepen evolving concepts.

Group 2:

Matthew: Picture F is also the same as C and H except that it is turned around.

Tania: See the faces in A and B? They look fatter than the others.

Gail: Some additional agreements: rather than say faces are fatter, "wider" might also be a suitable description.

Darrel: Well then, the faces in D, E, G and J are all thinner than the standard picture.

Gail: I wonder if there is a way to use the grid on the pictures to compare them. Talk in your groups about what you notice about the sizes of the pictures, using the grids.

Juwan: If you count the squares in the grid, you can find out how long each picture is.

Rebeccah: We can find the widths, too.

Gail: Work together to find the dimensions of these pictures. Let's put that information into the Picture Perfect table handout so we can look for relationships (see Figure 3.2).

Figure 3.2 Picture Perfect Table

Consider picture L to be the "original" picture.
1) Which pictures have the same relationship between the length and width as picture L has?
2) Which pictures are enlargements of picture L?
3) Which pictures are reductions of picture L?
4) Which other pictures have the same relationships between height and width?

Before counting the dimensions, reorient each picture so that it is facing up.

	A	B	C	D	E	F	G
HEIGHT							
WIDTH							

	H	I	J	K	L	M	N
HEIGHT							
WIDTH							

This is a perfect place for Gail to begin to talk about ratios and proportions. She has the students write an initial definition of ratio as a number that compares the size of one number to the size of another number. By using the lengths of the sides of the pictures, her students find that some pictures have the same relationships between the length and width, that is, they are proportional. She introduces the definition of proportions as a statement that two ratios are equal. This is also a convenient time to discuss enlargements and reductions, using the pictures as concrete examples. It is important that her students see that as one dimension of each picture changes, the other dimension must change using the same relationship, for the picture to be "in proportion." This rate of change will be an important concept when her students study algebra.

Activity 2: Absolute and Relative Thinking

In this activity, Gail presents three situations to help students consider a different kind of rate of change (adapted from Van de Walle, Karp and Bay-Williams, 2013). This time, instead of the lengths of a picture changing, students will be comparing mixtures, or growth rates. She wants them to think about the differences between looking at a situation using relative or multiplicative reasoning, versus using absolute or additive reasoning. She presents the situations one at a time and gives groups time to think, discuss in small groups, and finally share as a class. She has materials available for students to use to explore the situations, like rulers or tape measures for situation 1, and measurement containers for situations 2 and 3. She says to the class, "Let's now turn our attention to three situations that will help us grow in our understanding of proportions."

> Situation 1: Tom and Molly each planted a lima bean and recorded the growth of their plants. After 2 weeks, Tom's plant is 4 inches tall, and Molly's plant is 6 inches tall. After 4 weeks, Tom's plant is 12 inches tall, and Molly's plant is 14 inches tall. Which plant grew more?

Group 3:

James: Well they both grew by 8 inches in 4 weeks so there is no difference.

John: Yeah that was easy!

As Gail circulates, she is not surprised to note that students are applying only additive reasoning to this problem. She asks James to explain his thoughts.

James:	Well, Molly's plant started growing fast since it grew 6 inches and Tom's grew only 4 inches after 2 weeks. But then they both grew by 8 inches in 4 weeks so there is no difference.
Gail:	Does any one disagree or have another way of thinking about this situation . . .. [No response].
Gail:	Consider Tom's plant. You are right in that its growth from 4 inches to 12 inches is 8 inches more but let's think about using a comparison of growth to original size. What was its original and growth size?
John:	Its original size was 4 inches and it grew to 12 inches.
Gail:	4 and 12. OK. Other than addition, can you think of another way to compare these numbers?
Jose:	You mean, like 4 times 3 = 12 or . . . 12 divided by 3 is 4?
Gail:	What do you think? Talk in your groups about this.
Gail:	What do you think of when I say, "scaling up" or "scaling down?" When we think about multiplication, we can think about it as "scaling up." What do you think "scaling down" might be, in mathematics? Let's focus on scaling up for now.
James:	Tom's plant grew three times the height it started by end of 4 weeks.
Gail:	Would it be OK to say that Tom's plant tripled in size in four weeks? What about Molly's?
Tiffany:	It is not as easy to compare hers because 14 is not a multiple of 6.
Gail:	Well, *about* how many times did her plant grow?
Tiffany:	More than 2 but less than 3 so if we consider the relationships between the growths of the plants, then Tom's grew more.

Gail tells the class to write about the ways they could compare the growth of the plants in their notebooks. Because this way of thinking is so important, she changes the growth numbers for situation 1 and tells students to write the different ways of comparison in their notebooks.

Situation 1b: Tom and Molly each planted a bean and are recording the growth of their plants. After 2 weeks, Tom's plant is 4 inches tall, and Molly's plant is 6 inches tall. After 4 weeks, Tom's plant is 22 inches tall, and Molly's plant is 24 inches tall. Which plant grew more?

Gail:	What do you think about this situation? Talk in your groups.
Jelanna:	We noticed that Tom's plant grew over 5 times as tall this time, but if we multiply Molly's plant's starting height by 5, we get 30 inches. Her plant didn't grow that tall. We think Tom's plant grew faster.

Gail: So, you think we can describe how fast the plants grew? That is an interesting idea. We could call that the "rate" that they grew, couldn't we? Let's look at the next problem.

Situation 2: Sharon and Blake are making lemonade. Blake mixed 2 scoops of lemonade mix with a quart of water. Sharon mixed 6 scoops of lemonade mix with a gallon of water. Which lemonade has a stronger taste?

Myles: I have an answer. Sharon is making more lemonade, and she uses more of the mix than Blake does.
Gail: Let's return to the question: Is it asking about how much lemonade was made, or how many scoops were used?
Myles: No. It is asking which has a stronger taste.
Gail: I am going to make some samples of lemonade for two students to judge on which has a stronger taste. I already have a quart and a gallon of water here. I am now dropping 2 scoops in the 1-quart and 6 in the gallon. First, write a guess as to which you think will have a stronger taste and then let's get Cassie and Jeannette to taste and record their opinions on paper before sharing. Let's also do a quick poll to record on the board. How many think the quart will have the stronger taste? The Gallon?

Most of the students believe the gallon will have a stronger taste because they are putting more of the lemonade mix in that container.
Marcus: I know it will be stronger, because when I put sugar in my iced tea, the more I put in, the sweeter it tastes.
Andrea: But what about the sizes? The quart is a lot smaller than the gallon?

To clarify further, Gail tells the students to imagine a drinking cup, and the classroom's trash can, both filled to the top with water. She asks, "If I add a scoop of lemonade to my coffer and 10 scoops to the trash bin, which would have a stronger taste of lemonade?"

Megan: It would be stronger in your cup.
Gail: But I added more scoops to the bin!
Jerry: But it is more concentrated in the cup since there is less water.
Gail: Ahh. So you are thinking that we need to look at more than just how many scoops are used. You think we need to compare the amount of water in each container. Talk in your groups about that.

Marie: No. I agree. Suppose this whole room was a container filled with water and you added 50 teaspoons, the cup would still be stronger.

Gail: Let's return to situation 2. Please read it again to yourself and then answer the question in your notes and explain why. I want you to use some of the vocabulary we just applied in the other situations.

Gail allows some processing time and then starts to walk around. She notes that some students are flipping pages back and forth to look at previous examples for ideas on how to use the vocabulary and concepts appropriately. "When you are ready, just look up," she says and when almost everyone has done so, she says, "Let's share. I will just call some names randomly. Joseph, Jose and Tiana, please share what you have written."

Jose: I think that two scoops for a quart is like 8 scoops with a gallon. A quart is a fourth of a gallon so I multiplied the two scoops by four to get 8 scoops.

Tiana: I was thinking the same thing. I think the lemonade needs to be added at the same rate for them to taste the same. I don't think these are going to taste the same. I think the quart will be stronger.

Joseph: If the gallon had 8 scoops, it would taste the same, but it only has 6 scoops. For every quart of water, you need to add 2 scoops of mix. It needs more mix, so it will not taste as strong as the quart.

Gail shows the third situation, and gives students time to read and think about it. She asks table groups to share their thoughts, and is not surprised to hear several different interpretations.

Situation 3: Hannah and Jeria are mixing white paint with green paint. Hannah used more green paint than Jeria. Hannah used more white paint than Jeria. Whose paint is a darker shade of green?

Situation 3 can be considered many different ways. Some of Gail's students who are still thinking absolutely will only consider the amount of white paint (Hannah used more, so hers is a lighter shade), or the amount of green paint (Hannah used more so she has a darker shade). Other students, transferring what they learned from the other experiences, argue that there are two values to consider here, the green paint and the white paint. They are able to justify that either paint is a darker shade, or that they are the same shade, depending upon how much more of each color was used by Hannah.

Sylvie is explaining to her table that since Hannah used more white paint, her paint will be a lighter shade of green. Ben argues with her that since

Hannah used more green paint, her shade had to be darker than Jeria's. Gail calls the class together and presents the two ideas. She asks the class to consider what they think about what their classmates have said.

Rebekah: I think we need to think about both the white paint and the green paint.

Tomas: When we looked at the perfect picture faces, we used how long AND how wide they were when we compared.

Gerri: And when we compared the plants, we were thinking about how fast they grew compared to each other. I think we have to compare two things at the same time.

Rebekah: I agree, we need to think about both the green *and* the white paint.

Sylvie: So, if Hanna used more white *and* more green, maybe her paint . . . maybe her paint is the same shade as Jeria's.

Gail: How could that happen?

Tomas: If the amounts change at the same rate, then just like the lemonade, the mixture would stay the same strength.

Greg: And if she added a lot more white paint that she did green paint, then the paint she made would be a lighter shade.

Gail: This is an interesting idea, things changing at the same rate. Take a moment and write in your notebooks about how you can tell if two things are "proportional."

Activity 3: Index Card Ratios and Proportions Activity

Having laid the foundation for application of relative multiplicative thinking, and proportionality, Gail's students are now ready to take a closer look at proportions. She introduces the student to the index card and ratio activity to help then determine the characteristics of equivalent ratios. Below is her description of how she uses them:

> I direct students to fold an index card into four quarters, and have them write one of the four numbers in each section and tear the four sections apart. Putting the numbers on cards makes it easier for students to move them around to find different combinations, and also keeps them from using the same number twice in a ratio. I chose 2, 3, 6 and 9 because they have common factors that make some of the ratios equivalent to each other. There are many other sets of numbers that can be used, as well.
>
> Now I give students time to explore. I circulate as they move the cards around on their desks and record the possible combinations. After several minutes, I record their suggestions on the board. They

use ratio terminology ("2 to 3" and we decide to write them to look like fractions, to make the next step easier).

⅔, ⅖, ⅔, 3/2, 3/6, 3/9, 6/2, 6/3, 6/9, 9/2, 9/3, 9/6

Then I ask them to find pairs of ratios that are equivalent, and we write those on the board. 6/2 = 9/3. I explain that mathematicians call equivalent ratios "proportions." I ask my students what they notice about these proportions, and guide them to see that there is a pattern to the way the numbers are placed in the proportions. My students started by noticing that in the first and last proportions the 2 and 3 are side-by-side, and then extended that observation to note that the 2 and 3 in the middle two proportions were still side-by-side, only vertical this time. They decided the 2 and 3 were always adjacent, never diagonally placed. They also noted the same thing occurred with the 6 and 9. One student even noticed that if he started with the first proportion, he could rotate it right or left to make the second and third proportions, and just flip it to make the last proportion. At this point, another student remembered back to the pictures, and how some were exactly the same, just rotated or reflected.

To help students apply their patterns, Gail lists the following ratios on the board for her student to determine which can be written as proportions:

3/8 and 4/12   5/10 and 4/7   5/10 and 4/7   8/24 and 4/12 12/16 and 3/6

Students' responses leads Gail to believe that they really are getting the concept. For example, Glory says, "We noticed that in the first pair, 4 is a third of 12, but 3 is not a third of 8, so we don't think that we can form a proportion."

To continue reinforcing the concept of proportions, Gail has the students do the activity called Sense or Nonsense Proportionality Sort (see Figure 3.3), which can be also used as an assessment to see if students are making sense of proportionality. Some of the situations listed are not correct but can be fixed to make sensible proportions. Others are not situations that can be thought about in multiplicative ways. It is important for students to understand the difference between these situations. She has students work in groups to sort through the situations, talking about which ones don't work and what is wrong with them. Gail highlights some of the insights and misconceptions of her students related to these problems in Figure 3.9. As an extension activity she asks students to write some original examples and non-examples of proportional situations to share with classmates. "It is important

Figure 3.3 Sense or Nonsense Proportionality Sort

Directions: Sort the cards according to their reasonableness. Try to figure out what went wrong if the situation does not make sense. Be ready to explain your ideas.	
A. If six boys can deliver papers in three hours, then four boys could do that route in two hours.	B. Jasmine spends $4 on three tickets. That means she would spend $9 on 10 tickets.
C. If Raejean can text 20 characters in 15 seconds, then she can text 80 characters in a minute.	D. 8 oz. of lemon concentrate will make 12 cups of lemonade, so 20 oz. will make 24 cups of lemonade.
E. If it takes 20 minutes to bake a half a sheet of cookies, then it will take 40 minutes to bake a whole sheet of cookies.	F. 12 oz. of popcorn will make six cups of popped corn, so 20 oz. will make 10 cups of popped corn.
G. A cruise ship usually takes 30 people on a two-hour tour. If only 15 people take the tour, the ride will last one hour.	H. If one orchestra can play a symphony in one hour, then two orchestras can play it in half an hour.

that they are able to generate examples of their own, and the non-examples are an excellent way to demonstrate their understanding as well," she comments.

Next Gail introduces some real world situations for students to scale up and down to complete ratio tables. These problems are shown in Figure 3.4 where students are encouraged to find multiplicative relationships between the upper and lower numbers to complete the tables but there are also some blank spaces left for them to use to continue the patterns they find. In each case, it is important that students talk about how they completed the tables. Since this will be their first introduction to a variable, Gail helps them complete activities A–D in Figure 3.4.

Problem A with the jeep is one they can visualize, and if they want, use manipulatives to model: 2 sets of 5, 3 sets of 5, 4 sets of 5, etc. Some students are tempted to continue the pattern in the top line: 1, 2, 3, 4, 5, . . . but then they realize that 5 jeeps won't hold 35 passengers. They don't have much difficulty deducing that 1 jeep must hold 5 passengers, and are able to explain why they know that using models, drawings and words. One group is trying to figure out how to make 5 jeeps and 35 passengers work together when one of the students recognizes that she can use division to find the number of jeeps. Her table quickly agrees that this will work, and they use the

Figure 3.4 Ratio Tables for Problem Solving

Encourage students to use ratio tables to solve these problems. Do problems A–C with the students if necessary.

A. A jeep tour can accommodate five passengers. How many passengers can ride in n jeeps?

jeep	1	2	3	4			n
passengers		10			35	50	

B. 12 oz. of unpopped popcorn will make six cups of popped corn. How many cups of popcorn can n ounces of unpopped popcorn make?

unpopped	1		6	12	24		n
popped		1		6		20	

C. 8 oz. of lemon concentrate will make 12 cups of lemonade. How many cups of lemonade can n ounces of concentrate make?

concentrate		1	2	8	12		n
lemonade	1			12		30	

D. Three boys will eat four pizzas.

boys	1		3	6			n
pizzas		1	4		12		

same strategy to find that 10 jeeps will hold 50 passengers, since 50 divided by 5 is 10.

The use of a variable in the format of a table is new to many of the students. Gail talks about what it can mean to use a letter in math, and works through how to figure out what relationships in the table can help use the variable to determine how many passengers to expect for any given number of jeeps.

Gail: What do you suppose that "n" means at the end of this table? Think about it, and then talk with your group.

Maria: I think "n" means a number is missing.

Francesca: Like, we have to put something there.

Tiffany: "n" means that we can put any number there that we want.

Gail: Then how do we figure out what to put in the bottom part of the

	table, the number of passenger, if we can put in any number we want in the top? Talk to your group and think about the relationships we have been talking about.
John:	I think we could figure out how we get the other numbers of passengers, and do the same thing to the n.
Gail:	Explain further, John.
John:	In each case, we took the top number and multiplied it by five. So . . . we should take the n and multiply it by 5 to get n times 5.

Gail looks over John's shoulder and sees that he has written n times 5 using the letter "x" to stand for multiplication. She takes this opportunity to clarify why they will not use the letter x for multiplication with variables and introduces n(5) instead. She asks more questions to get students comfortable with writing it as 5n: "Could I write it as 5(n)? Which property for multiplication says that it's OK to do that? From now on, whenever we see a variable with a number and there is *no* operation sign between them, that will mean that the operation is multiplication. What would 4b represent if b were 3? What about 4+b?"

Now Gail decides that it is time for her students to struggle a bit more. She gives them the next two ratio problems to work on together as she circulates to listen to the conversations. She says,

> It is easier for my students to work horizontally to complete the tables, and often I find myself reminding groups to look for relationships vertically. I encourage them to draw a model, or use manipulatives to show how each amount in the top row changes in relation to the amount in the bottom row. The first two cells in each table are challenge activities for groups who have some extra time.

As she circulates, she notes the following discussion among the students: For problem B, she lets students begin work as she listens for their responses to the challenge problems. Joshua reads the problem: "12 oz. of unpopped popcorn will make 6 cups of popped corn. How many cups of popcorn can n ounces of unpopped popcorn make?"

John:	I don't know, what do you think Justin?
Justin:	I see that 12 is 2 times 6, so I think the unpopped number is twice as large as the popped number.
John:	But it doesn't make sense to me. Unpopped popcorn is little and popcorn is big. How can there be twice as much of the unpopped popcorn?

Marie:	The units are different, ounces and cups. Cups are a lot bigger than ounces.
John:	Oh, I see. So if we multiply by 2, we can find the number of cups of popcorn and that means 1 ounce of unpopped popcorn will make 2 cups of popcorn.
Marie:	I agree.
Sam:	I think 1 ounce of unpopped popcorn makes 2 cups of popped popcorn, and 1 cup of popped popcorn comes from 2 ounces of unpopped corn.
Marie:	But that doesn't make sense. I think you have to divide this time.
Justin:	Yes, and if we divide the popped popcorn amount by 2, we can figure out that it takes ½ ounce of unpopped corn to make 1 cup of popcorn.
Gail:	Does everyone agree? Please look at the table to verify what Marie and Justin said. What rule can we assign to "n" this time?
Stephen:	Each time, we double the unpopped number to get the popped number, so I think we should write "2n."

Problem C connects to the lemonade problem the class solved earlier: 8 oz. of lemon concentrate will make 12 cups of lemonade. How much lemonade will 1 oz. of concentrate make? How many cups of lemonade can n ounces of concentrate make?

Sarai:	I think we can figure out how many cups 2 ounces of concentrate will make by using the relationship between the 2 ounces and 8 ounces. 2 times 4 is 8, so we need to find a number that we could multiply by 4 to get 12 . . . which is 3.
Temby:	So, if 2 ounces makes 3 cups, then 1 ounce will make half as much, 1½ cups. That's the answer to the second question.
Sarai:	Yes, and to figure out how much concentrate it takes to make one cup of lemonade, we can go back to the 2 ounces for 3 cups. 3 divided by 3 is 1, so we need to divide 2 by 3 to get the amount of concentrate, 2/3 ounce.
Gail:	What rule can we assign to "n" this time?
Denah:	This time, for every 1 ounce of concentrate there are 1.5 cups of lemonade. Do we multiply or add this time?
Gail:	Talk with your group about Denah's question. What do you think we should do?
Brendi:	We think that we have been talking about multiplying, so we should keep multiplying.

Gail: What do the rest of you think?

Sarai: It is a multiplying relationship, just like when we looked at the pictures. We should multiply 1 times 1.5, and then multiply "n" times 1.5.

Gail: I wonder who notices something interesting in the tables we are making.

        She gives the students time to observe, and then to talk in their table groups.

Brandon: I noticed that in the first two parts of each table, the numbers that are with the "1" have the same digits, only upside down from each other.

Gail: Does that happen every time? I wonder why that is happening. Let's see if it happens with the next problem, as well.

Before moving on, Gail checks for understanding by giving students a chance to share their ideas for problems B and C. They look at the challenge problems as well. Next she assigns problem D as an independent practice, to give students a chance to try it with the opportunity to get help if needed. By this time, Gail is confident that students are beginning to recognize that there are multiple ways to scale the original ratio up and down to find the information they are looking for.

Her next activity has students in small groups to solve more of the ratio table problems, this time looking for one specific solution as an answer to a question, rather than completing a preset table. This application will help her students add to their problem-solving skills. As she circulates, she notes instances where students scale up, and then down, using the multiplicative relationships they are comfortable with. Some students, the ones who have a great facility with multiplication facts, are able to solve the problems using a minimal number of steps. Her students that struggle with facts use more steps, sometimes repeatedly using the same factor to scale up or down, but do arrive at the answers they are searching for.

When students are ready to work with percent problems, Gail directs her students in making what she refers to as "proportion slider" (see Figure 3.5) which is a wonderful manipulative she created to help students solve percent problems.

This proportion ruler has a top and a bottom ruler to relate to a part of the problem while maintaining the relationship needed between the two amounts. She comments, "My students enjoy making these proportion rulers. We call them 'sliders' because the brad fastener can be slid back and forth along the number line to indicate different amounts." Once the students have the sliders made, she assigns the following problems:

(1) Steven ran 80 percent of the way to school. He ran four blocks. How far is school from his house?

Gail: What numbers do we have to work with in this problem? Talk in your groups about where we should place them.

Vinnie: The 80 percent goes with the percents at the bottom.

Steph: The 4 blocks is the same amount as the 80 percent in this problem, just a different name for it. So the 4 should be written above the 80 percent.

Gail: So, if 80 percent of the distance is 4 blocks, what do we know about the whole distance? Talk with your group.

Vinnie: The whole distance has to be farther than 4 blocks, because 100 percent is the whole distance, and 80 percent is less than 100 percent, so 4 blocks is shorter than the whole distance.

Gail: Good start. Now, how can we use what we know about proportional relationships to find the whole distance from Steven's house to school?

Galen: If we divide 80 by 20 we get 4. I think we have to divide 100 by 20 to get the whole amount.

Figure 3.5 The Proportion Slider

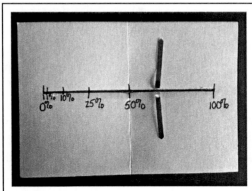

Start with an index card. Draw a straight line horizontally on the card. Label one end 0 percent and the other end 100 percent. Fold the card to find the location for 50 percent, and estimate or fold again to find 25 percent. Estimate to place 10 percent, 5 percent and 1 percent on the number line. Cut a slit along the line, and insert a brad, folding the ends up and down to hold it in place but still allow it to slide. Now the data from story problems can be entered onto the slider to find missing information.

Slip a piece of paper over the horizontal line so you can place corresponding story problem amounts on the number line as well.

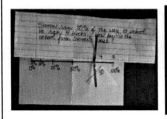

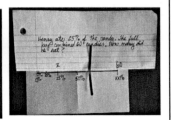

Figure 3.6 Slider for Problem 1

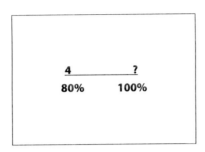

Steph: It would be 5 blocks. 5 times 20 is 100. (See Figure 3.6.)

Gail: Let's consider how to use the slider for the next problem:

(2) Sara has completed 12 of the 20 problems on her test.
What percent has she completed?

Tommy: Sharie and I got stuck along the way.

Gail: Share what you have done so far.

Sharie: 20 is the total amount of problems on the test, and 100 percent is another name for the whole amount so we agree that those two numbers need to be written together.

Tommy: 10 is half of 20, so I think we could put a 10 over the 50 percent.

Gail: How does knowing half help us?

Sharie: Then we know that 12 is more than half, so it is more than 50 percent.

Tommy: And a fourth of 20 is 5, so 5 goes with 25 percent, and 15 goes with 75 percent. Now we know the answer is somewhere between 50 percent and 75 percent, but that is as far as we can go.

Gail: Good work. Now that we have a good estimate, what can we do to find the exact answer?

Fawn: I think we can scale down from the 10 and the 50 percent. We know that 10 and 12 both have 2 as a factor. If I divide 10 by 5, I get 2. If I divide 50 percent by 5, I get 10 percent. That means I can fill in a 2 over the 10 percent. And 2 times 6 is 12, so I can use the factor 6 to find 10 percent times 6, which is 60 percent. (See Figure 3.7.)

Gail: I like the way all of you are thinking. Let's try the next problem.

(3) Henry ate 25 percent of the candy. The full bag contained 60 candies. How many did he eat?

Gail: How is this problem different from the first two? How can we use the slider with this problem? Talk with your group.

Frannie: The 100 percent goes with the whole bag, 60 candies.

Figure 3.7 Slider for Problem 2

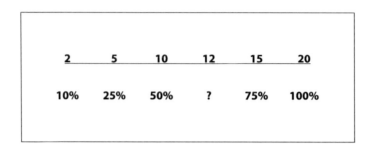

Figure 3.8 Slider for Problem 3

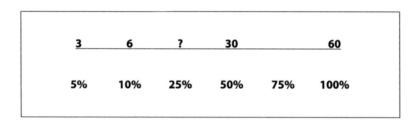

Tran: I can find 10 percent if I know 100 percent. You divide by 10, so 10 percent is 6. And 5 percent is half of that, 3.

Frannie: Why do you want to know 5 percent?

Tran: because I can multiply 5 percent by 5 to get 25, so I need to multiply 3 by 5 and I get 15. Henry ate 15 candies.

Brandon: Can we use fractions? I know that 25 percent is one fourth of 100 percent. I can divide 100 by 4 to get 25, so I could divide 60 by 4 to keep the same relationship.

Gail: Does that give you the same answer?

Tran: Yes, he can get 15 that way, too. (See Figure 3.8.)

Gail comments that her students are now able to look for relationships and use what they understand about proportions to estimate an answer, thinking about approximately where it falls on the number line, and to get an exact answer. The slider also reminds them of the relationships they found in the ratio tables, as well. What wonderful connections! Gail says,

Over time, my students become comfortable looking for and finding the relationships they will use to solve proportion problems. They recognize multiplicative relationships, and can use them to find missing lengths and to solve rates. Their proportional reasoning skills will help them as they work with linear equations in algebra and similar figures in geometry. They will be better equipped to explore rates, and to use ratios.

Discussion Between Colleagues

How do you accommodate for individual differences?

I use data from formal and informal assessments to design activities to help students move forward in their ability to understand mathematics. Some students earn the opportunity for extension activities while others need extra instruction on a topic based on their level of understanding.

What classroom procedures and arrangement foster your students' learning?

I find my students learn best when they work in interdependent teams. Their depth of understanding increases as they explain their ideas, listen to teammates and argue for their solutions.

Comment on the role of the teacher during this project.

It is very important for the teacher to act as a facilitator during these activities. If the teacher just tells the students how to solve the problems, and eliminates the need for students to grapple with the mathematics, vital connection will probably not be made, and students will not be able to transfer what they have worked on to other situations.

How do you assess the students as they participate in the discussions?

I listen to the team discussions for clues about what students are understanding, and misunderstanding. I ask for periodic self-assessments from my students (thumbs up, etc.) to gauge their comfort level, and I present students with an exit ticket that gives me a quick picture of what students take away from the daily lesson. I use the results of the exit ticket to prepare a "My Favorite No" activity for the following day (an error analysis). In this quick activity, I review one anonymous student's solution to the exit ticket, and have the class look first for what is RIGHT, then what went wrong. I select a common error, and make sure the focus is on how close the student came to a correct answer.

Which CCSSM institutes have you attended that you'd highly recommend?

I learned about the Common Core State Standards for Mathematics through professional activities connected to NCTM, and through participation in the Park City Math Institute, and summer residential program for mathematics educators.

Advice to teachers?

One of the most important aspects of proportional reasoning involves setting ratio problems up from word problems. It is often helpful to encourage students to include labels with the quantities for guidance, and to write the ratios and proportions in more than one way, to help students understand that it doesn't really matter how they set the amounts up, as long as they coordinate the amounts so that they correspond with each other. The most important idea to convey to students is that they don't need to remember how to write out the proportion equation and how to solve it—they can solve problems involving proportions by using common sense and noticing multiplicative relationships.

Commentary

As Gail's profile demonstrates, there is no single formula or universal set of steps used to solve every proportional-type problem because proportional reasoning can be found in many different situations, and presented in many different forms. According to NCTM, "the ability to reason proportionally develops in students through grades 5–8. It is of such great importance that it merits whatever time and effort must be expended to assure its careful development" (NCTM, 1989, 82).

In a study by Langrall and Swafford (2000), the researchers write, "Using proportional reasoning, students consolidate their knowledge of elementary school mathematics and build a foundation for high school mathematics and algebraic reasoning" (254). Gail's unit provides a conceptual basis for students to be able to understand the following topics requiring proportional reasoning abilities in the high school curriculum: linear equations, rates, rational numbers and expressions, similar figures, area and volume relationships. The researchers propose four categories or levels for classifying students' proportional reasoning abilities:

Level 0: Non-proportional reasoning
Level 1: Informal reasoning about proportional situations
Level 2: Quantitative reasoning
Level 3: Formal proportional reasoning

A review of Gail's unit shows that she has helped students to progress from Level 0 to Level 2 so that her students are now ready for the rigor of Level 3 reasoning.

Studies on conceptual understanding of U.S. teachers and preservice teachers show that both groups rely heavily on traditional algorithm and few are able to generate appropriate representations to explain why the algorithms work (Ma, 1999; Ball, 1998; Borko et al., 1992). It is clear that Gail's understanding of the fundamental concepts for proportional reasoning is solid and that she likewise wants to make sure that this is true for her students. In their research summary on multiplicative and proportional reasoning in middle school, Yetkiner and Capraro (2009) recommend that opportunities for students to develop a deep understanding of ratios and proportions be provided before the cross-multiply-and-divide algorithm. Throughout the teaching of the unit, Gail adheres to this recommendation by focusing on developing concepts rather than introducing an algorithm.

Gail's strategies also connect to research on the impact of the mathematical features that middle school students attend to or "notice" as they work on a topic and the effects of those features on problem-solving ability. Adapting work from cognitive science and applied linguistics, researchers Lobato, Hohensee, and Rhodehamel (2013) show that what students notice is, "a complex phenomenon that is distributed across individual cognition, social interactions, material resources, and normed practices" (809). An important outcome of their research is the role that teachers can play in directing or redirecting students to focus on the relevant features of a problem. As an example, because of Gail's extensive research on proportional reasoning, she expected and was quick to notice her students' focus on additive reasoning. She was thus prepared to pose questions to redirect their thinking towards the multiplicative aspects of growth which is crucial to proportional reasoning. The researchers also generalize that, "if teachers want students to understand covariation (for any type of function—linear, quadratic, exponential, and so on), then students need to notice two quantities, not just one" (285). Gail's sequencing of problems and skillful questioning strategies carefully guided her students to notice and understand this second important concept of proportional reasoning.

Unit Overview

Conceptual Foundation for Proportional Reasoning

Aim: What basic skills are needed for us to become "Proportional Reasoners"?

Objective: Students will complete a series of activities designed to help them gain insight into proportional reasoning.

Source: Van de Walle, Karp and Bay-Williams (2013).

Grade Level: 6th

Number of 45-minute periods: 7–8

CCSSM Content: 6.RP.A.(.1, 2, 3a, 3b, 3c, 3d); 7.RP.A.(1, 2, 2b)

CCSSM Mathematical Practices: MP1–MP4, MP6, MP8

Mathematical Content: Students develop conceptual understanding of proportions by: compare and contrast rectangles to find similarity; connect real life examples to rate problems, use factors to scale up or scale down; and create a tool to solve proportion and percent problems focusing on reasoning, rather than formulas.

Prerequisites: Students should have some familiarity with multiplication.

Materials and Tools:

- Picture Perfect—example sheet and accompanying worksheet.
- Index cards for index card ratio activity.
- Sense or nonsense proportionality sort.
- Ratio tables for problem solving.
- Index cards and brad fasteners for proportion sliders.

Management Procedures:

- Discuss basic information about ratios and proportions throughout lessons.
- Assign students to cooperative groups to facilitate student discourse.
- Have students:

    – complete the explorations and share their ideas.
    – make connections between activities to help them generalize about proportions.

Assessment: Informally check for understanding daily, and throughout each lesson. Periodically give a quick check/exit ticket assessment to gauge students' level of understanding more formally. Use problems on the handouts for homework and assessment.

Additional Resources:

Figure 3.9 Gail's Students Thinking on the Sense or Nonsense Proportionality Sort

---

A.   If six boys can deliver papers in three hours, then four boys could do that route in two hours.
    One group looked at six and three, and compared them to four and two, and decided right away that since three was half of six and two was half of four, this situation was fine. Another group challenged their thinking, asked them if they thought if fewer boys delivering papers would take more time, or less time to finish the job.

B.   Jasmine spends $4 on three tickets. That means she would spend $9 on 10 tickets.
    One group saw that one more dollar was spent on the tickets than the number of tickets purchased. They decided that it was all right to take the number of tickets, and add one to get the price. Another group said that three was close to four, so each ticket cost about a dollar, and 10 tickets for $9 was also about a dollar per ticket, so the situation was correct. One student countered that three WAS close to four, but it was less than four, and 10 WAS close to nine, but it was more than nine, so he didn't think they were the proportional. Then a student asked about the three tickets. She wondered what would happen if you bought groups of three tickets. She said, "One group of three tickets costs $4, two groups would cost $8, and three groups would cost $12. Three groups of tickets is nine tickets, and the price is already more than $9, so I think it is wrong."

C.   If Raejean can text 20 characters in 15 seconds, then she can text 80 characters in a minute.
    Students immediately wanted to check out their own rates of texting, but refocused on the problem and decided that 15 seconds was a fourth of a minute, and 20 was a fourth of 80, so that situation was correct.

D.   8 oz. of lemon concentrate will make 12 cups of lemonade, so 20 oz. will make 24 cups of lemonade.
    One student noted that $8 + 4 = 12$ and $20 + 4 = 24$. Another compared this problem to the ticket problem (B above) and wondered about 12 being half of 24, but 8 not being half of 20.

E.   If it takes 20 minutes to bake a half a sheet of cookies, then it will take 40 minutes to bake a whole sheet of cookies.
    This is one of those problems that might be easier to consider if students have had the life experience of baking. Whether the sheet is half covered or all the way covered, the amount of time needed doesn't change. Most of my students didn't have much experience with baking, but there was one young man who shared what he knew about baking cookies to convince his classmates this was not a proportional relationship.

F.   12 oz. of unpopped popcorn will make six cups of popped corn, so, we can get 10 cups of popped corn from 5 oz. of unpopped popcorn.

> This problem reminded my students of the lemonade problem. They noticed that 6 was half of 12, and 5 was half of 10. Then one student pointed out that if you had less unpopped popcorn you should get less popped corn, and they reconsidered the problem and realized that the units were reversed.

Figure 3.10 Additional Practice Problems

Encourage students to use ratio tables to solve these problems:

1) A rainstorm produced a rainfall of 6 inches during the 4 hours it stormed. How many inches fell per hour?

inches					
hours					

2) A snowstorm dumped 9 inches of snow in a 12-hour period. How long should it take at that rate for a foot of snow to accumulate?

3) A piece of wire 15 cm long weighs 100 grams. What should a 9-cm length of the same wire length?

4) A worker can complete the assembly of 15 DVRs in 6 hours. At this rate, how many can the worker complete in a 40-hour work week?

5) Christine spends 17 hours in a 2-week period practicing her trumpet. How many hours does she practice in 5 weeks?

6) If you can buy one box of cereal for $2, how much will 10 boxes cost you?

7) In a shipment of 400 computers, 14 are found to be defective. How many defective computers should be expected in a shipment of 1000?

8) Jamie worked at an electronics store and earned $2388 for the first 2 months during the summer. What can he expect to earn for the entire 3 months, at that rate?

9) Jonah bought 48 comic books for $16. How many comic books can he buy if he has $12?

10) Jonelle drives 125 miles in 2 ½ hours. At the same rate, how far should she be able to travel in 6 hours?

11) One cantaloupe costs $.85. How much will 4 cantaloupes cost?

12) One carton of strawberries costs $2.50. How many cartons of strawberries can you buy for $10?

13) To determine the number of fish in a lake, a forest ranger tags 144 and releases them back into the lake. Later, 405 fish are caught, out of which 45 of them are tagged. Estimate how many fish are in the lake.

14) In the Picture Perfect problems, if the size of a rectangle is reduced to a height of 2 inches, what is the new width of this similar rectangle, if it was originally 24 in wide and 12 in tall?

Figure 3.11 Answers to Table 3.3

Table 3.3 Ratio Tables for Problem Solving

Encourage students to use ratio tables to solve these problems. Do problems A- C with the students if necessary. **The starting relationship is indicated.**

A. A jeep tour can accommodate 5 passengers. How many passengers can ride in n jeeps?

Jeep	1	2	3	4	7	10	n
Passengers	5	10	15	20	35	50	5n

B. 12 oz. of unpopped popcorn will make 6 cups of popped corn. How many cups of popcorn can n ounces of unpopped popcorn make?

Unpopped	1	2	6	12	24	40	n
Popped	$\frac{1}{2}$	1	3	6	12	20	$\frac{n}{2}$ or $\frac{1}{2}n$

C. 8 oz. of lemon concentrate will make 12 cups of lemonade. How many cups of lemonade can n ounces of concentrate make?

$\div 4$

Concentrate	$\frac{2}{3}$	1	2	8	12	20	n
Lemonade	1	$\frac{3}{2}$ or $1\frac{1}{2}$	3	12	18	30	$\frac{3}{2}n$

$\div 4$

D. 3 boys will eat 4 pizzas.

$\times 2$

Boys	1	$\frac{3}{4}$	3	6	9	15	n
Pizzas	$\frac{4}{3}$	1	4	8	12	20	$\frac{4}{3}n$

$\times 2$

Figure 3.12 Answers to Practice Problems

ADDITIONAL PRACTICE PROBLEMS *Answers will vary depending on choice of factors.*

1) A rainstorm produced a rainfall of 6 inches during the 4 hours it stormed. How many inches fell per hour?

Inches	6	3	1.5		
Hours	4	2	1		

2) A snowstorm dumped 9 inches of snow in a 12-hour period. How long should it take at that rate for a foot of snow to accumulate?

inches	9	3	12		
hours	12	4	16		

3) A piece of wire 15 cm long weighs 100 grams. What should a 9-cm length of the same wire weigh?

length	15	3	9		
height	100	20	60		

4) A worker can complete the assembly of 15 DVRs in 6 hours. At this rate, how many can the worker complete in a 40-hour work week?

DVRs	15	5	50	100	
hours	6	2	20	40	

5) Christine spends 17 hours in a 2-week period practicing her trumpet. How many hours does she practice in 5 weeks?

hours	17	8.5	42.5		
weeks	2	1	5		

(continued overleaf)

Figure 3.12 Continued

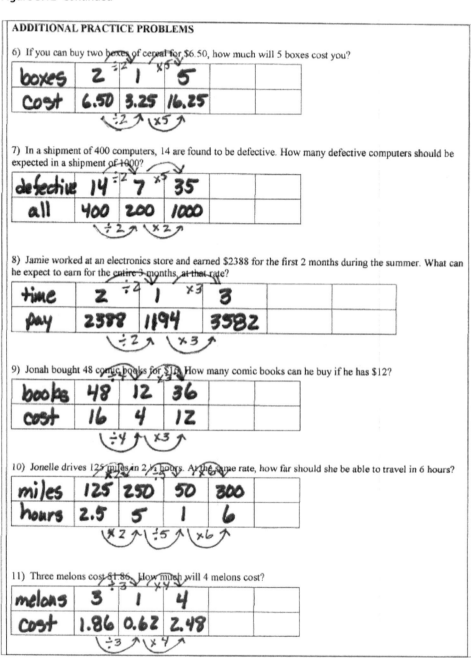

ADDITIONAL PRACTICE PROBLEMS

6) If you can buy two boxes of cereal for $6.50, how much will 5 boxes cost you?

boxes	2	1	5
cost	6.50	3.25	16.25

7) In a shipment of 400 computers, 14 are found to be defective. How many defective computers should be expected in a shipment of 1000?

defective	14	7	35
all	400	200	1000

8) Jamie worked at an electronics store and earned $2388 for the first 2 months during the summer. What can he expect to earn for the entire 3 months, at that rate?

time	2	1	3
pay	2388	1194	3582

9) Jonah bought 48 comic books for $16. How many comic books can he buy if he has $12?

books	48	12	36
cost	16	4	12

10) Jonelle drives 125 miles in 2 ½ hours. At the same rate, how far should she be able to travel in 6 hours?

miles	125	250	50	300
hours	2.5	5	1	6

11) Three melons cost $1.86. How much will 4 melons cost?

melons	3	1	4
cost	1.86	0.62	2.48

ADDITIONAL PRACTICE PROBLEMS

12) One carton of blueberries costs $1.25. How many cartons of blueberries can you buy for $10?

carton	1	2	4	8	
cost	1.25	2.50	5.00	10.00	

You can buy 8 cartons for $10.00.

13) One jar of hot fudge topping costs $1.50. How many jars can you buy for $12?

jar	1	2	8		
cost	1.50	3.00	12.00		

You can buy 8 jars for $10.00.

14) To determine the number of fish in a lake, a forest ranger tags 144 and releases them back into the lake. Later, 405 fish are caught, out of which 45 of them are tagged. Estimate how many fish are in the lake.

tagged	45	9	1	144	
all fish	405	81	9	1296	

There are about 1300 fish in the Lake.

15) Tremain reduced the size of a rectangle to a height of 2 in. What is the new width of this similar rectangle, if it was originally 24 in wide and 12 in tall?

width	24	4			
height	12	2			

The rectangle is now 4 in wide.

4

Laura Mullen: Learning Styles and Problem Solving

Oh it would be so nice if while doing all of this teaching I had more time to write about it in a form meaningful to others. I believe the NCTM and CCSSM Standards are here to provoke mathematical thinking in students and teachers alike. I chose this lesson because it generates a lot of information about the students' mathematical thinking that both students and teachers can discuss. In addition, this mathematical problem allows for many solutions that can be represented in various forms so that I can help all my students reach a level of success while engaging in lots of decision making.

(Lauren Mullen, seventh/eighth grade teacher,
Mount Nittany Middle School, Pennsylvania)

Imagine giving students a take home test on the very first day of class! How can any teacher do this and not promote or enhance whatever math anxieties students already have? Surprisingly, Laura's test is one that students appreciate and consider valuable to them, both during her mathematics class and years later. It is not a test to determine whether or not a student has a good or poor understanding of mathematics concepts. Rather, it consists of only one problem that aims to gain information on students' team role preferences as well students' approaches to solving a non-routine problem. The staircase problem (Figure 4.2) is one typically found in lessons on problem solving focusing on getting students to generate a table or list of examples for the purpose of finding a pattern or formula. Laura's application of this problem, however, has an important second focus. She writes,

> I use this problem on the first day of school to provide me with some personal information about my students' learning styles and cooperation gifts. Students often incorrectly assume that working as a group and a team are the same thing. However, when students are doing group work, I see them working towards a group goal. While they do individual and parallel work, they focus on solving a problem where they share ideas on interpretation, strategy and answers. On the other hand, students working as a team assume responsibility for solving a problem by sharing tasks and contributing a unique aspect to the process and presentation of the solution. I associate teamwork with role-playing and it is that which I hope to develop in my students so that they grow in their approaches to solving problems.

Preparatory Activities

To help students differentiate between groups and teams so that they can better play their team roles, Laura begins by explaining that not everyone is the quarterback on a football team, but everyone reads the same books in a book-sharing group. Also, she says that a team cannot go on without all its players, but a group can. She asks students to think of some elements that are critical to helping a team function successfully. Students mention that while members need to be patient with and respectful of each other, they must also be willing to contribute. "Contribution is certainly a critical factor. Knowing or understanding how you prefer to tackle a job is important to getting your best level of participation," she adds. "What are the ways that best help you to learn? How many of you learn best by reading the information from a book? How many of you prefer to try things out for yourselves?" she asks. Wanting to help students learn more about their preferred styles of learning so that they can develop skills necessary to successful teamwork, she engages students in a discussion on the seven styles of learning. A good resource she uses is the book, *Multiple Intelligences in the Classroom* by Thomas Armstrong.

Before assigning the staircase problem, she briefly describes each intelligence and asks students to identify which of seven multiple intelligences (MI) they think best promotes their own learning. She distributes a handout that describes each type:

1. Linguistic learners like to read, write and tell stories. They are good at memorizing details and learn best by saying, hearing and seeing words. They are, "Word Players."
2. Logical/mathematical learners like to experiment and explore patterns. They are good at mathematics and problem solving, and learn best by categorizing and working with abstract relationships. They are, "Questioners."
3. Spatial learners like to build things and look at pictures or movies. They are good at imagining things and making sense of charts and puzzles. They learn best by visualizing and working with pictures. They are, "Visualizers."
4. Musical learners like singing or playing a musical instrument. They are good at keeping time and picking up sounds. They learn best through activities involving aspects of music such as melody and they are, "Music Lovers."
5. Bodily/kinesthetic learners like talking or moving around. They are good at physical activities like sports, dance and acting. They learn best by touching, moving and interacting with space. They are, "Movers."
6. Interpersonal learners like to be around people and are pretty chatty. They are good at understanding and leading people. They learn best in cooperative sharing. They are, "Socializers."
7. Intrapersonal learners prefer to work alone and follow their own interests. They are good at being original and pursuing goals. They learn best working in individualized projects. They are, "Individuals."

It is not too difficult for students to quickly begin classifying themselves as "like this . . . but NOT like this." But some are confused because they find their style preference may depend on the subject. One student explains, "I think I learn well with visual representations in math, but I really prefer to learn by storytelling in social studies." Laura tells them that the human mind is too complex to be neatly categorized by any system. However, information on MI should provide them with a sense of their general learning preference and suggestions on how to cope when it may be in conflict with a teacher's instructional style.

Engaging Students

To exemplify for students the teamwork approach for applying MI to a task, Laura presents the following problem:

Five oranges and 10 apples cost $3.50, and one orange and one apple cost $.50. How much does an orange cost?

She asks: "Think of the ways different learners might approach this problem from a MI perspective." With her help, students suggest that the linguistic and interpersonal learners may prefer to begin discussing strategies; logical learners may begin working with the numbers first; spatial learners may prefer to draw a picture (as shown in Figure 4.1); kinesthetic learners may choose to use a manipulative to represent the apples and oranges and arrange them as in Figure 4.1; intrapersonal learners may ask for time to think alone before engaging in group discussion.

"But what about the musical learner?" a student asks. Students learn that not all styles can be easily represented all the time in all problems. However, Laura stresses that now that they have ideas about their preferred styles, they are empowered to think of ways to make learning and studying meaningful. Thus, having an idea of their preferred learning style should not be used as an excuse not to learn, but as an opportunity to learn more about *how* they learn. For homework, she has students write about the learning style they think best represents their way of tackling problems and to test this by doing Investigation 1 shown in Figure 4.2.

Investigation 1 – The staircase problem
  Given a staircase with five steps composed of 15 blocks, create a presentation for three ways to find the number of blocks required for

Figure 4.1

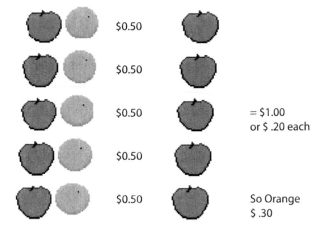

Total $2.50

Figure 4.2 The Staircase Problem

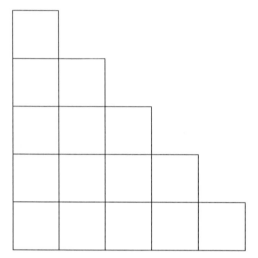

a staircase with 100 steps. Use whatever tools will help you: calculators, computer spreadsheet, or manipulatives such as rainbow cubes.

The next day, Laura collects the test so that she can gain as much information about her students' learning style as possible. For the next two classes, she uses this information to assign students to teams to work on an investigation. Whenever possible, she creates teams of seven students, one representing each intelligence. If this is not possible, for teams of six, she asks the intrapersonal and interpersonal students to choose one of those intelligences; for teams of five, the linguistic and musical are also combined. In all cases, students are asked to play the role of a type of intelligence and the first time they try, decision making is hard, even though Laura has clearly defined the roles as given below:

◆ The linguistic and musical students are in charge of determining the presentation of the problem.
◆ The logical/mathematical, spatial, and kinesthetic students are in charge of the three solutions. The students playing these roles begin to solve the problem, while the rest of the team discusses their contributions to the presentation and solution process.
◆ The interpersonal students are the taskmasters in charge of keeping everyone on schedule and happy. These students often pair up with one of the solution finders to help them work out a good solution. Sometimes they will explain what another student did. Sometimes

they may also decide who will be in what roles. Some students interpret this role as a secretary recording what is going on and who's doing what.

◆ The intrapersonal students are in charge of checking the validity of the three solutions.

Laura circulates around the room as the students work. She observes and notes quite a bit of interesting information about her students. She uses a checklist chart with the MI on the left and she records which role students choose on the right. This information will also help her in assigning students' roles throughout the year. She observes that students do not always stay true to the character of the role (which she thinks is fine) but she still holds them accountable for fulfilling the duties of the role. For example, if the solution person cannot solve it by drawing pictures, he/she may ask for help from others but is still in charge of recording the solution.

As she expected, students approach the problem from different perspectives. Some use numerical models and others use geometric ones; some create tables and search for patterns; others assume that the staircase is a triangle and apply the area formula to get (.5)(100*100); still others apply brute force by either adding all the numbers on a calculator or by taping many pieces of graph paper together to facilitate their count. Not surprisingly, lots of mistakes occur.

In all cases, Laura challenges students to try and find a general rule or formula that may justify their answer. Because the scoring rubric (see Figure 4.3) assigns points for varying degrees of success with the problem and the use of more than one approach, it plays an important part in encouraging students to pursue not only a solution but also to go the "extra mile" by continuing to think about the problem after they have found an answer. Thus, Laura observes that some groups do present multiple ways for getting examples to generate patterns. One group pleasantly surprised her by including the process of revising the work in the presentation. That group noticed that the sum of numbers from 1 to 10 is 55, and wrote "but 10 *55 will not give you the answer because 11 to 20 = 155 and so on." She writes: "Wow! By doing so, they actually realize that the thought process is worthy enough to be documented!" Other groups include prescriptive strategies helpful to deciding when a particular method works best. For example, contrary to what some students did, one group recommended using a calculator to find the sum manually only if the number of steps is *small*. Still others use the computer to write a simple basic program to recursively add the numbers, or to copy and paste squares to draw a staircase.

Figure 4.3 Assessment Scoring Rubric

---

5 Exemplary Response
- Successful strategy, complete, with clear explanations.
- Shows understanding of the mathematical concepts and procedures.
- Satisfies all essential conditions of the problem.
- Goes the "extra mile" by going beyond what is asked for in some unique way.

4 Complete Response
- Potentially successful strategy with clear explanations; may have minor miscalculation.
- Shows understanding of most of mathematical concepts and procedures.
- Satisfies all essential conditions of the problem.

3 Reasonably Complete Response
- Good start on a strategy, may lack detail in explanations.
- Shows understanding of most of the mathematical concepts and procedures.
- Satisfies some essential conditions of the problem.

2 Partial Response
- Start of a strategy; explanation may be unclear or lack detail.
- Shows some understanding of most of the mathematical concepts and procedures.
- Satisfies some essential conditions of the problem.

1 Inadequate Response
- Incomplete; explanation is insufficient or not understandable.
- Shows little understanding of the mathematical concepts and procedures.
- Fails to address essential conditions of the problem.

Laura observes how well students understand the concepts or follow through on their roles during each group's presentation of strategies and solutions. Depending on solutions presented, Laura follows with a second investigation consisting of a related example to enrich and highlight possible approaches to the problem.

Investigation 2
For each of the three examples to follow:

1. Read each team's approach to the staircase problem.
2. Describe the method in words.
3. Try to draw a model to represent the method.
4. Use the method to compute the number of blocks in 50 steps. Justify your thinking.
5. Try to use a pattern to discover a formula for the method.

Example 1

One team used the following method for finding the number of blocks in a 100-step staircase:

$(1 + 100) = 101$
$(2 + 99) = 101$
$(3 + 98) = 101$
$(4 + 97) = 101$

The team continued in a similar way to get $(50 + 51) = 101$ and concluded that $(101) \times 50 = 5050$. Thus a 100-step staircase has 5050 blocks.

Example 2

Another team represented the problem as shown in Figure 4.4.

In the review of the first two examples, Laura asks students to explain *what* the numbers represent and *why* the method works. This requirement forces students to think about the connections between the models and the numbers, a very crucial step towards algebraic thinking. In example 2, students are not quick to see that the numbers connect to the length and width of a rectangle. To help them understand why N steps has (N)(N+1)/2 blocks, she has students complete a table for simpler rectangles, count the number of blocks, compare the length and width of the sides, and then to try the area formula to see what modification is necessary to yield the number of blocks. Once students do so for four or five models, she focuses attention on the dimensions and has students represent the dimensions using N. Next she has them apply the area formula and finally compare the formula's answer to

Figure 4.4 One Group's Approach to the Staircase Problem

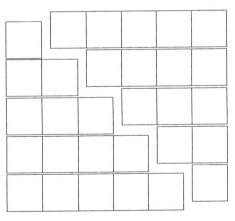

We created a rectangle by fitting two of the staircases together.
Therefore,

100 x 101 = 10100, and
10100/2 = 5050

the actual work done with the simpler models. She asks students to determine what should be done to the formula to get the answer (see Figures 4.5 and 4.6). Interestingly, even after having gone through this process, some students will still think that the answer for 50 steps results from simply taking the answer for 100 steps and dividing by 2. When this happens, Laura tells them to test their theories, write about their strategies and rationales in their journals and state how their ideas connect to what happened in class.

In example 3, she presents yet another application, but this time from an historical approach.

Figure 4.5 Table for Discovering Formula for the Staircase Problem

Complete the table (the first two rows are already done for you).

# Steps	Stairs	Rectangle	Width	Length	Area of rectangle	Number of blocks	Compare number of blocks to area of rectangle
1	□	□	1	1	1	1	$1 = 1$
2			2	3	6	3	$3 = 6/2$
3			3	4	12	6	$6 = 12/2$
4			4	5		10	
5							$15 = 30/2$
N	...N	..?	N			Call it B	

Does the formula you found for B also work for N= 1?

Figure 4.6 Answers for Table 4.5

# Steps	Stairs	Rectangle	Width	Length	Area of rectangle	Number of blocks	Compare number of blocks to area of rectangle
1	□	□	1	1	1	1	1 = 1
2			2	3	6	3	3 = 6/2
3			3	4	12	6	6 = 12/2
4			4	5	20	10	20 = 10/2
5			5	6	30	15	15 = 30/2
N	N	...?	N	N+1	N(N+1)	Call it B	B = N(N+1)/2

Verify your formula for N = 1 to 5.

Example 3

Here's a true historical story: To keep students quiet while the teacher completed work at her desk, young Karl Gauss' (1777–1855) class was given the task of finding the sum of all the consecutive numbers from 1 to 100. Karl stunned his teacher by quickly doing it in his head. How do you think he did it?

Students never fail to seriously suggest that Gauss probably used a calculator! Part of the next day's homework requires students to develop and test their conjectures, and to find the date for when a handheld calculator was invented.

Students' results show that most do not readily connect this problem to the staircase investigation. But Laura expects this and writes, "I want to get a picture of the student who does make connections and the student who does not, and to then use this information to help them continue to grow from their level of understanding."

It is evident that Laura is clear about what she wants to assess in her students and that the resulting information from their performances informs how and what she teaches next.

Discussion Between Colleagues

In general, what does a typical day in your class look like?

A typical day—this is middle school so not much is typical, but below are some general approaches I use:

(a) We discover some things through questions like: How would you add 100 numbers? How would you find the area? How would you compare video stores for the best price?

(b) I have them memorize some things: "Look how products of consecutive numbers are represented." "Oh, just memorize 1/4 = .25 because you'll see it again and you should not have to reinvent this every time. You deserve to have things easy." "Get to know five mathematicians because they merit it. How many are women?" "Memorize as many digits of pi as you can, because, you can."

(c) We tell some things: "How do they find deer populations?" How can we represent large numbers?"

(d) We try whatever works to understand some things: "Try it on the spreadsheet." "Use a table, graph it, draw a picture." "Turn it around ten times and try it again." All the while it is important to note that we make *decisions* about all things. It is also each student's job to contribute ideas to the class and discuss his/her choice of method. I often redirect class by asking kids to paraphrase and use statements like "Marie has contributed the idea that . . . is there anyone . . ." "What would you like to contribute?" "If we look at the ideas Tiana's and Justin's team contributed . . ." "I can't hear what Joseph is trying to contribute." To the extent students often raise their hands and start their sentences with "I would like to contribute . . ." these "contributions" are often what students can add to their written responses to get a five-point response on our rubric.

What classroom procedures and arrangement foster your students' learning?

On classroom procedures, students enter class and have assignments on an assignment section of the board. They are given a math notebook for each unit and complete a table of contents of their notebook with references to each numbered page. Notebooks include activities, notes, journals, homework etc. and are graded. Students have the option to organize the notebook in a way that will be useful for them. Students have bins of materials and computers available to them at any time. It is their choice to get up and get rainbow cubes, number cubes, multilink cubes, pattern blocks, string, scissors, rulers and/or tracers whenever they think it will help their pursuit of a mathematical question. The idea is for students to easily access material and information. Sometimes the seats are in a large circle and other times in groups. The seats are so arranged so that groups, partners and teams can change every two or three weeks.

Comment more on how your student's adhered to the roles connected to their learning styles.

Students do not always adhere to their roles while they work in their groups because some mathematical problems lend themselves to various roles. For example, musical talent was not easily applied to the staircase problem, unless you like "Building a staircase to Heaven" 45 times a day. However, students made those decisions and contributed in other ways, like helping another fulfill his/her role. Again the idea of roles is to allow students to value individual contributions and to try to view ideas from many angles.

How do you use the information you gathered on students' learning styles in future lessons?

Information of learning styles can help me make decisions about forming partners, or types of groups to cooperatively work on a project or task. It can also help me make decisions on how to present a problem so that more students can be successful.

What is your general approach to assessment? Do you use traditional assessment? If so, to assess which kinds of skills or concepts?

In general, I assess students through group presentation, participation with partner/class, journal reflections, and individual and group test. Students also use self-evaluation on journal entries, presentations (formal and informal) and homework using the scoring rubric. I do whatever I can to get information on student thinking to share with students, parents and any other interested person. I look to the objectives and outcomes of the Connected Math Project units and our units as guidance. We take individual tests to view problem solving, application and use of skills or concepts. We take group tests to learn test-taking strategies and assess ability to use team skills. We do group projects, partner projects, and individual projects to apply concepts and skills, make mathematical connections, and make real life connections. There are student-evaluated assignments, teacher evaluated assignments, and group evaluated assignments. We often create a system like the five-point response (scoring rubric) to assess these assignments. Since so much of the information on these assignments is in written form, I turn for help to the English Teacher. I learned that in my students' English class, they use FCAs (focus correction areas) to help assess writing. I think about FCAs that I am interested in when I assess in math. For example, one can see lots of math in the staircase problem but I try to focus assessment and comments on strategy, and process and not just calculation and answer. Those FCAs change for other problems.

I send home progress reports every four weeks, give students reports about every two weeks, and students have access to their grades at any time. The reports are organized by exams, group tests, homework, notebooks, projects, team projects, and other, so students can see strengths and weaknesses in these areas of performance. I use a grade program to organize these grades, I send home postcards for excellence in work or behavior, make celebration calls, contribute to the team newspaper, write math letters for each unit to better inform students and parents of our endeavor. In order to assess learning, we often seek answers to the question: "Is it not working because of lack of effort or lack of understanding?" With the help of my team of teachers, we try to create a "no excuses" environment. Students are held accountable for their success. My students will study and will be held accountable. If my students don't do homework, I call home. If my students forget their calculator, they come to tutoring and I sometimes rotely teach them the square root algorithm, long division, etc. Any single one of these things certainly has faults, but together it gives us a lot of interventions to help kids succeed.

Laura, this seems like a huge amount of work. What support do you get to do it all?
With the help of my interdisciplinary team consisting of teachers in the areas of math, science, English, social studies, art/music, a cooperative math department and district in-servicing for curriculum and technology, I can communicate with my students in a number of ways.

Where do you search for rich problems?
I use the NSF funded middle grades curriculum called Connected Mathematics Project (CMP) and some interdisciplinary projects. In addition, I attend at least one NCTM conference every year, read my

Mathematics Teacher and, Teaching in the Middle School journals religiously. We have one math meeting per six-day cycle to discuss ideas with math teachers and four team meetings to discuss ideas with other teachers. I coach MATHCOUNTS and sit down and do the problems with my team. I have math activities and chess club and play math games with my students. I take courses, join curriculum writing committees, and use my own problems sometimes to generate problems. However, my richest problems come straight from my students. For example, in the computer lab one of my students asked, "How could we show the population densities we computed on a map of the United States?" Students began the pursuit and were making dots, using shades, resizing states to represent population density size instead of square miles, and of course writing the numbers on the map too.

Can you suggest ways for extending this lesson to students in special populations?
These investigations are adaptable using models, and visual cues and partners. For my ESL students I find I often have to act things out or create a model. The staircase can easily be built for students and they can be led to organize sums in a table. One of my students helped Enrique understand the problem by numbering the blocks, 1, 2, 3, 4, etc. and using his fingers to take steps up the staircase. He created several staircases and asked, "How many steps?" Once the definition of steps was understood, the problem became accessible to Enrique.

Any further tips for readers?
I have a word of caution for the Gauss problem given in example 3. Most teachers might prefer to use it as a nice historical introduction to the staircase problem. The first time I tried to do so, there was one student who thought to do it like the staircase problem, and 123 students who merely applied brute force by trying to add the numbers. Gauss' story mentioned addition so students did just that—added. Next time around, I saved Gauss' story for last. Since the staircase form of the problem merely asks for the number blocks, students presented more than just addition as a strategy. Keeping Gauss' story last works better because I can then see which students can connect what we did in class to the story without inadvertently stifling creativity.

Tell us about your school's minority participation in your classes. Do you notice any differences in their performances in this lesson?
The largest barriers to high performance in my math class, especially since the adoption of CMP, has been language because of the amounts of

reading and writing. In addition to any adaptations I make, our school has an ESL teacher, a learning support teacher and a communication teacher to help adapt materials for students with reading or writing difficulties. I find any of the adaptations requiring more models, visual cues and partners, are helpful for every student and do not limit the use of these ideas to a select few. We thrive because of our differences, not in spite of them.

Commentary

Laura's dual application of a problem to gain insights not only on her students' problem-solving skills but also on their learning styles underlies how mathematics can be made accessible to all students. The different approaches taken by her students also reveal how necessary it is for students to have multiple representations of an idea in order to build solid conceptual understanding.

Her investigations have characteristics important to reaching all students because they are conducive to students' use of multiple ways to express their knowledge, thus tapping into students' preferred mode for learning. The fact that students can choose which manipulatives to use (MP4—use of models, MP5—use tools strategically) and are encouraged to express their formulas in words, numbers, or algebraic symbols, invites students to move from a concrete example to higher levels requiring greater and greater degrees of abstraction (MP2—reason abstractly, MP8—repeated reasoning). Letting students know that their ideas and learning preferences are valued increases the likelihood that lower achieving students will feel safe enough to share their own ideas, while encouraging higher achieving students to take greater risks (NCTM's Equity).

I was most impressed with Laura's use of knowledge of the learning styles of her students to guide her instructions. In a class of students with varying abilities, teachers adhering to the Standards typically create lessons with a variety of activities to accommodate different learning styles. But what does a teacher do when she/he knows the actual *specifics* of the learning preferences of each student in the class? How teachers use that knowledge may differ. Some may continue teaching in same manner and tell students that it is *their* responsibility to use that knowledge to enhance learning. This warns the student that if he/she has a teacher who lectures often, but he/she prefers to work hands-on, then some learning problems may ensue and it becomes the student's responsibility to apply strategies for coping and succeeding in the course. Others, like Laura, may decide to make a conscious effort to help students develop the coping strategies. When she says "I try to get them to see things from many angles," or when she purposely varies the roles they play in teams, she is helping students develop strengths in a different learning style. This practice is crucial if students are to succeed in becoming flexible thinkers with the ability to process information from various sources or modes of delivery (MP1—Problem solving). For readers interested in knowing about students learning preferences, there are web pages with learning style questions for students to answer online (e.g. www.berghuis.co.nz/abiator/lsi/lsitest1.html). The answers are processed immediately to give a student an idea of his/her styles together with suggestions on how best to learn under adverse conditions. These resources, together with Laura's approach for helping students understand particular learning styles, are necessary to helping students take responsibility for their own learning while simultaneously reducing the levels of mathematics anxiety.

An issue raised by Laura is language as a barrier to students' high performance because of the amount of reading and writing. Unfortunately, this is a problem for all students—not just LEP or low performing students. In his must-read book, entitled *The Problem with Math is English*, Molina (2012) writes,

> Language struggles are embedded in mathematics, which in many ways is its own language. These problems often occur at the critical juncture of math instruction and content. Two major issues that result for this merger and directly address MP6 which is precision: (1) the languages and symbolism of mathematics, which in turn greatly influence (2) the mathematics itself—the content we teach—and by association, how we communicate that content. (p. 1)

Molina writes that it is not only a math vocabulary problem, but also careless use of vocabulary; math symbolism; naked numbers—which is the use of numbers void of context, descriptors or units; multiple meanings and redundant terms, and, interpretation of a problem and its context. He provides research-based strategies for teachers to help students develop a deep understanding of the most troublesome areas of mathematics, as well as the mathematics language and representations so that students can "make enlightened connections" (p. 187).

Laura's students are fortunate in that she is attentive to and aware of their needs to understand the language of mathematics and that the school has support to help students do that.

Unit Overview

Problem Solving and Learning Styles

Aim: How can we solve a problem in more than one way?

Objective: Students will apply multiple strategies requiring different representations for solving a problem.

Grade Level: 6th, 7th

Source: Original

Number of 45-minute periods: 2–3

CCSSM Content: Number and Operations: 6.NS.4; 6EE. (1. 2. 3. 4. 9), 7EE.2. GEOMETRY: 6.G.1, 7G.6; Functions: 8.F.(.2.3)

CCSSM Mathematical Practices: MP1: Problem solving, MP2: Reasoning, MP4: Modeling, MP5: Use of tools; MP8: Repeated reasoning

Prerequisites: Students can perform basic operations and apply area formulas for rectangles and triangles.

Mathematical Content: Students develop, explain and apply strategies for adding consecutive integers through numerical, tabular, algebraic and geometric representations.

Materials and Tools:

- ◆ A description of the seven learning styles.
- ◆ A statement of the staircase problem.
- ◆ Assessment Rubric (Table 1).
- ◆ Spreadsheet program.
- ◆ Rainbow cubes or other cubes that lock onto each other.

Management Procedures:

- ◆ Discuss the seven learning styles.
- ◆ Ask each student to pick the style that best represents him or her.
- ◆ Present the staircase problem.

- ◆ Assign students to groups of four and describe their roles according to their learning style.
- ◆ Have students do the problem and present their approaches.

Assessment:

- ◆ Assign students to complete investigation.
- ◆ Note the processes they apply and how they communicate their ideas.
- ◆ Assessment rubric.

5

Thomas Wright: Making Sense of the Pythagorean Theorem

The many hats that I wear as teacher and chair of mathematics at my middle school as well as a university faculty of mathematics education courses, provide unique opportunities for me to transform theory into practice. I really believe that I have the best of both worlds. Working with adolescents grounds me through the day-to-day challenges and rewards of teaching middle schoolers while informing my teaching of university students from a practical level—it's not just pie-in-the-sky theory; I'm living what I teach every single day. The trends in pedagogical content knowledge that I embrace as a teacher and university professor all translate into the best practices for teaching mathematics to university students from early childhood through high school and college. My roles complement each other and I wouldn't want to do one without the other.

(Thomas D. Wright, Ph.D., Edward Hynes Charter School, New Orleans, Louisiana)

Thomas is what one calls a real "go-getter." He entered as a full-time student in the Ph.D. program at the University of New Orleans and earned his degree by the end of his second year. I was fortunate to be his major professor and to have him as my research assistant during that time. Coming from the software development world and wishing to have real-life experiences as a teacher before seeking an administrative or university position, Thomas applied for and received an appointment to teach at Hynes Charter School.

He loves doing that! His care for students and exemplary teaching soon earned him the teacher of the year award for Orleans Parish. This unit on the Pythagorean Theorem demonstrates how he structures his lessons and class to maximize learning.

At the beginning of the school year, Thomas began reviewing the Common Core State Standards for the eighth grade and decided that he would take an investigative approach to teaching lessons on the Pythagorean Theorem that drew upon the students' creative and artistic abilities. "Many of my students are in the talented art program so I frequently like to do investigations that will draw on these aptitudes and interests," he says.

Thomas designed the unit to answer the following question: How can we use properties of right triangles to compute areas? Note that he did not mention Pythagorean Theorem since he did not want to give the concept away. The students already had an understanding of square roots and how to find the area of rectangles and squares so he began the lesson with a do-now or warm-up activity that served to review these necessary skills for understanding the theorem (see the Unit Overview). After discussing formula for both the area of a rectangle and a square, Thomas had the students use graph paper to construct a square of side 6 units so that they were ready to think about the formula for finding the area of a square as side-squared (s^2). He guided them to see this abstractness with the following discussion:

Thomas: What is the simplest way to write the formula of a rectangle?

Clintt: The simplest way is length times width.

Thomas: Using variables only, what is its formula?

Mallory: The formula of a rectangle is l times w.

Thomas: Do we have to use the letters l and w?

Clintt: No, we don't have to use those letters, but it makes sense since they represent the rectangle's length and width.

Thomas: That makes sense. Since we have options on which letters to choose for a variable, we might as well choose those that connect to the problem. Ok, what about the formula of a square, using only variables?

Caroline: The formula of the square is also l times w.

Thomas: D'Accord. Do we have to use l and w? Does a square have any different or more unique characteristics than a rectangle?

Clark: The square's sides are equal . . . so . . . we could use s times s, for "side."

Sydney: But instead of saying "s times s?" we could say, "s-squared."

Thomas: Okay. Now follow me here: Again, *could* we use any letter we want?

Clay: Yes because it is a variable.

Thomas: So we could call it something like *a*-squared, or *b*-squared, or *c*-squared if we had three separate squares for which we wanted to denote the formulas.

Thomas next focused attention on the class's vocabulary wall of words that will facilitate students' use of the important vocabulary terms for the day: leg, hypotenuse, right triangle, area. At the end of the lesson, the Pythagorean Theorem would be included. Thomas organized his students in teams and discussed the specific roles of: Task Master, Organizer, Recorder and Checker. (Each student's role changes weekly and is based on the student's desk number.) Students were ready to begin their exploration project. The team Organizer retrieved the buckets which were arranged ahead of time. Included in the buckets were the lab sheet with directions for the activity; the lab packet, on which the students would record their work and answer probing questions at the end; construction paper; glue; and markers.

Launch

Once the Organizers returned to their tables and distributed the materials, Thomas had a student read the launch for the lesson which was on the board:

> The new triangular garden in the neutral ground outside our classroom window measures 15 yd by 20 yd. The contractors want to pour a concrete square that runs the length of the hypotenuse. If they have enough cement for 600 sq.yd. of concrete, do they have just enough, too little, or too much? Draw a picture and solve the problem. Answer the problem using complete sentences.

He told the students that the investigation is about comparing areas on the sides of a right triangle, and that they'd have to decide which two media would work best for this investigation in order to explore and answer the launch. The choices were Cheez-Its, washers, Cheerios, flat marbles, Base-10 unit blocks, and graph paper. The teams discussed which they would like to use and came up with a first choice and an alternate. Thomas also instructed them to discuss their reasoning: "Why are you choosing this for your first choice, and your second choice?" In order to remain fair, he used the random number generator on the Promethean board to select the order teams would go to choose materials. Once done, Thomas questioned the teams to determine the reasons for their choices.

Thomas:	Blue Smurfs, why did you choose the Cheez-Its?
Lori:	We chose the Cheez-Its because they were square, we were measuring squares, and we could snack on the leftover materials as we work.
Thomas:	[*Astonished that middle schoolers would be hungry right before lunch*] Thank you for sharing. Jolly Green Giants, why did you choose Base-10 Unit blocks?
Will:	We chose Unit blocks because we were filling in the areas of squares. That means that if we're filling in squares, we ought to use squares.
Thomas:	Thank you for sharing. Red Rangers, why did you choose Cheerios?
Brenda:	We chose Cheerios because we knew that they would be small enough to completely cover the area of the square, and that we could break them into pieces if we needed to. Oh, and we're hungry too; we wanted a snack.
Thomas:	[*Not believing his ears that adolescents have a high metabolism and eat often and a lot*] Thank you for sharing. Purple Pirates, why did you choose the graph paper?
Rosalyn:	We chose the graph paper because we wanted to have our 90-degree angles drawn for us. We also knew that the graph paper's squares would be more accurate. We can also cut the squares into smaller pieces if needed.
Thomas:	Thank you for sharing. Brown Bandits, why did you choose the flat marbles?
Clintt:	Well, since we were second-to-last, we figured the flat marbles were better suited to the project than those big washers.
Thomas:	Why is that?
Clintt:	The flat marbles were better suited to the project than the washers because they are smaller than the washers. We think the smaller the media are, the more control we have over how they cover the squares we cut. I mean, we can use more and fit them in more tightly. Also, they're closer in shape to a square, whereas the washers are clearly round.
Thomas:	Thank you for sharing.

The Task Master of each team began reading the lab directions and questions to each of the members. After each member reviews the team rubric expectations (see Figure 5.3) and the rubric for group presentation (see Figure 5.4), teammates began working on their project. Again, the Task Master will ensure that everyone stays on task; the Checker will ensure that everyone in the group has participated and comes to a consensus, and that what is being evaluated is recorded for the oral presentation at the end.

Figure 5.1

Lab Directions

1. Using your straight edge, construct a right triangle on the graph paper and cut the triangle out. Label one leg *a*, one leg *b*, and the hypotenuse *c*. Using your glue stick, paste the triangle on the middle of your construction paper. Write your name in marker at the top of your construction paper.

2. Using the length of each leg and the hypotenuse of the right triangle, construct three squares that correspond to the length of each side of the triangle. Make sure you use your straight edge. Cut the squares out and paste them on the construction paper, *connecting* them to their matching side of the right triangle.

3. Using a marker, label the squares and their matching sides of the triangle "a," "b," and "c."

4. Arrange your medium (e.g., Cheez-Its, Cheerios, washers, flat marbles, Base-10 unit cubes, squares from the graph paper) on the smaller two squares so that the squares are completely covered. Next to each square, write the number of objects it took to cover each square.

5. Reseal the source container (Zip-Lock) and return it to your team bucket before going on to the next step.

6. Move as much of the media as you can from the smaller two squares to the largest square. Next to the largest square, write the number of media it took to cover the square.

Figure 5.2

Lab Questions

Discuss the answers to these questions with your team members. Using your 3×5 index card, write a few key points from your Team Talk discussion and be prepared to present your investigation findings to the entire class.

1.   Why did your team choose that particular medium for this investigation?

2.   What is the hypotenuse always labeled? Which leg is "a" and which is "b"? Does it matter which is which? How do you know which is the hypotenuse? Does it matter if you use another label (or variable) for the hypotenuse?

3.   What are we demonstrating when we cover the squares with the media? What do we do if the medium doesn't completely cover the square or if the medium hangs over the side? Mathematically speaking, how do we account for that? What does that have to do with the preciseness of answers in mathematics?

4.   Think back to Do Now problem #7 at the beginning of class. Think about the length of each of the three squares. What can you conclude? In specific, how do the areas of the two smaller squares relate to the area of the largest square? What is your evidence?

Figure 5.3 Rubric Student Engagement During Team Talk Rubric

	3	2	1	0
Team Work	Almost always listens to, shares with, and supports the efforts of others. Tries to keep people working well together.	Usually listens to, shares with, and supports the efforts of others. Does not cause disturbances in the group.	Often listens to, shares with, and supports the efforts of others, but sometimes is not a good team member.	Rarely listens to, shares with, and supports the efforts of others. Often is not a good team player.
Contributions	Routinely provides useful ideas when participating in the group and in classroom discussion. A definite leader who contributes a lot of effort.	Usually provides useful ideas when participating in the group and in classroom discussion. A strong group member who tries hard!	Sometimes provides useful ideas when participating in the group and in classroom discussion. A satisfactory group member who puts forth minimal effort.	Rarely provides useful ideas when participating in the group and in classroom discussion. May refuse to participate.

(continued overleaf)

Figure 5.3 Continued

	3	2	1	0
Quality of Work	Provides work of the highest quality. Provides concrete examples as evidence.	Provides high quality work. Usually right on target. Usually provides evidence.	Provides work that occasionally needs to be checked/ redone by other group members to ensure quality. Occasionally needs reminding to provide concrete evidence.	Provides work that usually needs to be checked/ redone by others to ensure quality. Does not provide evidence for conclusions.
Problem-solving	Actively looks for and suggests solutions to problems.	Refines solutions suggested by others.	Does not suggest or refine solutions, but is willing to try out solutions suggested by others.	Does not try to solve problems or help others solve problems. Lets others do the work.
Attitude	Never is publicly critical of the project or the work of others. Always has a positive attitude about the task(s).	Rarely is publicly critical of the project or the work of others. Often has a positive attitude about the task(s).	Occasionally is publicly critical of the project or the work of other members of the group. Usually has a positive attitude about the task(s).	Often is publicly critical of the project or the work of other members of the group. Often has a negative attitude about the task(s).
Focus on the task	Consistently stays focused on the task and what needs to be done. Very self-directed.	Focuses on the task and what needs to be done most of the time. Other group members can count on this person.	Focuses on the task and what needs to be done some of the time. Other group members must sometimes nag, prod, and remind to keep this person on-task.	Rarely focuses on the task and what needs to be done. Lets others do the work.
Preparedness	Brings needed materials to class and is always ready to work.	Almost always brings needed materials to class and is ready to work.	Almost always brings needed materials but sometimes needs to settle down and get to work.	Often forgets needed materials or is rarely ready to get to work.

Figure 5.4 Presentation Rubric

Think-And-Connect Rubric for Team Presentation

Points	Indicator
100 points	The presentation findings are correct and the students show evidence from the experiment. The presentation is given in full sentences with appropriate question stems included.
90 points	The presentation findings are correct, but non-compelling/incorrect evidence is given. The presentation is given in full sentences with appropriate question stems included.
70–80 points	The presentation findings are correct, but there is no evidence that supports the findings.
60 points	The presentation findings are incorrect.

Comments:

Explore

The teams set to work creating their right triangles following the instructions and as Thomas circulated, he noticed that this was not easy for many of them. Some read and re-read the directions to make sense of what the variables actually meant and how to construct a square, in spite of the initial class discussion. Doing their best to cut and paste their squares on the graph paper, some realized after having pasted the squares on legs of their right triangle, there was not enough space to place the square on the hypotenuse; others begin wishing that they had chosen a different medium because they saw too many gaps in their squares; some were on their way to seeing the relationships that would lead to the theorem. In addition to monitoring the rubric for each group, helping students understand that the term "a^2" represented the area of the square on the leg labeled "a" was Thomas's goal as he circulated.

Data Sharing

After teams gathered their data, Thomas invited each person to visit each of the different teams. His goal was to have them see the results for the different materials and to have students questions and communicate information. He said, "When I call numbers, move to the team I say and visit that team.

Figure 5.5 Table Summarizing Team Results

Medium	Number of Objects in Square A	Number of Objects in Square B	Number of Objects in Square C	$a^2 + b^2$
Cheez-Its	9	16	≈25	25
Cheerios	≈45	≈23	≈72	≈68
Flat Marbles	≈18	≈18	≈32	≈36
Washers	None of the five teams chose this medium.			
Base-10 Unit Cubes	81	36	≈117	117
Graph Paper	36	49	85	85

Each of you should pick a different person to ask for information. Record what you've found in the table on the board. Start with your own information" (see Figure 5.5, which also contains student data that was not there for students). As the exploration drew to a close, the students were asked to make sure that each of the items in the presentation rubric was addressed (see Figure 5.4). Each of the teams presented their findings and responded to questions about their data. The question-and-answer dialog follows.

Thomas: Okay, let's just go in order, starting with the Cheez-Its. I know you've had time to collaborate with your team members to come up with a consensus of your findings and conclusions.

Brendan: We covered our first square with 9 Cheez-Its. We covered our second square with 16 Cheez-Its. We found that $a^2 + b^2 = 25$. It took approximately 25 Cheez-Its to cover the largest square.

Thomas: Why do you say "approximately?"

Lori: We said "approximately" because some of the Cheez-Its varied slightly in size. Plus, since we had to construct the hypotenuse of the triangle based on the two legs, its length didn't turn out to be the exact length of x-number of Cheez-Its. So we had to break them to fit as best as we could.

Thomas: Thank you for sharing. Next, we have the Cheerios.

Rosalyn: Cheerios taste great but don't have a very consistent shape. Even with breaking them to fit inside the crevices and between the circular shapes, we still were only able to estimate how many it would take to *actually* cover the first two squares.

Thomas: Let's hear from another team member. How many did it take to cover the two smaller squares and then the largest square?

Brenda: It took about 45 to cover Square A and around 23 to cover Square B. We found that $a^2 + b^2 \approx 68$. We said "approximately equal to" because neither 45 nor 23 were exact.

Thomas: That makes sense. As long as you have a sound mathematical reasoning for justifying your steps. Someone else, how many Cheerios did it take to cover the largest square?

Clintt: It took around 72. Even though we had to break the Cheerios into pieces to cover all of the space, we think that we made a good estimation—at least the best we could do given the Cheerios.

Thomas: You mean you wouldn't have chosen Cheerios if you'd been able to go first?

Clay: No, we wouldn't have. The Cheerios were circular and we were measuring squares so that was not easy.

Thomas: Thank you for sharing. Next let's hear from the team with the flat marbles.

Caroline: We wouldn't have chosen these either had we had the chance to choose first.

Thomas: Why is that?

Caroline: Just like Clay said: We're filling up squares and we're using circular flat marbles to fill in a square shape. It didn't give us a very accurate measurement.

Thomas: Fair enough. Sounds like it made you do some thinking though. Let's hear from someone else. What did y'all find?

Clark: Well, it took us around 18 flat marbles to completely cover each square. We drew a scalene right triangle. Like they were saying, we had some of the marbles hanging over the side of the squares we'd drawn.

Thomas: Why didn't you lop part of them off to make them fit?

All: [*blank stares*]

Thomas: Or, better yet, what could you have done to make sure at least two of the squares would have allowed the flat marbles to fit perfectly?

Will: We could have used the marbles to figure out the length of the first two legs and then drawn them to that length?

Thomas: What good would that do?

Will: We wouldn't have had the marbles hanging out of the squares or not completely filling up the lengths as much as possible.

Thomas:	Sounds like you're on to something. Maybe taking your time in the beginning and do a little extra planning. Let's hear from someone else. Explain to me what you wrote in the last two columns of the table.
Laurie:	We found that $a^2 + b^2 = 36$. But, it only took 32 of the marbles to completely cover the largest square.
Thomas:	So how do you account for that?
Laurie:	We couldn't break the marbles into pieces so we filled in as best we could and guessed how many marbles there would be to fill in the extra space.
Thomas:	Thank you for sharing. And what about the Base-10 Cubes?
Jamie:	We measured ours out and made a 9-by-9 unit square and a 6-by-6 unit square giving us 81 units to cover square A and 36 units to cover square B. We found that $a^2 + b^2 = 117$ square units.
Thomas:	Hang on. Yours fit perfectly?
Greg:	Yes. Just like you've told us before, "Measure twice, cut once." Since we were going to use the Base 10 unit squares as our measurement tools, we knew we wanted them to be equal.
Thomas:	When I was walking around, y'all were frustrated about the hypotenuse. What was up with that?
Rob:	We were frustrated because we wanted to measure out the hypotenuse on the front-end also so that it would come out perfectly.
Thomas:	Why didn't it?
Rob:	Because we had to *construct* it based on the other two sides. It wasn't coming out equally based on the Base-10 Units. So we did like you said, we connected the two endpoints and hoped for the best.
Thomas:	And . . . Let's hear from someone else.
Julia:	We had to use an approximation. Since we couldn't cut the Base-10 Unit cubes to fill in the spaces, we had to estimate. We knew that it *should* take 117, so we say it will take about 117 to fill in the area of the largest square.
Thomas:	Why approximation? If the other two squares were measured out, doesn't it stand to reason that the other will fit perfectly?
Juno:	Yes, but we don't think it was going to turn out exactly right anyway.
Thomas:	Really? Why not? What other things may have happened that caused some impreciseness?

Bianca:	[*Thinking and discussing with her team*] Well, we could have been a little off when we drew the shapes . . . or when we cut.
Thomas:	So, user-error then? No matter how perfect we try to be, because we lack the ability to construct things perfectly all the time, we know that there's room for some margin of error. And for the purpose of what we're doing, that's perfectly fine! I just want you to think about those things.
Thomas:	Okay, last but not least, let's hear from the team using the graph paper.
Raymond:	I think we chose the best medium of all—even if we couldn't snack on it.
Thomas:	Oh? Why's that?
Raymond:	Because the gridlines were drawn for us. All we had to do was cut them out as straight as possible. And then count how many squares each was.
Thomas:	That sounds good. What'd you find?
Monroe:	We had 36 squares covering A and 49 squares covering B. We found that $a^2 + b^2 = 85$.
Thomas:	I notice that you didn't write "approximately equal to 85" in the cell for Number of Objects in Square C.
Rosetta:	Just as someone said, we used pieces and parts of our graph paper to fill in all of the gaps. Since we knew how many *could* fit, we cut them up as best as possible and filled in the gaps. We had exactly what we needed.
Thomas:	Good work, class. Now, please look carefully at our results table to see if you can find a relationship between these squares. Look carefully and justify your conjecture (see Figure 5.5 with student data).
Julia:	If you look at our results, you can see that adding the number of base-10 blocks in the two small squares almost equals the number in the bigger one.
Raymond:	The other numbers show almost the same thing except they were off a little.
Rosetta:	In our case, they were equal.
Caroline:	I think we would have gotten the same thing if we had chosen graph paper.
Thomas:	So . . . what are we agreeing to? Can some one use mathematics to summarize this relationship? Look at our vocabulary wall.
Juno:	I think it is okay to say that, if we measured exactly, we would get that $a^2 + b^2 = c^2$.

Thomas: Does anyone disagree with Juno? [Pause]. Who can tell us the name of this very famous theorem and . . . what does this have to do with our launch?

Brenda: It's the Pythagorean theorem. I remember that from one of my classes, I think. We can get the area of the two legs and add them up to see if that is equal to or more than 600sq. yd. of cement.

Raymond: Let's see . . . 15 × 15 is . . . 225 and 20 × 20 is . . . 400 and added up gives 625 so that will be enough!

Thomas: I am very impressed with your work, teams. You will get your rubric assessment tomorrow.

To wrap up the lesson, a student was chosen at random to read the History of the Content from the Promethean Board. Thomas believes that not only is it a good practice to connect the lesson with an historical perspective for the sake of doing so, it also partially satisfies the spirit of the CCSS to plan and implement lessons that blend the lines that once separated content areas. Another student was chosen to read the career link—so they could clearly see how using the Pythagorean Theorem is used explicitly in some careers.

In order to show the students multiple representations of the same content, Thomas played three videos from YouTube on the Pythagorean Theorem. One was "The Pythagorean Theorem Rap" by 2 bitty and crew/CORE math Productions. This especially appealed to the students because the catchy chorus stuck with the students to the extent that they were rapping with the video as the chorus repeated. The second video, "Pythagoras in Two Minutes" by Educational Solutions was an excellent way of demonstrating using animation what the students had just discovered for themselves. The final video, "Pythagorean theorem water demo" by 00000000130, proved the theorem through liquid being poured from two square containers the length of the two smaller squares into a third, larger square, that when the water was poured from the two smaller squares into the largest square, there was just enough—no more, no less—to completely fill the largest square.

Thomas distributed a homework sheet (Figure 5.7) with problems for applying the theorem and reminded students to complete the Exit Tickets from their lab packets (Figure 5.6). The organizers collected supplies and returned them to their respective containers. All took a moment to write their responses on the exit tickets and handed them to Thomas as they exited the room.

Figure 5.6 Exit Ticket

Name_____Date_____

Exit Ticket

1. Why did your medium work better or worse than another team's medium? Explain.

2. Given a right triangle whose sides are 5, 12, 13, tell me all that you know about it.

Figure 5.7 Homework

Practice Problems/Homework
due tomorrow during homeroom

Directions: Talk with your team members about how the Pythagorean Theorem might be able to help you solve the following problems. Complete problem #3 for homework.

1. Can you form a right triangle with the three sides 3 cm, 4 cm, 5 cm? Explain using complete sentences and question stems.

2. Can you form a right triangle with the three sides ,8 in., ,10 in., ,12 in.? Explain using complete sentences and question stems.

3. Use the ordered pairs to construct the triangle. Find the value of the hypotenuse in the following diagram. {(-3,1), (-3,-5), (1,1)}. Explain your answer using complete sentences and a question stem.

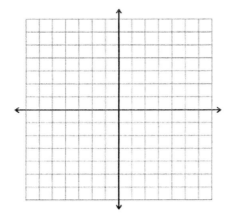

Discussion Between Colleagues

Please describe your school.

We are Title I school of approximately 650 students in grades Pre-K through 8. We are an A+ school—based on our school performance score—and have been designated one out of 41 high poverty/high performing schools in Louisiana. For our school-wide reading curriculum, we use the Success For All® program. Using its rubrics of responding to questions, justifying answers throughout the day, and working during Team Talk throughout each of the content areas, the teachers and students are able to speak in one common language when exploring and discussing topics student-to-student, student-to-teacher, and teacher-to-students.

What is your general approach to assessment?

I appreciate the value in using multiple measures when assessing my students. I do use traditional assessments, but they are neither the sole nor main way of determining what my students know. Through our daily classroom discussions, I am able to get a sense of what a student understands and what he or she is having difficulty with. I also walk around during Team Talk discussions to gauge the level of understanding. Choosing students at random to answer questions is another non-traditional way of assessing students that is vital for painting a clear picture of which concepts have been mastered and which may need a little time so that no one is left behind. Only from collecting data from the students using multiple measures can I truly assess what my students know and what areas may need a little more work before moving on.

What you would you change or keep next time you teach this unit?

I would have more choices of media for the students. I limited them so that that we could have a variety of answers. However, in doing so, it prevented some of the students from seeing how precise their measurements could have been with other material. Another idea may be to have each team experiment with one medium that is able to give relatively precise measurements (like the graph paper), and another that isn't (like the large washers). Then the students could compare/contrast the two and draw conclusions on what a difference the media makes.

Which resources for the CCSS have you found most helpful?

As the math chair at a PK through 8 school, I've attended many workshops that have given different pieces of the puzzle regarding the

CCSS. Some of them were useful, others weren't. The most useful thing that I've done is to become very intimate with them, on a personal level. Rather than going to a workshop, I had to first read as much as I could about the CCSS—not just in the grade levels that I teach, but those before and those after. That way I know what the students *should* know when they get to me, and what I need to make sure they know before they leave me. I have found the EngageNY website particularly useful. It has a vast comprehensive curriculum filled with project ideas; letters and other reproducibles; and videos of implementation, discussion, and expectations.

I notice the lights are dim in your class and that there are plenty of plants.

The atmosphere in the room factors into my class climate as well. We have dimmable fluorescent lights which usually stay off, a wall full of windows—so natural light shines in, the water flowing into the aquarium from the filter adds a soothing white noise, and the music that continually plays softly helps as well. I think plants make the kids feel at home and thus comfortable enough to make mistakes, I hope. All too often I think it's the fear of making mistakes that prevents them from rising to their fullest potential.

What about your classroom management?

I'm a huge fan of Harry Wong and I re-read *The First Days of School* often. I think that by implementing procedures from day one—and taking the time to implement them with fidelity—the middle school students are able to manage themselves when it comes to routines.

What suggestions can you give teachers so that students do the most of the work as was true in your class?

I had a very wise mentor who instructed me in the ways of constructing a student-centered environment. There's a lot of work that goes into building this environment on the front-end—planning, setting up lab packets, organizing, etc.—but the end result is that the students truly take control of their own learning. And, that mentor—you, Yvelyne—always says, based on an article you always had preservice teachers read, "Never say anything that a student can say." I take this to heart. For as much as possible, I want the students to construct their own knowledge because in doing so, as research shows, their *conceptual* understanding is much deeper and they can apply what they know to many different circumstances.

Tell us a bit about preparing preservice teachers.

After teaching a great lesson, I used to think that one day a student is going to recall a teacher teaching them the Pythagorean Theorem, or how to complete the square, or take a derivative. Because of my experience with preservice teachers, I think this may not always be true. Each semester I begin with a prompt asking my masters and doctoral students to think of a favorite teacher that they had—whether math or otherwise, whether as a kid or as a college student. "Describe why you remember this teacher as being your favorite." I have found that my students remember their teachers for *how* they made them feel, mentioning nothing about the specifics of what they learned. Since this is the case, I discuss this phenomenon with my teachers and try to impress upon them throughout the semester how important it is that we make a personal connection with our students, that through our enthusiasm we draw them into the world of appreciating meaningful mathematics, and that we are, first, there to help develop the child—not merely teach them mathematics. I believe that I am there for the children first, and sometimes the mathematics lesson that I spent so much time must go by the wayside for me to discuss problems that they may be having. It doesn't happen very often, but when it does, I am ready to go that extra mile to reach them where they are and get them the help they need.

I also tell my teachers that a problem they may face is that there aren't enough textbooks yet written based on the CCSS. Relying solely upon any textbook or any resource does a disservice to our students and greatly impedes the effectiveness of our teaching on our students. Get out there! Find your own resources! Taylor-make them to fit the specific needs of a particular group of students for a particular day of the week for a particular year.* Gone are the days when we use the same boring activities over-and-over. We owe it to our students to keep a journal and track what works well and what doesn't. Then we must tweak our plans as we practice self-reflection. Only when we do this—and make it a part of our teaching routine—will we grow as teaching professionals and better enable our students to learn to the best of their abilities.

* The article Thomas refers to is in NCTM's *Mathematics Teaching in the Middle School* (April, 2000) by Steven Reinhart. Reinhart shares the ways he was able to actively engage his students that included: replacing lectures with sets of questions; asking good questions, and using more process questions than product questions. These strategies and more helped participants in an NCTM Common Core High School Institute to rewrite textbook problems to closely align to the CCSSM. See Chapter 8 in this book.

Commentary

Thomas's lesson requires students to manipulate squares and triangles so that they can make the connection between the algebraic and geometric interpretation of the Pythagorean Theorem. The activities will help students develop a solid foundation and appreciation for the theorem, which in turn will better prepare them for algebra, geometry and trigonometry. His launch serves to provide a real-life connection so that students are problem solving, communicating, utilizing models and looking for patterns while learning about the theorem. Noteworthy are the multiple resources he brings to the lesson: problem solving, history of math, connections to careers, interesting videos, a rap song and manipulatives. He models what NCTM's Teaching Standards describe as elements necessary to developing mathematical power for all students:

1. Selecting mathematical tasks to engage the interest and intellect of students.
2. Orchestrating classroom discourse in ways that promote the investigation and growth of mathematical ideas.
3. Using, and helping students use, technology and other tools to pursue mathematical investigations.
4. Seeking, and helping students seek, connections to previous and developing knowledge.
5. Guiding individual, small group, and whole class work. (NCTM, 1991, 1)

He is thus successful at capturing his students' attention so that they are motivated to learn.

Unit Overview

Making Sense of the Pythagorean Theorem

Aim: How can we use properties of right triangles to compute areas?

Objective: The students will informally discover a well-known proof of the Pythagorean Theorem.

Grade Level: 8th

Duration: Three one-hour sessions.

CCSSM Content: Geometry: 8.G.B.6, 8.G.B.7

CCSSM Mathematical Practices: MP1: Problem solving, MP2: Reasoning, MP3: Viable arguments, MP4: Modeling, MP5: Use of tools; MP8: Repeated reasoning

Assessment Tasks: Students will be assessed on how well they perform in their teams based on their Numbered Heads responsibilities (see rubric), their participation during their activity (see rubric), and their oral presentations at the end of the lesson (see rubric).

Prerequisite Skills: Students must be able to identify right triangles, square numbers, compute square roots and graph points on the Cartesian plane.

Materials and Tools:

Construction paper, colored pencils, scissors, glue sticks, base-10 unit cubes, washers, flat marbles, graph paper, Cheez-Its, Cheerios.
Pythagoras 2 in minutes 2 video: www.youtube.com/watch?v=uaj0XcLtN5c
Water Proof of Pythagorean Theorem: www.youtube.com/watch?v=CAkMUdeB06o
Pythagorean Theorem Rap: www.youtube.com/watch?v=DRRVu-RHQWE

Do Now: Simplify.

1. $7^2 + 9^2$
2. $9^2 + 3^2$
3. Simplify $\sqrt{121}$
4. Simplify $\sqrt{625}$

5. Find the area of these rectangles (square=specific type of rectangle).

17 cm

3cm

6 in.

6. What is the simplest way to write the formula of a rectangle?
7. What is the simplest way to write the formula of a square?
8. Using graph paper, how would you construct a square whose side is 6 inches?

History of the Content: Today, historians know that Pythagoras and his followers were not the first to make use of this theorem, although it bears his name (Karamanides, D. (2006). *Pythagoras: Pioneering mathematician and music theorist of ancient Greece.* New York, NY: The Rosen Publishing Group, Inc.) There is evidence that the Egyptians made use of it for many centuries before the Pythagoreans. Archeologists have found cuneiform tablets (an ancient writing system used by the Babylonians), suggesting that the Babylonians knew of the Pythagorean Theorem as early as 1800 B.C.

Milesian philosophers, including Pythagoras's teachers, Thales and Anaximander, were familiar with Babylonian science. Some historians believe that Pythagoras learned about the theorem while studying with these men. Scientists have also found evidence that the people of India and China knew about the theorem as far back as 500 B.C. One modern historian has even suggested that the theorem should be named the pre-Pythagorean theorem. Although Pythagoras and his followers may not have been the first to make use of the theorem, they were the first to attempt to explain it scientifically. Thus, we can sleep well at night understanding why it bears his name.

Career Link: When we think of airline safety, many of us think of pilots. But there is also a network of people, air-traffic controllers, who work hard to ensure the safe operation of aircraft. Using radar and visual observation, they closely monitor the location of each plane. They coordinate the movement of air traffic to make certain that aircraft stay a safe distance apart. They also coordinate landings and takeoffs to keep delays at a minimum. In their jobs, air-traffic controllers use angle measurements in some of the same ways you do when you solve problems in algebra and geometry. Annual Median Pay: $108,040/$51.94 per hour. (http://stats.bls.gov/ooh/Transportation-and-Material-Moving/Air-traffic-controllers.htm)

Management Procedures:

◆ Review the Do Now. Be sure students understand how to cut a square given one side.

- ◆ Have the students solve the Do Now individually and then share.
- ◆ Introduce the launch for student to explore and share. Summarize results.

Assessment Rubrics: See Figures 5.3 and 5.4.

Homework: See Figure 5.7.

6

Madeline Landrum: Modeling Real World Problems with Multi-Step Inequalities

I like to introduce my lessons with an academic challenge by choosing problems that relate to the lesson and simultaneously challenge the students. Such problems allow the students an opportunity to discover some math concepts on their own. While the challenges usually create a state of frustration for students, students have come to accept this state as precursor to great mathematical discourse that will eventually guide them through the major parts of the day's lesson.
(Madeline Landrum, Lusher Charter School, New Orleans, Louisiana)

Madeline's students enter her class and immediately sit around tables that are arranged for group work. Students normally sit in pairs, but for this lesson, she tells them to sit in any group of three. "I thought three in the group would promote more discussion and brainstorming," she says. For this lesson on inequalities, she chooses a challenge from the text that reads:

Artists often use the golden rectangle because it is considered to be pleasing to the eye. The length of a golden rectangle is about 1.62 times its width. Suppose you are making a picture frame in the shape of a golden rectangle. You have a 46-inch piece of wood. What are the length and width of the largest frame you can make? Round your answers to the nearest tenth of an inch. (Fair, 1997, 193).

Included with the problem is a picture of the Parthenon, the ancient Greek temple that was designed so that its dimensions formed a golden rectangle. As the students begin tackling the problem, she observes different approaches and areas of misunderstanding arising. As examples, one group uses trial and error, and another uses the perimeter formula and substitutes 1.62w for the length. In one group, students have no idea what to do with the 46 inches information given about the wood because the problem makes no mention of the wood's length or width. After questioning the students in one group, she realizes that this group of students doesn't have a clear picture of what a 46-inch piece of wood looks like or what they are to do with it.

It is interesting to hear the initial brainstorming about the problem and see how Madeline facilitates discussions as she walks around. Her interaction with a group that couldn't start the problem follows:

Magan:	Ms. Landrum, if the piece of wood looks like this [she uses hands to form a rectangle] why don't they give us length or something?
Madeline:	No, No. It's just one piece of wood that is 46 inches long. You are going to cut that up so that the rectangle you make . . . so that the frame you make . . . fits the requirement that the length is 1.62 times the width. But, the wood, is just 46 inches long.
Magan:	Oh . . . so we just have to . . . like . . . cut it into four different pieces to do that?
Madeline:	Right!

As Madeline leaves, she hears Magan explaining to others in her group, and they then begin the planning process. Another group has progressed from understanding the problem to making a plan, but is having difficulty translating the key ideas into algebra. The following discussion reflects how students do not easily understand the variable concept.

Tony:	OK. It's going to be 6.2 times x or something like that because you have to use a variable.
Bernadine:	Why don't we try a big number first to see how much . . .
Tony:	It's 46 inches right? If it's 46 inches, then that means it's 46 inches long—right?
Sergio:	I'm not sure but I think it's 1 point 62 times, or maybe, plus, x equals . . .
Bernadine:	46!
Sergio:	Yeah, 46.

Bernadine: I think you divide it by 2, times its width, because the rectangle is twice its width long as it is length.

Sergio: So it would be 1.62 times . . . 2? Then it would be like, x, or something like that?

Tony: Look at the Parthenon picture—It would be 1.62x, times 2.

Bernadine: So wait . . . 1.62x, twice, times x squared = 46?

As Madeline approaches this group, she demonstrates how to keep students thinking. When Bernadine asks her if the group has set up the equation correctly, the following dialogue ensues:

Madeline: What are you trying to find?

Bernadine: Wouldn't you use 2L + 2w which would give you P?

Madeline: And what is that?

Bernadine: The perimeter . . . which is . . . 46? Is that right?

Madeline: Ask the others in your group.

This quick interaction is enough to get the group to correctly apply the perimeter formula. Another group does not understand how to represent the length in terms of the variable. Madeline's line of questions shows ways to help students gain increased understanding on the use of variables: "What are you trying to find for the rectangle? What does your x represent? What is the length? What does the 46 represent in terms of this? Let's go back to the problem. You need to write down what your width represents. . . . OK, so you think the width is the variable—Then what will the length be equal to?". . . . As this group begins to apply the perimeter formula, she moves on.

    Madeline walks around to be sure that the groups have reached an answer and thus asks each group to check answers. Helen calls her over and says that she has checked her work twice with a calculator and says, "but when I check, I'm over the 46 inches yet I know my answers are correct." Madeline replies, "But is that possible?" She walks over to another group and after a few more minutes of grappling, calls the class together and has one group go up to the board to set up equations:

Let w = width and 1.62 w = length

2L + 2W = 46

       2(1.62 W) + 2W = 46

       3.24W + 2W = 46

       5.24W = 46

       W = 8.8

W = 8.8 and to get L, L = (1.62W)

       L = (1.62)(8.8)

       L = 14.256

       L = 14.3

Answer: W= 8.8 and L= 14.3

It's interesting to see how this group partitions the task of reporting. While one student writes on the board, the other two take turns explaining what is being written and why. It is clear that this group had all its members actively involved in determining the solution. Students then ask questions of the group members, who again take turns explaining their reasoning. A student challenges the group by saying, "But when you check the answer, you get more than 46." The members of the group check the results and show that they get 46.2, but admit that they don't see any errors. Madeline calls on Pablo, who had taken an alternative approach to the problem, to show his work at the board. Instead of an equation, Pablo writes the inequality, $2(8.78) + 2(14.22) \leq 46$. When asked why, he explains, "You want the largest dimensions possible without using more than 46 inches. He also explains that he rounded the width (8.77) to 8.8, but that he rounded the length (14.25) to 14.2 so as not to exceed the 46 inches. The class agrees with his reasoning, but Liz says, "If you use those signs and those dimensions, than Pablo's inequality is more than 46 so that is still not true. He'd have to put: $2W + 2(1.62W) \leq 46$." Madeline looks at Liz's work and notices that the numbers she substitutes for length and width are rounded to the tenth place. She tells Liz, "Compare his numbers to yours and then check his work again." A more careful check satisfies Liz's group and Madeline asks the class to reflect on why the other inequalities did not work for home-work.

For the next activity, she tells the class that the Greeks not only used the golden rectangle in their architecture, but they also believed that some human body proportions were divinely proportional provided they fit the character-istics of the golden rectangle. She instructs students to measure two distances, the first being the measure of the distance from the head to the navel, and the second being the measure of the distance from the navel to the feet. "Use the first result for the numerator of the fraction; and the second for the denomi-nator. Determine how close the result is to 1.62 or, to having a what Greeks thought to be a divinely proportional body," she tells the class.

With tape measures and calculators in hand, students enthusiastically set out to measure each other to find the perfect body. They were saying to each other, "Take your shoes off; stand up straight; this doesn't seem right; let's do it again; divide that with the calculator." After about 15 minutes, students move around and happily share their measurements with other groups. One group reporter, Laura, gives a quick summary: "While Lisa has a divinely proportional body, I am the least divine person in my group!" Laura is very tall, and is disappointed in her ratio because it is over 1.7. Madeline asks students to think of why her ratio might be higher than others. Kendra suggests that it is probably because her legs are long so that her torso probably has yet to catch up with them. Others agree. Madeline adds, "No need to worry about not being divine—few of us are!"

Madeline assigns students to practice solving multi-step inequalities from their text. Again, she walks around and monitors the student's progress as they work in groups. For homework, she assigns additional problems from the text and tells students to gather measurements to compute the divine ratio for one member in their family.

The next day, she begins the lesson by asking students to explain the discrepancies in the inequalities from the previous day's lesson on the piece of wood. Nicette says, "In both of Pablo's equations, he had numbers in the hundredths but we rounded off our numbers to the nearest tenth. Maybe that's the problem." Students return to their calculations and verify that Nicette is indeed correct. Joseph chimes in, "Sure! We shouldn't have rounded off until we reached the end!"

"Does that make sense?" asks Madeline as she looks carefully at students' faces for signs of confusion. As students nod, "yes," she distributes a sheet of paper with a table on it for students to enter the family data gathered for homework and the corresponding divine ratio calculation. She asks, "Do you think that most people will have that characteristic? Let's see what the data tells us. After the class has entered the results, I will make you a copy to analyze on a spreadsheet." While the table is passed around, Madeline reviews the assigned homework from the text and then proceeds to have the class analyze the data gathered on family member's divine ratio calculation.

Discussion Between Colleagues

What made you decide to teach mathematics?

I have always enjoyed math because I had success with it. My dad was also a math teacher. However, it was my methods course instructor who influenced me to consider math. She took me aside one day and said that she thought I would enjoy continuing with math so why not become a math major—I did—It was one of the best decisions I ever made!

What is your philosophy for teaching mathematics?

I believe that NCTM is right: All students can learn mathematics—maybe at different rates or different levels, but they can all learn it. I try to help students become comfortable with mathematics because so many come to me afraid of it. By giving students time to work with a concept or through use of different techniques, I find that I slowly break down the walls that hinder their learning.

How do you generally assess students?

I use both traditional and alternative ways to assess students. For example, I find test scores, quizzes and grades for notebook useful. I also have students do both individual and group projects and allow students to show improvement on any score that is equivalent to a low grade.

What resources do you use other than the text for instruction?

I use calculators, computers, the internet and manipulatives. The third lesson in this unit, for example, uses the art of Davinci's Vitruvian Man to investigate ratio of arm span to arm length, which I downloaded from the net.

Middle grade students are so body-sensitive. Do you find that the data analyzed is enough to show that it's OK not to be divinely proportioned?

Yes, because I discuss this issue at length after the second lesson because the data do support this. This is the primary reason I assigned students to collect data on family members. In the past, I have had them collect data on teachers too.

What would you keep or change next time you teach this lesson?

I liked both activities and I will use them again. Before this lesson, the students had solved some multi-step equations. I found the academic challenge to be just what I needed to introduce the lesson in a way that demonstrated to students the close parallel between solving equations and inequalities. Students had difficulty seeing the shape of the 46-inch piece of wood. Maybe a general class discussion clarifying the given information might help. Students also began rounding off their decimals too early in the process. I left it as a challenge for students to determine why their equalities did not work but other times I may just give them a warning and move on.

Commentary

Madeline's lesson provides opportunities for students to use algebra to model and solve problems—a most difficult task for many students to grasp even with each other's help. From his research on students attempts to apply variables while solving non-routine problems, Reeves (2000) writes, "Students will not automatically learn to use variables even after hearing their class mates use them as shortcuts. The use of variables will have to be encouraged by the teacher if that outcome is a goal of an algebraic-thinking strand" (401).

As she listens to her students grapple with applying a variable to a problem, Madeline applies Reeves' advice through questions that reflect a sound method for helping students focus on the essential aspects for applying variables. Her questions show students that they too can get fruitful answers if they ask themselves and each other similar questions—questions that focus on understanding the variable's role in the problems and which Madeline asks over and over again as she lays the foundation for students' deeper understanding.

Madeline's lesson also connects geometric ideas to art and everyday life. The difficulty students have understanding what to do with the information given on the 46 inch-long wood illustrates how necessary it is to give problems requiring analysis of relationships between 2-D and 3-D figures. Such problems help students learn that real-life problems may not have the key words that readily connect to algorithms they know (MP1, MP2, MP4, MP6).

Her homework requiring that students find measurements for a family member has an important outcome extending beyond students' practice of skills. It is a good way for informing families about the content students are learning through a fun and meaningful activity and may help families make some meaning of mathematics reform. Such assignments often get parents to say, "Wow! As a student, I never had this much fun doing math!" This sort of information-sharing between classroom and home is important to assuaging some parents' fears of mathematics reform being synonymous to a watered-down-fun-curriculum, or of one having little connection to traditional basic skills.

In their article on Algebra, Phillip and Schappelle (NCTM, 1999) write, "The way in which a teacher views algebra has important implications for their instructional goals. A teacher who believes that algebra is primarily about manipulating symbols will teach algebra differently from someone who sees algebra as a language for generalizing arithmetic" (315). Madeline's approach clearly demonstrates that she believes in the latter.

Unit Overview

Solving Multi-step Inequalities

Aim: How can inequalities help in solving real-world problems?

Objective: Students will model and solve a real-world problem from geometry using multi-step inequalities.

Grade Levels: 7 grade Algebra

Number of 90 minute periods: 2

Source: Prentice Hall (1997), *Algebra: Tools for a Changing World*, p. 42

CCSSM Content: Expressions and Equations (6.EE.(A.1, A.2); 7.EE.(A.1, A.2, B.3, B.4, B.5)

Numbers 7.NS.(A.2, A.3)

Mathematical Practices: MP1: Problem solving, MP2: Reasoning, MP4: Modeling, MP6: Precision

Mathematical Concepts: Students apply the perimeter formula for rectangles to solve a real-world problem using multi-step algebraic inequalities.

Prerequisites:

   ◆   Solving one-step inequalities.
   ◆   Concept of ratio and proportions.
   ◆   Ruler measurements.

Materials and Tools:

   ◆   Tape measure.
   ◆   Calculator.

Management Procedures:

   ◆   Assign students to groups of 3–4 to work on finding golden proportion dimensions for a rectangle whose perimeter cannot exceed 46 inches.
   ◆   Have students share results.

- ◆ Have students measure length of body parts to seek the 1.62 divine ratio stemming from: length of navel to foot, divided by length of head to navel.
- ◆ Assign multi-step inequalities for practice.

Assessment: Circulate to observe and question students' work. Check multi-step problems assigned for homework and check students' search for divine ratio in a family member's measurements.

7

Merrie Schroeder:
Statistics with Snack Food

I created the Snack Food Unit partly to satisfy one of the missions of my school, which is the generation of new teaching materials and strategies to help colleagues implement Standards-based teaching in K-12 classrooms. The unit is for middle grades students and centers around solving a problem comparing our own eating habits of snack food with other countries. I try to find ways to teach students to develop their own thoughts and ideas because the mathematics classroom is a room full of people, not machines. And people have emotions, and people learn differently, and they feel differently on different days, and most important—they THINK. And they LOVE to think. They love to feel important. This kind of teaching gives students a chance to think and to feel important.

(Merrie Schroeder, Price Laboratory, University of Northern Iowa, Iowa)

Merrie Schroeder uses numerous resources to create lessons based on real-world data for her classes. She created the Snack Food Unit from statistics reported in magazines published by Snack Food Association (Google: snack food statistics for latest data), or by Shapiro (1992, p. 31).

To begin the unit, she describes and clarifies the goals and activities to come, noting that the first activity—learning all the concepts and gaining the necessary tools—will be done as a whole class, and the application of the concepts and skills will be done in teams. To introduce the first part, she presents real-life questions for students to pursue about snacks: "I have found some statistics about the amount of snack food that people eat in a year in several other countries. I was curious. . . how do WE compare as sixth graders to these statistics? What are we going to have to do to compare ourselves?" Some students quickly respond that students should start recording how much they eat. In a short time, someone asks, "What IS snack food? Does an orange count? Or do we keep it to chips and candy and stuff like that . . . stuff our moms don't want us to eat?" Another student counters, "I snack only on healthy foods. I like those banana chips and the dried stuff instead of potato chips. I think my healthy snacks should count." "Yes" another student says, "but most of us don't eat that stuff. Ms. Schroeder, did they say what they counted as snack food?" Merrie answers by quoting from the book: "From potato chips to pretzels, popcorn to pork rinds, the United States leads in snack food consumption among all countries for which data is available. What can you infer from that?" A student says, "Sounds like they're talking more along the junk food line." This discussion ensues for a few more minutes until a call for a vote on the definition is made. Students agree that they are going to define snack food as items like chips, candy bars, etc. and not so much like the healthy foods. The next problem is figuring out how to record it. Given that the book's data is given as the number of pounds of snack food consumed per capita annually, Merrie asks the class to determine how they will make comparisons. Students' comments include:

John:	"We could weigh ours each time and add it all up."
Mimi:	"We could use the information on the bags and jars . . . like if the bag says it holds a pound and I eat half of it, then I record a half pound."
Justin:	"Can we include our family? They eat a lot!"
Merrie:	"No. Let's keep it for our class. Besides, we want our numbers to be smaller, don't we? Won't that make us look like we're healthier?"
Joseph:	"Are we going to do this for a whole year?"
Tiana:	"I think that, if their data is for a whole year, we have to do something to compare it right . . . I know! Let's divide theirs by 12 and it will be for a month. Then we can do this for a month."
Joseph:	"Or we could find out how much we ate in a day and multiply it by 365 to be a year."
Germain:	"Yea, but what if you have an off day and really pig out because you got a bad grade on a test or something and you know your parents are really gonna be mad?"
Julian:	"Well, somebody else might not eat anything because they are sick, so won't those make up for each other? We're comparing as a class, aren't we?"

After a few more minutes of debate and discussion, the class decides to estimate their snack food eating habits for a year, since that is what they would compare against. Merrie assigns homework requiring students to record what they normally eat for snacks in a day and to check package labels and do whatever weighing is necessary to determine an estimate of their daily consumption. They are to then compute the estimated yearly consumption. Before they leave, she tells students to make an estimate in their journals of their yearly average. She informs the class that the next couple of days will be devoted to a better understanding of how to best organize and present the data they will produce. She describes and clarifies the goals and activities to come, noting that the first activity—learning all the concepts and gaining necessary tools—will be done as a whole class, and the application of the concepts and skills will be done in teams. She distributes a handout outlining the goals and procedure of the lessons to follow (see Figure 7.1).

Figure 7.1 Goals and Instructions for Data Gathering and Analysis

1. Be able to understand, use and make
   ◆ tables
   ◆ graphs: bar and circle (pie charts)
2. Be able to understand and compute averages (measures of central tendency)
   ◆ mean   ◆ median   ◆ mode
3. Use estimation skills
4. Work as a team

To reach the goals, you will
1. work as a class to learn about and use tables, graphs, the measures of central tendency, and estimation skills. Topic: Snack Food
2. create a project as part of a team to extend your knowledge and skills. Topic: Your Choice

Assessment:
1. Evaluation of the team project.
2. To show how well you have reached the goals, you will be given an inventory to complete on your own.

Project:
1. You and your team will choose a topic for which you will gather data from your classmates.
2. You will organize the data in tables and graphs.
3. You will draw conclusions from the data.
4. You will make a presentation to the class.
5. You will be critiqued (in a very kind way) by your classmates to help make your understandings and skills the very best possible.
6. Each of you will hand in your own tables and graphs, even though you developed them as a team. The quality of what you hand in will depend solely on you.

The next day, students come prepared with estimates and are eager to compare what they consume with others in the class. Before class officially starts, students are already drawing conclusions about why their number is so different from others. The data's wide range, 40 to 370 pounds, stems from body size to inaccurate estimates. Merrie asks students to compare their numbers to the ones in their estimations in their journal. "How close are you?" she asks. Fun discussions fill the airwaves. She asks students to think of reasons for such a range of estimations. As students report some data, she asks them whether the data is for daily or yearly consumption. While some students are unsure about the process for conversion, others, like Eugenie, are eager to share thoughts:

> I looked on the chips and cookies boxes and they said that a serving was one ounce. I figured I ate about 3 servings of that stuff a day, so I took 3 ounces times 365. That was 1095. But when I told my mom what we were doing, she said I'd better go on a diet or divide it by 16. That gave me about 68 pounds.

To be sure that all students understand the various steps, she asks Eugenie to explain why she divided by 16. Merrie then instructs the class on the steps to follow and emphasizes the key concerns on unit measures:

> All of you need to be sure that your answers are in pounds. Before we can compare, our data must all be in the same units. Double check your work: did you add up all the same unit measures—ounces to ounces, pounds to pounds, etc. If you added up all ounces, did you divide by 16? Remember that our goal is to compare our class to the world, rather than YOU personally. Do you think that your own number will end up being the one that represents our class?

Students are quick to make suggestions and eager to see what the "average" will be. Merrie invites suggestions on how to proceed. A student suggests that they call out numbers for Merrie to record on the board. She selects a student to do so and once done, asks them to find an average. Students are not comfortable with numbers being randomly recorded so one comments, "They should be written in order, like from smallest to largest." With lots of help from everyone, the numbers are re-written, but Merrie is careful not to erase the original list. As they think of data processing, most students begin to remember from earlier grades how to compute an average. "That's an awful lot of digits to add. Is there a faster way to do this?" Merrie asks. Some students decide it is OK to have different groups of people add up different sets of numbers, and then compile them for a grand total. Merrie divides the data among different groups and an average for the class is computed. "Could we have done this without re-organizing our list?" she asks. Students do see that the organized list was not necessary. Merrie next asks what she calls, the *big* question: "What does this mean? You say our class' average is 59 pounds a year. But Eugenie's is about 68. What does average mean?" This is a most difficult concept for middle grade students to understand. It is very easy to compute, but because it is not understood, students have a difficult time recalling from one occasion to another how to do it. As soon as they are reminded, they quickly jump to the mechanics of computing this mysterious number. Reviewing the properties of the three measures of central tendency (average, median and mode) is Merrie's next focus.

To help students differentiate between the measures, she creates a situation requiring students to compare and contrast the information given by each measure. She tells them: "If three statisticians from *Snack Food* magazine came in here and looked at our numbers on the board, all of them might declare a different "average" and they would all be correct. One might say the average is this one (circling the one in the middle of the organized list), the second person might say it is this one (circling the most often recorded number/s), and the last person might agree that it is the one we came up with. How do you think they each came up with their answers?" It is here that fun with mathematics ensues. Because students are great at hunching how people arrived at their conclusions and love to try to think the way others do, they enjoy imagining reasonable responses. After a little time is spent on students deducing the methods, Merrie guides them to the definitions and meanings of the three measures of central tendency. Returning to the original and the organized lists of yearly averages, Merrie asks a series of questions to help students distinguish between the measures: "How important is it to have our numbers organized from smallest to largest to determine the mean? The median? The mode?" "How hard would it be to determine the median from our first list?" Students are able to state that the order of the numbers is unimportant to determine the mean; to determine mode, the order is not critical but it helps; to determine median the numbers must be in order. However, Merrie comments,

> With all this discussion, it is still possible for students NOT to understand the meaning of the mean average. Students must be able to verbalize that it is the equal sharing of amounts. We call it the Robin Hood theory: we take from the rich and give to the poor so that everyone has the same amount. (Students call this 'mean' to the rich.) How many people are treated meanly? Half? Less than half? More than half? Why does it vary? Why isn't it always half?

These kinds of discussions dominate the numerical portion of the lesson. Students are then assigned several smaller sets of data to practice calculating and describing the mean, median, mode and range.

Focusing on students' attention once more to the variability in the data, Merrie next plans to highlight other factors that may contribute to the differences. She asks the class to consider if differences might exist between the measures of central tendency for boys and girls. "How can we answer that question?" she asks. Students are quick to suggest dividing the data in two columns for listing boys' and girls' data, and then computing the three averages.

Having viewed the data from a numerical perspective, Merrie's next goal is to move students towards presenting a graphical approach. She asks, "Some of us are very visual interpreters. How can we make the data more visual for us all to understand?" Some students suggest making a bar graph, but aren't terribly sure how to start. Merrie suggest that they cluster the averages, like 0–20, 21–40, 41–60, and determine the number of clusters necessary. Students begin to play with the numbers, and discover that there are *lots* of clusters. They suggest making the clusters bigger, like 0–50, 51–100, and enter in the table the number of boys and number of girls having data in each cluster. Because most students have had experiences creating bar graphs in earlier grades, very little review is necessary to get them to do so. Merrie invites discussions to interpret the data and then asks students to think of other categories that would be suitable for comparing the data. She comments, "My next steps depend on what they choose to do." Because students suggest height, shoe size, age, involvement in extracurricular activities, and hair color, she gives students a recipe card and tells them to record each of these attributes and to return the card to her. These cards will be used for the second part of the unit: the team project.

Analysis of the data on snack food eaten in other countries is the next lesson. Her major goal is to help students understand how to create and interpret pie or bar graphs so that students will be able to extend the interpretations to the class' data. It is now that she gives students a handout with data of snack consumption from other countries (Figure 7.2). Data is omitted on five countries that will serve as the comparison group and a blank pie graph representing their amounts is given. Merrie tells students that the total amount of food for all five countries is about 40 pounds. In the blank near each country, she instructs students to write an estimate, and come to a team decision on the amounts and placements on the pie chart. She asks students to first estimate the amounts for each country and to next guess which country a given wedge represents. (Note that the Figure 7.2 numbers in parentheses are the actual data and are not shown to students at this time.) Each team chooses a recorder to explain the team's decision to the class. After all groups have shared results, Merrie shows the actual data. She asks questions about the data to reinforce students' understanding of decimals: "Notice that these data are reported to the nearest 10th, but our own class data were not. What suggestions do you have for making the data look similar? How would you round the data to be usable?" Depending on the class's response, she reviews decimal computations as well as when and how to estimate decimals.

Figure 7.2 Snack Food Graph Unit

This unit is based on the statistics reported in *We're Number One*, Andrew L. Shapiro, as reported in various issues of *Snack World* magazine, Snack Food Association, Alexandria, VA. Data for five of the countries we will study are not given.

Pounds of snack food consumed per person per year, 1987–1991:

Australia	4.4	Denmark	3.5
Finland	—	Germany	—
Italy	17.6	Japan	3.7
Netherlands	2.5	Norway	8.0
Spain	2.9	Switzerland	2.7
Sweden	—	United States	—
United Kingdom	—		

The five countries listed below will be the focus of our study. Given that the total amount of food for all five is about 40 pounds per person per year, estimate the snack consumption for each and enter result on the blank line.

A. United States ___ (19.2)   B. United Kingdom ___ (10.0)   C. Sweden ___ (4.4)
D. Finland ___ (2.2)   E. Germany ___ (6.1)

In the pie graph below, the estimated size of each wedge represents one of the five countries. Guess which of the five countries is represented by each wedge. Use a letter from A to E to represent a country.

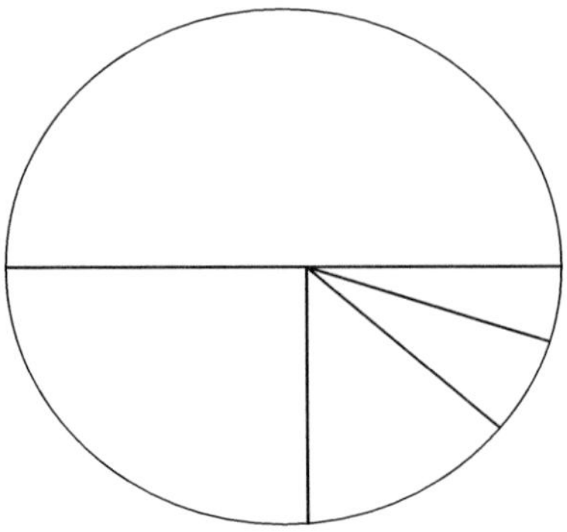

To help the class connect circle graphs to bar graphs, she distributes graph paper, and has students create a bar graph representing the same data. Students individually think of a suitable scale for the vertical axis and then plot the graph. They return to their teams to develop a single team graph and Merrie asks each group to draw and present one graph. Once a group has decided which scale is best, the rest is easy and after each group has presented its graph to the class, Merrie moves on to help students see how a bar graph can be converted to a circle graph. She gives students scissors and instructs them to cut their bar graph, connect the pieces and shape them into a circle with tape. She then shows the original pie graph and the circular bar graph on the same transparency, and then asks the class to look for connections between the two graphs. "There are no wedges on the bar graph's circle," she says, "Can you suggest a quick way to draw them?" Some students will suggest estimating the point of the center and drawing wedges to each end of the taped graphs. She has the class verify that both pie graphs are now the same and then asks, "Is it possible that different sized bar graphs for this data will result in the same circle graph? How can we test this idea?" Students suggest checking each other's graphs and Merrie tells them to do that and to reach a conclusion.

How bar graphs compare and contrast to pie charts is Merrie's next discussion point. At this time, she asks the class for their ideas and lists them in two-columns. Students say that they are alike because:

- bar and circle can both be used as a percentage of a whole;
- you can tell the same information in two ways;
- both are graphs;
- both use physical size to determine the largest number;
- both use symbols to identify which amount is how much; and
- you can use both to compare countries.

Students say they are different because:

- one looks like a pie and one looks like a rectangle;
- bar graphs have a scale of measurement, but circles don't;
- bar graphs have x and y axis, circles don't;
- circles are good for finding out how much more you need to fill up to a whole (100%); and
- circle is easy to do percent for each wedge . . . you can estimate the percent easier than with bar.

At this time Merrie has students practice changing bar graphs to pie graphs. Students are put in teams of four to select any four countries to record their data in a table, transfer it to a bar graph, and then transfer that to a circle graph.

The second part of the unit is to be done in teams. Merrie instructs students to choose their teams and select criteria from the recipe cards to make graphs of their own. For example, a group chooses to analyze the class snack food data by hair color: how much snack food did each blonde eat? each brunette? each redhead? Another group looks at snack food consumption by range of shoe size. Students are to develop tables, bar graphs, circle graphs, and discuss their findings and are expected to use sound mathematical language when discussing the project before the whole class. They should plan to tell not only what the three measures of central tendency are, but to describe the meaning of each and what the implications are. In essence, students are to tell a story about their findings, not to simply report them. The class has the job of helping teams by telling the presenters what they like about their work, and asking important questions from which everyone can learn.

Merrie distributes a handout summarizing the team project and assessment criteria (see Figure 7.3). She emphasizes that all presentations should

Figure 7.3 Team Assessment Instruction

1. **Planning:** You will use the information from our class to make a presentation about snack food consumption. As a team, discuss which category you wish to present and how sophisticated you want your project to be. Decide on number of categories, how you will report your statistics, narrative, etc. You will have two/three days to complete this part of your work, and one more day to add on any extras that will enhance your project. Although you will work as a team, you will each produce your own copy of the product for your folder.

   When all projects are completed, your team will present its data to the whole class. Class members will be given an opportunity to respond to your work and to ask questions of your team. Be prepared to be in charge! You will hand in your work as a team. It will be scored individually, and will be added to your work folder.

2. **Project delivery:** Hand in the project by teams, with each person handing in their own data. Include one copy of the team's raw data.

3. **Teamwork assessment:** "How did your team do? How did you do?" Include this reflection with the project in the folder.

4. **Presentations:** Each team will tape its graph on the board and conduct the discussion. Be prepared to respond to questions, comments or ideas from the class.

5. **Assessment will be based on:**
   A. Degree of accuracy in presenting what was intended.
   B. Degree to which circle and bar graph data match.
   C. Completeness of supporting information
   - graph title
   - labels on data in circle
   - where the data comes from
   - neatness and appeal
   - labels on bar graph axes
   - description of what you try to show
   - measures of central tendency

clearly demonstrate the items listed. She adds the discussion requirement because she believes that while the presentations help students prepare for the final exam, the discussions of the presentations allow students a chance to polish their skills.

A unit written exam consisting of 5–6 questions, which is to be completed by individual students, is the final activity (see Figure 7.4 for sample exam with a student's answer). Because some of the questions may depend on an answer from a previous question, Merrie allows partial credit to reward valid

Figure 7.4 Student's Work on Individual Assessment

The following circle graph shows how many liked the named fruit best, out of 120 people. Given that 40 people liked apples, estimate the number of people for other fruits and make a bar graph to match the information on the circle graph. Label the axes.

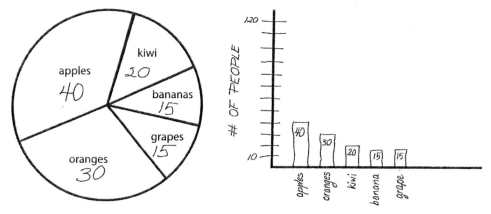

1. How many degrees would be in the wedge labeled "grapes"?

    45°

2. Write a calculator sentence that would give the number of degrees in the wedge labeled "kiwi."

    20 × 360 ÷ 120 =

3. "The average American loves kiwi." This statement is statistically true. Explain.

    The average of the pie graph is 24, the closest number to that graph is 20, which is about how many people said they liked kiwi.

4. Name three ways circle graphs and bar graphs are alike.

    Both are graphs; they can be used to find percents; they use size to show the largest number.

5. Name three ways circle and bar graphs are differ.

    Circle graph is a circle and bar graph has axes. To add more groups to a graph without making each group too small, width of bar graph increase but area of circle stays the same.

thinking that may be based on a false premise. For example, problem 1 presents data with a circle graph of five wedges, each representing a type of fruit. The amount of fruit in one wedge is given and students are to deduce the number in the others and to make a bar graph based on their estimations. If a student incorrectly estimates the sizes of the wedges but has a bar graph that corresponds to the incorrect wedges, then the student loses credit for the wedge part but receives credit for the bar graph.

The examination covers the entire range of Bloom's taxonomy of levels of thinking: Remembering, Understanding, Applying, Analyzing, Evaluating, and Creating.

Discussion Between Colleagues

What are the reactions of the students to your unit?

They always love this kind of teaching and learning. My students know that they are teachers, valued members of the group, and that I too, learn from them. They don't hesitate to offer a new idea, ask a different question than was expected, or try to derail the class. Many are still pubescent, too, and love to play and joke and horse around. That is part of growing up. We take that in our stride, give the appropriate chagrined looks, regain some control, and move on. Some days are smoother than others, if for no other than a change in barometer. Sometimes it's more serious. The math classroom is a room full of people, not computers. And people have emotions, and people learn differently, and they feel differently on different days, and most important—they THINK. And they LOVE to think. They love to feel important. That is what this kind of teaching does. We have fun while we learn. I try to create opportunities for students to "show off' their knowledge. I want my students to realize that the side trips we take to understand a topic are as valuable as the main trip itself.

Question 2 in the individual assessment requires the calculator. How was it used in the project?

They were not only used, but also studied extensively enough to promote the notion that there are many forms of number sentences that allow us to reach an answer, and that students must have some knowledge of order of operation, number sense, and how programmers design calculators to compute. I also use it to connect making wedges by finding fractional parts of the circle. We do stop to do the explorations needed to be able to write the calculator codes that will allow students to find the degrees for the wedges. We use the Explorer calculators, and we really DO explore.

For brevity of this lesson, the actual transition to the mathematics of the circle graph, using calculators, fractions and 360 degrees, was eliminated. But the same types of investigations and inquiry continue to bring students to calculating the actual degree sizes of each wedge for the countries chosen to examine.

How do you weigh the various responses on the exam?

Responses are scored in a variety of ways: the short-answer completion questions net a point each; the essay-style questions are scored at one point for each correct and unique answer. Thus, the exam has no anticipated top score prior to administration. I anticipate the quality of answers and corresponding point value prior to the exam and expect that the average understanding of the concepts and skills would net a student around 8–12 points. Students who have a high level command of the concepts might score about 17 points. The mark of a student in trouble would be one who does not achieve as many as six points. As it turns out, the class' scores generally does well: The scores range from 9 to 17, with a mean of 15.9, a median of 14, and modes of 12, 13, and 14.

How often do you do this kind of project with class? Do you ever lecture?

I do this type of lesson most often. Lecturing is woven into the lesson where students cannot possibly discover something that is contrived or defined by mathematicians. I think one of the errors some make in mathematics reform (or any other) is to make blanket rules, like "kids should discover meaning." Sometimes kids can't possibly discover meaning because the guy who invented the rule or algorithm or relationship spent his/her whole life doing it in the first place. Then we think we can have a 12 year old do it, too, because someone did it. Kids can make connections, given the right set of ideas to examine. And kids can look for patterns, and they can predict and conjecture and test their ideas. But there are lots of places where teachers have to do some lecturing to bring traditional knowledge to the students. Then it is the teacher's job to craft the use of the knowledge so that students can latch it to what they know and to make new mental structures to accommodate the new information. And then there is the reality that sometimes just doing plain old arithmetic computation is flat out fun! Students like a change of pace, and to be able to sit down and just compute is fun. In a way it is like being a musician . . . it is greatly rewarding to be a part of a band, adding to the whole piece of music. And other times, it is a real kick just to go off on your own and play a bunch of notes however you wish, just for the joy of doing it. I think math is the same way.

Do you give traditional exams?

I'm not sure anymore what a traditional exam is. Therefore, I guess the answer is, no. However, I do have pieces of exams that have some tradition in them, such as a section where students just compute . . . naked math, as it were. When I assess traditionally, it is in down and dirty quick-check quizzes to give me some needed information prior to a skill or concept. At one point I thought it would be important to give students traditional exams so that they could practice this type of activity for success in later courses. But it is such a waste because the traditional (meaning matching or fill-in-the-blank or only quick computation) exams don't give ME any information worth spending the time and energy on. They certainly are easy to grade, but it's about as meaningful as counting all the food in my cupboards to determine how much I weigh. And my students love the other types of exams so much that they don't like the traditional style.

Do you assess your teaching?

I assess my teaching through reflecting on the lesson after I have done it, as well as through revisiting the tests and projects. Another factor is conversations with colleagues. It is important to have opportunities to share with others and to have them provide feedback and ask questions to take the quality of teaching a step further. My colleagues always ask good questions. Those people are hard to find! Having a colleague who looks at my teacher's materials, gives it a cursory glance, and grunts, "Cool," is not helpful. I am fortunate to have colleagues willing to devote the extra time to help me improve my teaching. Another way to keep assessing my teaching is by getting on programs for conferences with a colleague who wants to share my techniques. Preparing for public scrutiny with a colleague REALLY makes you polish your work and think hard about why you do what you do. It's different than doing a "show" by yourself. You can bluff your way through a presentation when you are by yourself, but sharing the teaching with a colleague makes you try harder to look good for both of you, and so you find yourself assessing yourself more. Case in point: Having to write the unit for this book really made me do some re-assessing. Snack Food wasn't very well written, especially for publication. Most of my writing is just to give myself reminders of what I do. When it becomes public, I have to get critical of what I do.

Comment on the units you teach in class. Any reactions from parents?

I have developed all my units. I cannot teach primarily from a text. However, I do use texts for resources of practice problems. I share my units through conferences, and some are earmarked to be written for publication. Our feedback from parents has always been very positive and supportive.

Tell us a bit about your school's minority participation in your classes.
Our school has minority students and they participate as successfully, if not more so, than the others.

Any advice for readers trying your project for the first time?
Many times beginning teachers are learning the mathematics along with their students from very good texts. This is an important learning period in the early teaching years. "Teaching on the fly" comes when there is a great command of the content as well as great comfort in management. Students get excited about topics that relate to them, and their excitement shows physically. A teacher has to be very relaxed about both behavior and ideas that are unexpected. Advice for beginning teachers: know your mathematics. This project may not be written carefully enough for a beginning teacher to venture into it. A beginning teacher may need the help of an experienced teacher.

Commentary

In keeping with the process for engaging students in MP1 (problem solving), Marie begins with a real-life connection of interest to her students that leads them to collect data so that they can make a presentation to compare and contrast their snack-eating habits to those of other countries using statistical analysis and basic skills for fractions and decimals (Focus, Rigor, Coherence). Students had to organize their data and choose appropriate measures of central tendencies to represent the data (MP4—models) and then justify why this measure is appropriate in terms of the context (MP6—precision).

The project is one that demonstrates students' strengths, weaknesses and ability to make connections between different modes of representing data (MP4—Models). Building on that information, Merrie guides students in making their own representations of data and presenting them to the class. She fully integrates problem solving, reasoning, communication, and connections in mathematics as the vehicles for reaching the goals of her unit. But how sound is the unit's mathematical content? Little scrutiny quickly reveals that its mathematical content is very rich. Merrie craftily gets students to unravel the concepts and connections of pie and bar graphs while they review computations for averages, uses of ratios, and the rounding of decimals to make better sense of data (Focus, Coherence and Rigor). Noteworthy is the fact that she does not present the practice of traditional basic skills as isolated skills for students to memorize. Rather, they arise as skills that need to be mastered because they are useful for completing a problem of interest to students (Fluency). In short, her instructional approach reflects CCSSM's placement of problem solving and precision as overarching math practices to teach content because the unit stems from a need to resolve a problem requiring attention to precise measures.

Marie's mastery of the content is reflected very early in the unit when she asks the class to suggest ways for organizing their own class' data set and says, "My next steps depends on what they choose to do." This constructivist response shows Merrie's confidence in her mathematical knowledge and her belief that it is her responsibility to understand and appreciate the needs and capacities of her students. Her comment on how collaboration with colleagues is helpful for generating and polishing her ideas, shows that she adheres to all the suggestions for reformed-based teaching listed in Chapter 2.

For those interested in using similar but more accessible data for comparison, go to http://content.healthaffairs.org/content/29/3/398.full. There are summaries and graphs from national surveys of food intake in U.S. children that kids can explore to support trends such as: more than 27 percent of children's daily calories are coming from snacks.

Unit Overview

Statistics with Snack Food

Aim: What measures can we use to compare our class' consumption of snack food to that of other countries?

Objective: Using data from the Snack Food Association, students will compare and contrast data from other countries to their own by using measures of central tendencies, bar graphs and pie graphs.

Grade Level: 6

Prerequisites:

- ◆ Ratio and proportions.
- ◆ Degree measures in a circle and related sectors.

CCSSM Content: Number and Relations (ratios, fractions, decimals)

Statistics and Probability: 6.S.P.(.1– .5)

CCSSM Practices: MP1: Problem solving, MP2: Reasoning, MP4: Modeling, MP6: Precision

Mathematical Concepts: Students will apply concepts of mean, median, and mode, to create graphs for real-life data. They will determine and apply relationships between pie and bar graphs to transform one into the other.

Materials and Tools:

- ◆ One copy of Snack Food Graph Unit sheet per student (Figure 7.1).
- ◆ Masters for transparencies.
- ◆ Recipe cards for recording information about self and estimated snack foods.
- ◆ Graph paper, scissors, tape.
- ◆ Student journals.

Management Procedures:

Major sections of unit:

A. Using statistics on world consumption of snack food (*Snack World* magazine, various issues, published by Snack Food Association, Alexandria VA or *We're Number One*, Andrew L. Shapiro, Vintage Books, N.Y., 1992, p. 31), students will gather their own personal data on snack food consumption as a class and compare it to other countries. To determine how different their class is, students will learn to record data in tables, use measures of central tendency (mean, median, mode, range) to discuss the data, and will represent the data visually in graphs (pie and bar).

B. Students will work in teams to create a statistical project to show to the class, based on data collected from classmates. Topics will be chosen by students and will be presented to demonstrate their knowledge of gathering, recording, and analyzing data. Classmates will help critique the presentations.

C. Students will take a final examination by paper/pencil, individually. The final examination will reflect the knowledge, skills and concepts gained through studying as a class about snack food consumption and through creating team projects.

Assessment: See B and C under management procedures above.

8

Teachers Adapting Tasks to Closely Align to CCSSM

Consider this quote from a student:

> "Math is either boring or hard. If I get it, it's boring. If I don't it's hard."
> We want to challenge students but not in the wrong ways.
> The question for teachers is: How de we challenge students so that students find math satisfying and challenging in all of the right ways?
>
> (Dan Meyer, http://blog.mrmeyer.com/)

One of the things I (Yvelyne) do to continue growing in my understanding and application of the CCSSM is to attend CCSSM institutes. I participated in an NCTM online course for high school teachers which was facilitated by Kristin Keith. While the course, "Engaging Students in Learning: Mathematical Practices and Content Standards: Extended Online Professional Development—Grades 9–12," was a continuation of a summer face-to-face institute which I could not attend, the Fall topics did not require the summer's prior knowledge and if so, webinars, readings or PowerPoint's from the summer were readily accessible. The extended sessions were also taped and available to participants during the term of the course. Kristin's ease with navigating Moodle and the Adobe Connect interfaces to present her work or those of other presenters, helped teachers from across the United States to form a community of learners.

In addition to meeting teachers who care about teaching, what I greatly enjoyed was the opportunity to listen to and chat with presenters whose work I had read or seen applied many times in workshops. For example, rather than talk about the work of Bill McCallum, who is a lead writer for the CCSSM, or of Dan Meyer's strategies for creating engaging tasks, Kristin invited them as speakers and had participants view a recorded NCTM presentation by Meyer. We posed questions by typing or using a microphone so that we and the presenters could quickly respond. Noteworthy is that online discussions included many participant-to-participant sharing that modeled what we wished students would do in our classes rather than the traditional teacher-to-student discourse. The presenters provided helpful strategies for integrating worthwhile tasks in lessons which I will describe next.

An assignment for the course was to view Dan Meyer's summer presentation on how to create or adapt problems to engage students at high cognitive levels. Dan showed examples of tasks that do a disservice to students because they:

1. Reduce math to filling-in the blanks and referring to worked-problems as examples.
   In such problems, students are given all the information necessary to problem solve: the numbers, formula, a leading visual, etc . . . and . . . if they get stuck, there are hints of where to find a sample worked-problem in the chapter.
2. Abstract the problem for the student.
   Textbook problems are typically decomposed into several parts that students have to process in order to answer the main question.
3. Hide the statement of the main problem from students until the very end.
   This is a consequence of doing the abstractions for students. Because students are first guided with the important questions leading to the main problem, they do a lot of reading before coming to the statement of the problem.

Dan showed visuals and examples to illustrate the value of transforming problems to engaging ones that add abstraction and reasoning. Below are his recommendations for doing so:

1. Don't hide the task from the student. Present the challenge question first and allow students the opportunity to decompose the problem.
2. Have students abstract the problem. Don't do it for them.
3. Separate the tasks—just like they are in real life, then, have conversations to help determine what should follow next since in real life we often will not know what to do ahead of time.
4. Provide next steps *only* when students are ready for them.
5. Use visuals that are worth abstracting—that means the visual is interesting and has information that does not reduce students' opportunity to reason about which information is important or necessary to obtain.
6. Keep a camera or camera phone handy and be ready to take interesting shots of the math that is encountered unexpectedly.
7. Look for problems that already have these characteristics or good visuals that you can easily transform.

A list and examples of engaging videos produced by Dan are at threeacts.mrmeyer.com. A presentation by Dan similar to what we viewed is *Math Class Needs a Makeover* and is at www.ted.com/talks/dan_meyer_math_curriculum_makeover.html

After viewing Dan's presentation, Kristin assigned the following:

Dan speaks about the types of questions that are available in the textbooks and why they limit students' thinking. What has been your experience with the questions that your students are completing? What can you take from Dan's presentation that can help you with the types of problems you find provided in the textbook? How do you think these changes will benefit your students? Adapt a task using sample textbook problems, former assessment problems, or problems that have been used previously by:

- ◆ Choosing a partner to work with you in the area of: Algebra 1, Geometry, Algebra 2, Pre-Calculus/Calculus, Trigonometry.
- ◆ Adapting a task using sample textbook problems, former assessment problems, or problems that have been used previously.
- ◆ Working with your partner to adapt the task.

- ◆ Posting your adapted task assignment to the appropriate section below. Include the following:
  - − a copy of your original task (including source information);
  - − a copy of the adapted task; and
  - − your written summary.
- ◆ Reading through your classmates assignments and commenting on at least TWO other participants' adapted task.

Teachers' Adaptation of Tasks

Believing that it is difficult for many teachers to reinvent and create tasks due to time constraints, I received permission to include some of the tasks adapted by the teachers that may prove helpful to middle grades teachers. I present the tasks below without any comments but I must say that the first one by Kristin and Megan (Figure 8.1) embodies Dan's suggestions and is a wonderful example of "less is more."

Figure 8.1

Partner Task-Algebra

Kristin Mullins and Megan Farrelly

Original Task

Years of Education, x	Annual Salary, y
0	28
2	40
4	52
6	64
10	88

13. SALARY The table shows a person's annual salary y (in thousands of dollars) after x years of education beyond high school.

a. Graph the data.

b. Write a linear function that relates the person's annual salary to the number of years of education beyond high school.

c. What is the annual salary of the person after 8 years of education beyond high school?

Revised Task

According to this data, would 8 years of education after high school be worth the annual salary you would earn? Explain your thinking using numbers, symbols, words or pictures.

Years of Education After High School	Annual Salary in Thousands of Dollars
0	28
2	40
4	52
6	64
10	88

Dolores Espinoza: Building a Ramp

Source: McDougal Littell Algebra 2

Prerequisite Knowledge: This task is appropriate for students who know similar triangles, proportions, and the Pythagorean Theorem.

Mathematical Content: Students determine the length of a wheelchair ramp using two different state standards. They will investigate the effect of slope on the length of the ramp. They need to identify necessary information, draw a scale model, use appropriate labels, and answer the questions in context with appropriate units of measure.

CCSSM Content: Process Standards: Problem Solving, Connections, Representations.

Mathematical Practices: MP1–MP8.

Materials: A copy of the task, graph paper, ruler, and a calculator.

Original Task

Figure 8.2

Original Problem

54. MULTI-STEP PROBLEM You are in change of building a wheelchair ramp for a doctor's office. Federal regulations require that the ramp must extend 12 inches for every 1 inch of rise. The ramp needs to rise to a height of 18 inches.

▶ Source: *Uniform Federal Accessibility Standards*

18 in.

a. How far should the end of the ramp be from the base of the building?

b. Use the Pythagorean theorem to determine the length of the ramp.

c. Some northern states require that outdoor ramps extend 20 inches for every 1 inch of rise because of the added problems of winter weather. Under this regulation, what should be the length of the ramp?

d. *Writing* How does changing the slope of the ramp affect the required length of the ramp?

Adapted Task

You are in charge of building a wheelchair ramp for a doctor's office. Federal regulations require that the ramp must extend 12 inches for every 1-inch of rise. The ramp needs to rise to a height of 18 inches.

1. Draw a diagram to represent this situation. Label the diagram with the appropriate measurements.
2. Determine the distance of the base from the building to the end of the ramp.
3. Find the length of the ramp.
4. Some northern states require that outdoor ramps extend 20 inches for every 1-inch rise. Under this new regulation, what would the length of the ramp be?
5. What affects the lengths of the ramps? Use the graph paper provided to compare the ramp from the doctor's office to the ramp of the northern states. Explain your reasoning in detail.
6. Why do northern states have different regulations than southern states? What affects the decision to have different regulations?

Summary

I chose this problem on Slope because I felt comfortable with the content and the level of the problem. It was a familiar problem and it made it easier for me to make changes on it. I liked this problem because it starts with a real-life situation. It also provides a set of standards to build a wheelchair ramp.

The questions require or reinforce the following:

Question 1: Students can decide to draw two similar triangles information given.
Question 2: They need to write a proportion in order to find the length of the base.
Question 3: They have to use the Pythagorean Theorem to find the length of the ramp.
Up to this point students have used prior knowledge.
Question 4: This question reinforces questions 2 and 3 because in order to find the length of the new ramp they will have to use again proportion and the Pythagorean Theorem.

Question 5: In order to answer this question, students make scale models of both ramps using graph paper. Students should realize that what affects the length of the ramp is the height and the base of the triangle. This question helps students develop further their concept of slope based on their knowledge of geometry.

Question 6: This is a class or group discussion question. In order to answer this question, students need to put the concept of steepness (slope) in the context of the problem.

Kristin Mullins: Algebraic Representation of Perimeter

Holy Spirit Regional Catholic School, Huntsville, AL.

Source: Holt McDougal Algebra 2

Prerequisite Knowledge: This task is appropriate for students who know similar triangles, proportions, and the Pythagorean Theorem.

Mathematical Content: I chose to do my Adapted Task using a perimeter activity from Chapter 1 in my Algebra I text: Holt McDougal Algebra I with my eighth graders who are in a ninth grade Algebra I curriculum. As I was preparing this lesson, I wanted a way to be certain my students recalled perimeter before we used the variables because they often confuse Area and Perimeter.

Process Standards: Problem Solving, Connection, Communication, Representation.

Mathematical Practices: MP1–MP6.

Materials: A copy of the task, graph paper, ruler, and a calculator.

Original Task

Figure 8.3

 # Perimeter

Connecting Algebra to Geometry

The distance around a geometric figure is called the *perimeter*. You can use what you have learned about combining like terms to simplify expressions for perimeter.

A closed figure with straight sides is called a *polygon*. To find the perimeter of a polygon, add the lengths of the sides.

Example 1

Ⓐ Write an expression for the perimeter of the quadrilateral.

Add the lengths of the four sides.

$$P = (a + 3) + (2a - 8) + (3a - 3) + (a - 1)$$

Combine like terms to simplify.

$$P = (a + 2a + 3a + a) + (3 - 8 - 3 - 1)$$
$$= 7a - 9 \qquad \text{This is a general expression for the perimeter.}$$

Ⓑ Find the perimeter of this quadrilateral for $a = 5$.

Substitute 5 for a.

$$P = 7(5) - 9 \qquad \text{Multiply, then subtract.}$$
$$= 35 - 9$$
$$= 26 \qquad \text{This is the perimeter when } a = 5.$$

Try This

Write and simplify an expression for the perimeter of each figure.

1.

2.

3.

Find the perimeter of each figure for the given value of the variable.

4. $k = 3$ 10

5. $n = 10$ 68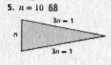

6. $y = 4$ 34

Adapted Task

FIRST: Instead of beginning with, "Open your text to page 52," I gave each student a piece of scrap paper and wrote on my Promethean Board: "Create a polygon with a perimeter of 26." I think this was an example Jo Baeler had given in her "How to Learn Math" online webinar. I chose to use a "simpler" known perimeter. I set the timer for two minutes and let them work without answering any of their questions until the timer went off.

FIRST RESULTS: The results were very interesting. I was pleased to see my eighth graders excited about going to the boards to draw "their" shape. I think this was because it was a different type of activity. I found that my students' hands were up far more than usual that day.

Some students made triangles with whole number values, but there were also rectangles and trapezoids as well as a 26-gon with each side of 1, which led to a 13-gon with each side of 2. I invited students to use the chalkboard, whiteboard or Promethean Board to show their polygon. I also have an ELMO projector, but each student was more eager to redraw their shape rather than show their original drawing.

QUESTIONING: "Create a polygon with a perimeter of 26" on the board, I asked, "What would make this task more difficult?" My goal was for the students to come to the idea of what my lesson was about: the polygons with algebraic expressions as side lengths, but the students actually suggested different ideas such as: "Use decimals in the side lengths." "Instead of a perimeter of 26, use a perimeter with a decimal."

SECOND: Then, I said, "Well, I have a challenge for you! How about this?" and I erased 26 and made the task read, "Create a polygon with a perimeter of $6x + 3$" and I set the timer again. After two minutes, I asked for volunteers. I was thrilled to see so many students eager to share! I think this is because they knew there was more than one answer. What I found most interesting was that every single student picked a value for x before finding the perimeter. They STILL did not do what was in the text, which I was aiming toward. Some, after creating a value for x found $6x + 3$ and used that number to create whole number valued side lengths on their rectangle.

QUESTION: Some students said $x = 2$ or 4 or even a decimal, but one stated that $x = 0$ and I asked, "How would they represent the sides of their polygon?" And, "Were there any other shapes you could use?" Another student asked if they could use a circle and I responded, "Is a circle a polygon?" That started another conversation in which I encouraged them to find a resource in the room to get the definition of polygon. They used a textbook glossary and then one asked to borrow my Mathematics dictionary on my desk to see if the definition was any more complex.

THIRD: I said, "Let me share with you another way to show a perimeter of $6x + 3$. Open your texts to page 52 and look at #1." I heard lots of "Oh!"s and "Oh yeah! I didn't think of that!" I pointed out the fact that, as many had chosen to do, the variable values were given for some problems, but not for others. As I passed out a final piece of scrap paper, I ended with, "Here's your final challenge: try #2 and #5." I set the timer for two minutes one more time and at the beeping of the timer, about half the students' hands were up, wanting to share!

Summary

This was a very involved, whole-class activity and I am excited to try another task like this in partners and/or small groups. I was thrilled with the fact that I didn't even open the book until the end when I made opening the book this "A-ha!" moment for everyone. And, I believe I would not have known that every single one of my students needed to assign a value to x when I gave them "Create a polygon with a perimeter of $6x + 3$." That really surprised me, reminding me that the way I expect them to think and/or respond may not be the way it actually goes! I think the students enjoyed this approach to the topic MUCH more than a typical, "Open your book to page ___. Today, we'll be learning about ___." I also feel like I learned more about my students teaching the idea this way, too!

Cynthia Trotman: The Actual Cost of Owning a Vehicle
Victory Christian Academy, Richmond, VA.

Source: Original

This is a problem that I wrote to help my students connect solving linear systems by graphing to the real world. They will need to discover a pattern, write a general rule and make a prediction for 7-year and 10-year costs of two cars based on miles driven.

Prerequisite Knowledge: Writing and evaluating algebraic expressions, graphing coordinates and linear functions, determining rule for a function given its table.

Mathematical Content: Functions 8.F.A.1., 2; 8.F.B.4., 5

NCTM Process Standards: Problem Solving, Reasoning and Proof, Communication, Connections, Representations.

Mathematical Practices: MP1–MP6.

Materials:

Students will receive five-year data for a Nissan Altima and Ford Fusion from
http://autos.yahoo.com/ford/fusion/2013/se/cost.html

http://autos.yahoo.com/nissan/altima-sedan/2013/2–5-sv/cost.html

Original Problem

The initial cost of Car A is 10,000 and the initial cost of Car B is 20,000; with
the actual cost of owning these cars respectively accumulating at the rate of
$.50 and $.40 per mile.

a) Calculate the actual cost for each year that the cars are driven 10,000
20,000 and 30,000 miles.
b) Graph each relation and predict the year in which the accumulated
costs are equal.

Adapted Problem

Often a lower sale price appears to be the better deal. However, the actual
cost of owning a car has more determining factors than the initial price of the
vehicle.

a) Compare the actual cost of owning a Nissan Altima with the actual
cost of owning a Ford Fusion of the same year and predict each cost
over a seven-year period.
b) Compare the actual cost per mile if the owner plans to drive the
Nissan 20,000 miles each year and the Fusion 12,000 miles each year
for seven years.
c) How do the actual costs compare after five years if the owner of the
higher priced car received a $1,000 rebate? 0 percent financing?
d) Write at least two function-rules to generalize your findings.
e) Illustrate your findings on the coordinate plane.

Summary

The students separated into four groups of two; each group coming up with
a different strategy. Group A: Took the published five-year cost, divided by 5
then multiplied by 7 to estimate the seven-year cost. Group B: Looked at the
different growth rates between each year and made a seven-year estimate.
Group C: Estimated the seven-year cost using the published cost per mile

ratio and estimated annual mileage. Group D: Made a scatter plot with the yearly totals for each car.

I was pleasantly surprised at the discussion and techniques that each group used and most surprised with the group who chose to create a scatter plot. Students were unfamiliar with some of the terms like depreciation and rebate and they did not understand why their calculation of loan interest did not match the published loan interest for each year. This led to me giving them a brief overview of compound interest vs. simple interest. They were uncomfortable about making estimates; they were looking to determine one way to find one answer. As I reassured them that it was okay to work through the strategy that they created and that there was no one right answer, they seemed to enjoy the task. Students worked 20 minutes on this task. As time passed, Group A and Group D were the groups to accomplish writing a function rule. Group A estimated an average rate of change in cost using the first-year's cost as the y-intercept. Group D asked to use a graphing calculator to calculate the lines-of-best fit.

Class ended before students could graph their results. However, we will complete the graphing portion of this task for the next class. This task is rich with knowledge, fosters questions and is very engaging. As a teacher, the questions that students posed let me know that they were interested and excited about what they were doing. In addition, students who showed little interest or recall when completing textbook problems were very engaged in their groups and were able to contribute strategies.

Stacy Remphrey: Introducing Linear Equations
Charles F. Patton Middle School, Kennett Square, PA.

Source: Original

My students come to my class with some experience in linear equations already so I just have to review the concepts. I typically start my linear equations unit with the notes in Table 1. There are more problems but I think you get the idea. We discuss the ideas and how they work and then I have students graph two equations similar to $y = 2x + 1$ and $2x + 3y = 6$.

Prerequisite Knowledge: graphing coordinates and linear functions, determining rule for a function given its table.

Mathematical Content: Functions.

NCTM Process Standards: Problem Solving, Reasoning and Proof, Communication, Representations.

Mathematical Practices: MP1–MP6, MP8.

Materials: 4–5 cups per group, two rulers for each group, graphing calculators or use desmos.com.

Original Problem

See Figure 8.4 overleaf.

Adapted Task

I used an idea from Dan Meyer's blog and changed it a bit to make it my own. This is the website: http://blog.mrmeyer.com/?p=692

Cup stacking:

◆ Began by holding up 2 cups and asking them to write down an estimate of how many it would take to match my height.
  – Asked students to give an example of an estimate that is way too low and then one that is way too high.
  – Then said, "OK, well what do you think you need to figure this out?" They said they wanted cups, my height, a ruler, a calculator, paper and a pencil.
  – Gave each group 4–5 cups and 2 rulers and told them my height.
  – Each group worked to calculate an answer. I wrote all of the answers on the white board then each group brought up their cups and started adding them to the stack next to me. At times I would stop and say, "So how are you feeling about your answer now?" When we got close I would say, 'Want more? Less?" Until they decided it was right and then we compared with answers on the board.
  – Asked students to tell me how they found the number of cups. I wrote all of their different work on the board and we discussed if they meant the same thing and why different operations were done and different numbers were used.
  – Asked the groups to come up with an equation so that we could find out how many cups we would need for anyone in the class.
  – Split the class in three and picked one person from each group. Students used their equation to find the number of cups needed for the person in their group and then we tested to see if they got it right.

Figure 8.4 Stacy's Notes to Review Linear Functions

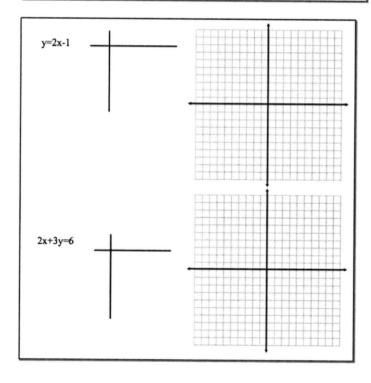

> 7-3 Functions-Tables-Graphs
>
> - The coordinate plane is filled with an infinite amount of lines. Each line has characteristics that make it stand out among all the others. You are unique and have characteristics that make it possible for me to pick you out of a group of 10, 100, or 1000. The same is true for a line. Through this unit we will learn about these special characteristics.
>
> - Table: Each function has a table of values that is unique. Sometimes another function may have one or two matches in the table but it will never have all of the same values.
>
> - Graph: Each function has its own unique graph related to the table of values. Again, another function may go through one or more points but it will not share all of the points.

- Questions on the board: What varied when we did the cups for me and the cups for the new person? What stayed constant?
- We looked at our equation and identified where the constants were and what they meant and what the variables meant.
- We wrote all of the functions on the board and again discussed if they meant the same thing and discussed differences so that we could decide on one to use as a class. This was a discussion where I simply moderated because I didn't want to tell them which was right. They had to defend which one they wanted to use and which ones they didn't think were right.
- Create a graph with the variables on the axes.
- We put all of the points on the graph and the students saw they made a line.
- Used desmos.com to show them the graph and other points on it.
- Interpreted the meaning of other points.
- Was it OK to have a decimal in the height? What about in cups?
- Discussed why they only needed the first quadrant instead of all 4 (as the free graphing calculator from Desmos.com showed).
- Looked at some interesting points and what they mean (x and y intercepts but we didn't call them intercepts).
- What does (3, 0) mean? And one of my students even said, "That means you are smaller then the cup so you can't have a cup to measure you!"

Notes:

◆ Make stacks of 20 and mark them with a marker. This makes it easier and faster to count them out when you are stacking them to measure.
◆ If this is done in multiple periods, only do the teacher measurement in one class. In the next period, pick a student. (Otherwise they will hear the answer from the students in the class before and just blurt it out.)

Summary

By starting with this task, the students were definitely more engaged. Because it was set in a context, the students were very quick to see a relationship between the cups and the height. After each group had gotten their number for how many cups tall I was, they took turns adding to the stack. As we got closer to my height, I had students standing up out of their seat because they were so excited to see if they got the answer! They then debated things such as "I don't think it is perfectly straight!" or "I don't know that the cups are pushed all the way together!" Talk about attending to precision!

I loved the discussion piece too because we definitely had some arguments break out about different pieces. For example, the height of one cup was 3.5 inches and the rim was 0.5 inches. Most of the students got an equation such as cups = (height −3) × 2. However, some students subtracted 3.5 instead of 3. I did not tell them which one I thought was right, I just said, "I'm not sure. Convince us to believe what you believe." The comments were amazing.

I plan to keep coming back to this activity as we look at intercepts and slope and talk about what they meant in this particular situation. I think this helps them apply the ideas of slope, intercepts, and just analyzing equations for the parts that are valid in certain contexts.

One interesting piece is that the seventh grade Algebra teacher did the same task with his students. His students did not have any background in linear equations and found the line that he created with Desmos to be almost magical.

Megan Farrelly: Real-life Application of Integers
Mark Twain Middle School, Alexandria, VA.

Source: www.scoe.org/files/mars-grade7.pdf

Prerequisite Knowledge: Integer Operations.

Mathematical Content: Integer Operations.

NCTM Process Standards: Problem Solving, Communication, Representation.

Mathematical Practices: MP1.

Materials: Give students a copy of Figure 8.6.

Original Problem

Figure 8.5 Megan's Original Task

MARS Task Grade 7. Mathematics Assessment, n.d. Web. www.scoe.org/files/mars-grade7.pdf.

Quiz

This problem gives you the chance to:

◆ Interpret a table of data

◆ compare results of calculations

Steve, Marty, Zac, and Liz take part in a quiz.
The quiz consists of ten questions.
Here are their results.

	Steve	Marty	Zac	Liz
Number of **correct** answers	5	4	6	5
Number of **incorrect** answers	4	4	3	1
Number of questions **not attempted**	1	2	1	4

A **correct** answer scores **3** points.
An **incorrect** answer scores **minus 2** points.
A question **not attempted** scores **0** points.

This is how Steve works out his total score:
$5 \times 3 = 15$ points, $4 \times -2 = -8$ points, and $1 \times 0 = 0$ points = 7 points

1. Who scores the most points?
   Show how you figured it out.

2. One of the rules is changed.
   A question not attempted scores minus 1 point.

   Who scores the most points?
   Show how you figured it out.

Adapted Task

Figure 8.6 Megan's Adapted Task

Grading Policies

Steve, Mark, Zoe, and Liz complete a quiz. Their quiz consists of ten questions. Here are their results:

	Steve	**Mark**	**Zoe**	**Liz**
Number of correct answers	6	4	6	5
Number of incorrect answers	2	4	3	1
Number of questions not attempted	2	2	1	4

Ms. Lee grades quizzes according to these rules:	Mr. Powell grades quizzes according to these rules:
◆ A correct answer scores 3 points.	◆ A correct answer scores 3 points.
◆ An incorrect answer scores negative 3 points.	◆ An incorrect answer scores negative 2 points.
◆ A question not attempted scores 0 points.	◆ A question not attempted scores negative 1 point.

Which student(s) would prefer to be in Ms. Lee's class and which student(s) would prefer to be in Mr. Powell's class?

Support your choice with using numbers, symbols, words and/or pictures.

Whose class would you rather be in? Explain why.

Summary

I found the original task on a website that I had found as a resource for finding tasks. After reading the task I knew I could adapt it, so it did not have as much scaffolding. The Math 7 team has decided to implement one task each unit this school year, and as the math coach I am supporting them in this goal. Teachers implemented this during the first unit of the curriculum, Integer Operations. I co-taught with a teacher in order to see how students reacted to this task.

This adapted task helps students to practice the first mathematical process standard; make sense of problems and persevere in solving them. Students have to analyze the given constraints and form meaning of the solution. I work in Virginia, so we do not use the common core standards. This mathematics helps students to complete the Virginia standard MTH.7.3.b.

Students completed this task at the end of the unit, as a way to review for the unit test the following class period. I handed out the task and asked for the students to read it over and gave them five minutes of individual think time. After five minutes of individual quiet think time, students separated into groups of three or four and were given the opportunity to talk about the task. The students had difficulty understanding the term "not attempted," but with this exception most students had a plan on how to organize and complete the task. If done again I may try it at the beginning of the unit to see what they can do before learning the procedures or exploring the operations. When given a real-life context students can usually complete the mathematics, even if they had not yet learned the topic in math class, at least at the middle school level.

9

Jim Specht: The Last Great Race

The Iditarod Trail Sled Dog Race is as much a part of the culture of Alaska as Mardi Gras is of New Orleans. The high school principal in McGrath, one of the race checkpoints, once said that their town only observes three holidays—Christmas, the Fourth of July, and Iditarod. When I learned that the race is covered on the Web in real time for two weeks every March, I thought it would be a great project for my general math students. Caught up in following the race, they could learn how to interpret data in various kinds of tables and graphs, and at the same time we could explore the geography and culture of Alaska.

(Jim Specht, Hillsboro High School, Hillsboro, Oregon)

Jim Specht tries to use real-world activities as much as possible in his math classes. For his general math students, he finds it's also important for the activity to be intriguing; otherwise, it's just another word problem. Before he assigns a lesson, he tests it on himself: Is it interesting? Will he enjoy seeing the students' work, or will it be just another set of papers to grade? For a long-term project, is the math component real or contrived? The idea of following the Iditarod—the "Last Great Race"—with his class struck him as "just so cool" that he decided to give it a try.

Jim's preparation for the project was extensive. One concern was that he has only one online computer; in addition, he may get a busy signal as he tries to access the Iditarod Committee's homepage during class (www.iditarod.

com/). He planned to use his home computer as a backup, downloading the latest data before he comes to school each day.

He collected, and placed on reserve in the school library, periodicals with reports on previous races. He purchased from the Iditarod Committee a videotape of the race; from AAA, a map of Alaska; and from an airport, an airline chart showing rivers, elevations, towns, airports, and radar beacons across the state of Alaska. Based on the data available on the homepage, he devised a number of appropriate and interesting questions for his students to investigate. One week before the race, he taught (or reviewed) how to create and interpret bar graphs, line graphs, and box-and-whiskers plots, using a graphing calculator.

Engaging Students

Now he is ready to introduce the project to his students. He starts with a general discussion. "Who has heard of the Iditarod Trail Race?" (Some share bits and pieces of information.) "How did it get started?" (No one knows.) "What's a musher?" (The person who handles the sled and the dogs.) "What must it be like to travel by dog sled for 1,131 miles, from one coast of Alaska to the other?" And, having piqued their interest, "How can we find out more about the Iditarod?"

He tells the class that they will be immersed in the race for the next two weeks. They will download the latest information from the internet every day, and prepare graphs, tables, charts, and maps from the data. Each will choose two individual mushers to follow, keeping a daily log of their adventures and analyzing the race data to explain their performance. Each student will compile a folder for the project (see Figure 9.1).

The first assignment is to research the background of the race. For many, this project was their first experience gathering data from the Web. Sharing what they find, they submit their reports. Most have some version of the following story:

> In the winter of 1925, the Alaskan community of Nome was threatened by a diphtheria epidemic. The townspeople feared that, without help, the settlement would be devastated. Pack ice had frozen the harbor, and in an era of biplanes and model-T cars it appeared that there was little hope that help might arrive before the spring thaw. When the people in the town of Anchorage learned of the threat to their fellow Alaskans, heroic mushers volunteered to use dog sleds to take the necessary medicine across the 1100 miles of roadless mountains and

Figure 9.1 Iditarod Folder Requirements

All work completed for the project will be organized in a folder. Check all calculations and hand in neat work.

Please organize your work according to the sections below.

1. Title page
2. Table of contents
3. History of the Iditarod
4. Biographies of two mushers
5. Map of Alaska with the trail outlined
6. Graphs of:
    a. Male vs. female competitors
    b. Veterans vs. rookies
    c. Elevation of sites
    d. Daily high and low temperature in Anchorage
7. Daily log sheets
8. Evaluation of project

frozen tundra. Their hazardous journey through blizzards and ice storms over the Iditarod Trail saved the settlement of Nome. To this day it is honored yearly by a dog sled race that covers approximately the same route. Many people in Alaska follow the Iditarod closely with great pride, as it is a part of the culture unique to this 49th state.

Next Jim downloads the list of the racers, also called mushers (see Figure 9.2), which gives their names and home states and identifies first-time Iditarod racers. From the board, students record facts and statistics about the racers and Jim asks preliminary questions:

◆ How many of the mushers are Alaskan? What percent of the total is that?
◆ How many of the racers are Iditarod rookies? Veteran racers?
◆ How many women are competing this year?

Working in pairs, students examine the data, calculate the answers, and sketch circle graphs by hand to represent the results (see Figure 9.3).

From the table of biographical data, Jim tells each student to choose two mushers. (Some take the time to research past race results in *Sports Illustrated*, *Newsweek*, and *Time* before choosing "their" racers!) From the data, they write profiles of the two for their Iditarod folders.

The next task is to sketch the race trail on copies of the AAA map of Alaska. Jim downloads the table of checkpoints and tells students to use that

Figure 9.2 Adapted List of Musher Facts

Last Name	First Name	Home Town	Status	Sex	Last Ran	Best Finish	Year
Buser	Martin	Big Lake, AK	Veteran	M	2000	1	1992-4-7
Cotter	Bill	Nenana, AK	Veteran	M	2000	3	1995
Gebhardt	Paul	Kasilof, AK	Veteran	M	2000	2	2000
Halter	Vern	Willow, AK	Veteran	M	2000	3	1999
Hahn	Nils	Germany	Rookie	M	0	0	0
Ramstead	Karen	Perryvale, Canada	Rookie	F	0	0	0

Figure 9.3 Student's Circle Graphs

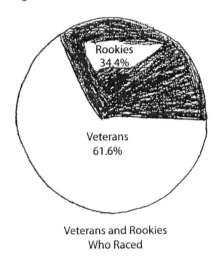

Veterans and Rookies
Who Raced

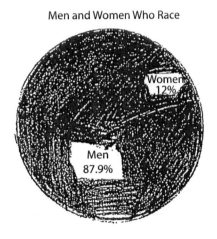

Men and Women Who Race

as a guide (see Figure 9.4). But although the map shows Alaska's roads and towns, students soon discover that the Iditarod Trail crosses vast stretches of wilderness, and many of the checkpoints are not actual communities of any size. How can they determine the approximate locations of the checkpoints that are not shown on the map?

Jim introduces the idea of interpolating between two known checkpoints to approximate the position. The students have studied ratio and proportion

Figure 9.4 Checkpoints and Distances
(EVEN YEARS)

Checkpoints	Distance Between Checkpoint	From Anchorage	To Nome
Anchorage to Eagle River	20	20	1131
Eagle River to Willow	50	70	1081
Willow to Yentna	45	115	1036
Yentna to Skwentna	34	149	1002
Skwentna to Finger Lake	45	194	957
Finger Lake to Rainy Pass	30	224	927
Rainy Pass to Rohn	48	272	879
Rohn to Nikolai	93	365	786
Nikolai to McGrath	48	413	738
McGrath to Takotna	23	436	715
Takotna to Ophir	38	474	677
Ophir to Cripple	60	534	617
Cripple to Ruby	112	646	505
Ruby to Galena	52	698	453
Galena to Nulato	52	750	401
Nulato to Kaltag	42	792	359
Kaltag to Unalakleet	90	882	269
Unalakleet to Shaktoolik	40	922	229
Shaktoolik to Koyuk	58	980	171
Koyuk to Elim	48	1028	123
Elim to Golovin	28	1056	95
Golovin to White Mountain	18	1074	77
White Mountain to Safety	55	1129	22
Safety to Nome	22	1151	0

before, but Jim knows they have not mastered these concepts. He guides them through the steps, the answers for which are in parentheses:

1. We need to find approximate locations for White Mountain and Safety. What information from Figure 9.4 and from our map can help

us? (The checkpoints are between Golovin and Nome, both of which are on the map. Figure 9.4 shows the distances.)

2. Let's start with White Mountain. How far is White Mountain from Golovin? (18 miles.)

3. The scale of our map is one inch for every 60 miles. How can we use that information? (18 miles is about 1/3 of 60 miles, so the distance from White Mountain to Golovin on the map should be about 1/3 of an inch. Draw a one-inch segment; place compasses (the kind used for geometrical constructions) on the segment and adjust them to a little less than 1/3 of an inch. On the map, use the compasses to draw a circle with that radius around Golovin.)

4. What other clues can we use to locate White Mountain? (Students find this aspect interesting. The map shows that Golovin is on the seacoast, with mountain ranges to the north. The name "White Mountain" is a hot clue.)

5. What should we do next? (Follow the same procedure for Safety, which is 22 miles from Nome. Use the compasses to approximate a little over 1/3 of an inch, and mark that distance. Any other clues? Nome is also on the coast, just south of the mountain range; the trail should stay out of the ocean!)

6. Finally, check to see if the distance between White Mountain to Safety, as we have located them on the map, is consistent with the information in Figure 9.4.

Having completed their trail maps, students are ready to think about situations that might affect their mushers on the trail. Jim presents this problem on the overhead projector:

Suppose a musher makes it from Koyuk to Elim in 6 hours. The same musher goes from Elim to Golovin in 7 hours. Is this surprising?

Using the information in Figure 9.4, the students set to work. Koyuk is 980 miles from Anchorage; Elim is 1,028 miles from Anchorage. The difference is 48 miles; they divide by the time, 6 hours, to find the rate, 8 mph.

Now they look at Elim and Golovin. At this point, one student remembers that the table shows "miles to next checkpoint," so they can save the step of subtraction. (Jim is pleased; one of his goals was to encourage students to seek patterns that will reduce computation as they read the charts.) The students calculate the musher's rate from Elim to Golovin and find that it's only 4 mph.

A discussion ensues. What might be the reasons for the difference in speed? Students offer ideas: Maybe the same dogs were used in both legs of the race and are getting tired; maybe the musher had to leave some dogs in Elim. What about the geography? Was the team climbing a mountain, or traveling through an area where there is very little snow? What about the weather? They conclude that they need more information. Jim is ready to oblige.

He downloads weather reports. Students make line and bar graphs of daily high and low temperatures in Anchorage and other sites along the trail; this gives them an idea of the trail conditions for the different teams. They use their map of Alaska and the weather reports to draw conclusions about wind direction and clear and cloudy skies.

Another table gives the elevations of the checkpoints which students use to plot the position and elevation of each checkpoint on the airline chart Jim has taped to the wall. On this larger map, the geography of Alaska is vivid— they note the vast mountain ranges, huge tracts of wilderness, great distances between populated areas, and very few roads. No wonder the AAA map doesn't show all the checkpoints! They prepare line graphs showing the elevation changes along the trail (see Figure 9.5), and it becomes obvious why some stretches of the trail go more slowly than others.

Figure 9.5 Student's Graph of Elevation Points

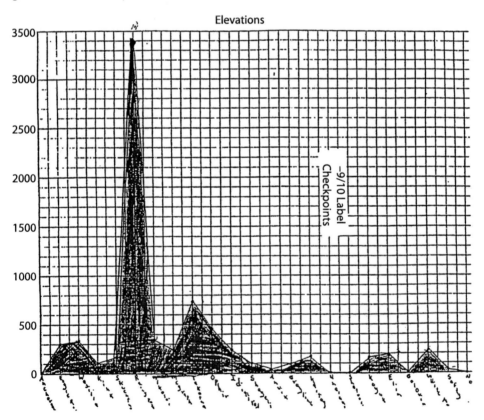

The highlight of each day, of course, is checking the racers' daily standings (Figure 9.6). About 15 minutes before class, Jim downloads the latest data and prepares it for distribution. Eager to see how their mushers are faring, the students are soon familiar with how to read the table—place standing, bib number, latest checkpoint, with the arrival time, number of

Figure 9.6 Adapted List of 63 Daily Checkpoint Standings

#	BIB	MUSHER	ID	Check Point Now	IN Date	IN Time	# Dog	Rest Time	ID	Check Point Before	Out Date	Out Time
1	34	Jeff King	21	Elim	3/16	13:28	8	00:35	20	Koyuk	3/16	7:42
2	3	DeeDee Jonrowe	20	Koyuk	3/16	10:25	9	06:18	19	Shaktoolik	3/15	13:41
3	32	Doug Swingley	20	Koyuk	3/16	3:22	9	06:16	19	Shaktoolik	3/15	19:45
4	37	Martin Bauser	20	Koyuk	3/16	3:17	9	06:22	19	Shaktoolik	3/15	19:48
5	58	Charlie Boulding	20	Koyuk	3/16	4:12	10	5:29	19	Shaktoolik	3/15	19:51
6	4	Mitch Seavey	20	Koyuk	3/16	4:52	11	4:58	19	Shaktoolik	3/15	22:18
7	17	Vern Halter	20	Koyuk	3/16	5:09	11	5:01	19	Shaktoolik	3/15	21:40
8	36	Rick Swenson	20	Koyuk	3/16	5:18	9	5:14	19	Shaktoolik	3/15	21:42
9	18	Linwood Fiedler	20	Koyuk	3/16	6:14	9	4:23	19	Shaktoolik	3/15	22:45
10	64	John Baker	20	Koyuk	3/16	6:11	10	***	19	Shaktoolik	***	20:38
11	49	Ramey Smyth	20	Koyuk	3/16	8:38	8	***	19	Shaktoolik	3/15	23:27
12	27	John Barron	20	Koyuk	3/16	8:38	7	***	19	Shaktoolik	3/16	00:38
13	38	Paul Gebhardt	19	Shaktoolik	3/16	6:16	10	6:07	18	Unalakleet	3/16	00:50

*** Blank line indicates that no reading was registered.

dogs, and rest period, followed by the departure time from the previous checkpoint (given in "military time"). Jim may zip out in the middle of class and download even more current data, usually with three or four changes in musher position—information the students pounce on and quickly process. Jim keeps the questions perking: "Is your musher at the halfway point? Past it, or not there yet? A third of the way? Are the dogs making better time today? Is your team gaining on the others?"

Jim distributes daily log sheets (see Figure 9.7), on which students record, compute, and reflect on the information about their two particular mushers. One of the entries is the musher's average speed in the last 24 hours. Students know the formula, but correctly entering the real-time data from Figure 9.6 into their calculators presents a challenge. In Figure 9.7, for example, the first step is to estimate the rate. But as the students perform the actual calculations, Jim notices some wildly different results on their calculator screens; in addition to 6.8, he sees 49.5, 65, or 8.2, depending on where students inserted parentheses, or whether they remembered to change minutes into hours.

Jim reminds them to check against their estimations—"Does my answer make sense?"—and to check their entries in the calculator. He takes the opportunity to review the order of operations, writing the most common incorrect results on the board and asking students to guess the kinds of errors that produced them.

In another challenging exercise, Jim's students use a graphing calculator to prepare a box-and-whiskers plot of the current standings within a nine-interval range. This requires that they find "friendly" interval lengths before entering the range data. To do this, they subtract 5 from the least number of miles, then try interval lengths in multiples of 25. For example, using un-adapted versions of Figures 9.4 and 9.6, students see that Jeff King leads and is at Elim, which is 1,028 miles from Anchorage, and the last-place team is at mile 364. They calculate: $365 - 5 = 360$; $50 \times 9 = 450$; $360 + 450 = 810$. They see that 50 is too small an interval to cover the range, so they try 75 or 100. Those using intervals of 75 set the range of their calculators for 360 to 1,035.

In List 1 on the graphing calculator, they enter the current "miles from Anchorage" standings of all the racers, based on the information in Figures 9.4 and 9.6. (Although they could have shortened the process by entering the frequency in List 2 (see Figure 9.8), all quickly enter the data in List 1 without a frequency count.) The calculator generates a box-and-whiskers plot and looking at the graph, students are surprised to see the box without the typical median line inside (see Figure 9.7). "Why did this happen?" they ask.

Figure 9.7 Daily Log Sheet with Sample Entries

Daily Log Sheet (with Sample Entries)

Today's Date: _March 16_

Musher #1   Name: _Vern Halter_   Bib# _17_

Position in the field: _7_

Latest milepost: _Koyuk_   Trail Miles: _980_

Last milepost listed: _ShakToolik_ Trail Miles: _922_

Distance since yesterday: _58 mi_ Time elapsed to travel that distance: _8:31_

Average speed in mph: _6.8 mph_ Calculation: _58mi/(8+31÷60)hr_

Musher #2   Name: _Paul Gebhart_   Bib# _38_

Position in the field: _13_

Latest milepost: _ShakToolik_   Trail Miles: _922_

Last milepost listed: _unalakleet_ Trail Miles: _882_

Distance since yesterday: _40 mi_ Time elapsed to travel that distance:

Average speed in mph: _5.6 mph_ Calculation: _40mi/(7+6÷60)hr_

Box and Whiskers Plot of Distances (Calculator Printout is ok)

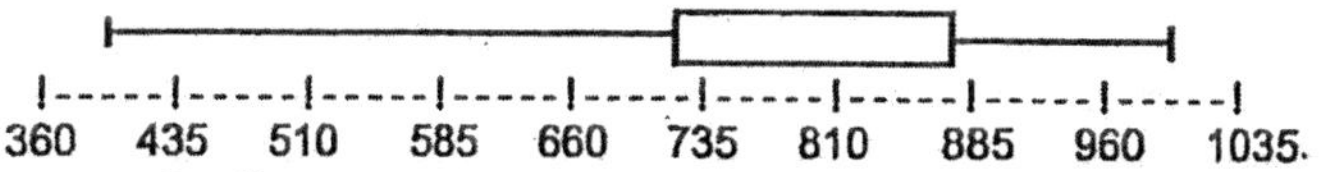

```
      |-----|-----|-----|-----|-----|-----|-----|-----|-----|
      360   435   510   585   660   735   810   885   960   1035.
```

Average Distance: _818_   Last Place Distance: _1028_

Median Distance: _792_   First Place Distance: _364_

Anecdotes of Interest: _Paul and Vern are doing better than most. The road to Kaltag is easy for many muskers because most of them get there at about the same time._

Figure 9.8 Loading Daily Standings

L1	L2	L3
1028	1	
980	11	
922	7	
882	7	
792	24	
698	9	
646	1	
413	2	
365	1	

From Jim's preparatory lessons, they have a general sense of how the lengths of the various sections depict clusters and spread of the data. Now, taking advantage of their curiosity, Jim seizes the opportunity to explore the concept of quartiles. Examining the data in Lists 1 and 2 and the Stats + Calc menu of his overhead calculator, he reviews box-and-whiskers plots, introducing new language. For example, in addition to saying, "Half of the mushers are clustered between these two checkpoints," Jim shows that they can also state, "Between 50 and 75% of the mushers are clustered between these two checkpoints, or quartiles."

As they continue to apply the quartiles, students gradually understand that the "lost median" actually overlaps with the first quartile line, at the left end segment of the box. Jim asks them to interpret this information. Their most common response is that 25 percent of the racers are at milepost 792, where 24 of the 63 racers have checked in. "Can you justify that from the data?" he asks. Doing the calculations, they find that 25 percent of 63 is less than 24. Now they realize that they should have said at least 25 percent were at that point. Finally, working together, students copy the graph and report the data from the Stats + Calc menu of the TI–82/83 calculator in their log sheet (see Figure 9.7).

Based on the maps, graphs, and charts they are compiling, together with the current weather reports and their daily log sheets, they keep a journal reflecting why they think their mushers are progressing as they do. Some class time is also devoted to storytelling; students share interesting items from their research, and Jim downloads anecdotes published on the website each day by a reporter who is following the race. These find their way into the journals and stimulate class discussions. For example, Jim asks students for their opinions on the blog topic, SPCA protests that race is inhumane. The class watches a video of last year's race, and sees the harsh conditions under which the mushers and dogs persevere. A lively debate ensues.

By the end of the project, students are dropping in during lunch and their free time to ask Jim to print out the latest update. "Having followed their mushers across the wilderness," he says, "they have a very real sense of ownership." As the race ends, they complete their reports and graphs, and submit the project folder for evaluation. The next day, Jim distributes a form for their assessment of the project. Students are also required to write a personal summary of the project (see Figures 9.9 and 9.10).

Figure 9.9 Student Assessment Of Project

On a scale of 1 through 10 (10 being highest), how would you rate the Iditarod project in the following areas:

1. Maintained your interest. _____

2. Taught you things you did not already know _____

3. Applied math and graphing skills in a meaningful way. _____

4. Helped you practice organization of materials. _____

5. Was worth the time. _____

6. What part of the project did you like best? _____

7. Offer suggestion for improving the project.

_____

_____

_____

8. Did you choose to share any of this project with your folks? If "yes," what part?_____

_____

9. In 3–5 sentences, why do you think it is called "The Last Great Race"?

_____

_____

_____

10. For homework, write a personal summary of the project describing what you have learned. Would you want to see it someday? Why or why not?

Figure 9.10 Student's Reflection on the Project

Personal Summary

When we first began this project, I had no clear idea of what the Iditarod Race was, how it got started or any knowledge of the accompanying details associated with this quest. Three weeks later, I now have a clearer idea of all, and though I still feel that it is taking advantage of dogs in one form or another, I do have a certain amount of respect for the race. It takes a strong person, mentally and physically, with a great trust in just a handful of dogs, to brave the Alaskan climate and terrain in hopes of not only winning the prize money of such a small amount, $50,000, but also being able to have the satisfaction of saying one completed it. Besides the knowledge of the statistical information gained, I found the race more interesting considering that I had two of my own mushers to have a certain amount of personal interest in. Even though neither one even finished in the top 30, the suspensefulness of the race was heightened because I had my mushers to root for.

I had peace of mind to some extent, also, knowing that the dogs were being treated wonderfully. There should not even be consideration of treating them any other way considering the feat they are forced to undertake. I say 'forced' because the dogs really don't have any other choice. It has been said that they just love to run and go crazy if they can't, and it could be so, but I wonder who exactly has asked them and if they carried on an in depth conversation with the dogs to obtain their opinion about the Iditarod.

However, overall, the project was less grueling than I thought it would be. Sometimes it was tedious and incredibly frustrating, mainly the first two days, but it got easier with time. I had an enormous amount of help from two incredibly kind fellow students who recorded my information for me when I became very sick. That was probably the single most stressful part of the whole project next to finding the elevations of all the checkpoints.

When the Iditarod comes around next year, I wonder if I'll tune in to it. Either way, my perspective on it will no doubt be different. I could say I might even be interested in it, but the more appropriate word, I believe, would be accepting!

Discussion Between Colleagues

What does a typical day in your class look like?

We integrate the use of graphing calculators into instruction several times a week. I often have to give oral instructions or handouts to help students work with the calculator. On projects like the Iditarod, I encourage students to rely on each other for help.

Students likely had gaps in their mathematical knowledge. Comment some more on how you prepared them to tackle your project.

Having them work in teams of two was very beneficial—the gaps were not so great that two of them together couldn't help each other understand the work. I do believe that children are born curious. My first responsibility is to kindle that curiosity into a desire for learning. If they know that I am truly working on it, they will generally try to work with me. When the students are engaged, everything else solves itself—discipline, attendance, attitude, and work ethic. What generally erodes students' enthusiasm is the burden of number crunching. I apply a judicious use of technology to keep the momentum going.

How did you assess the folders?

I graded them one page at a time. It was nothing profound. Every page was worth a maximum of 10 points, and 18 pages were expected, for a total of 180 possible points. I valued:

◆ mathematical accuracy;
◆ completeness—Did they finish the page? Include all entries?; and
◆ neatness and correctness in following directions.

What can you say about what students learned?

I think they valued what they learned. I require them to include some projects as part of their course portfolio. Every student selects the race for inclusion. All students also choose to include this project as an entry for their semester portfolio. Their reflections showed that they learned how mathematics can serve as a vehicle for exploring another place and culture. When you asked me to send you copies of students' work, I contacted five of my former students and asked them if they still had their folders. All five had not only kept them, but could easily locate them! Finally, when I read reflections that say "the project was sort of interesting," or "that wasn't bad," I take it as very high praise of a math project from these students.

What about your role as teacher during this project?

This activity was fun for me. As the race progressed, it was amazing to think that up in Alaska one of the judges at a checkpoint would log onto the internet with a laptop and a cell phone, and 10 minutes later I was able to place a downloaded copy of that data on an overhead transparency in my classroom. We truly live in an age of wonder.

My role in the classroom also contributed to my enjoyment—not a boring moment for me because students did not all work on the same thing at the same time. This was partly due to students' preferences, and partly due to logistics—for example, not everyone had a graphing calculator. Once students had the current downloaded information, I felt more like a coach. I would do a bit of refereeing to make sure that materials were shared fairly, or point out that several students could work from one box of colored pencils if the colors were shared wisely, and that protractors could be used as straight-edges if the line was less than six inches long. . . .

What did you learn from your students about projects of this sort?

Unfortunately, it did not prepare them for the climate of some of the traditional courses that came later. When they expect class to be interesting and intriguing, a traditional textbook course doesn't hold much interest.

Since the Iditarod Committee now has all the information necessary for your lesson nicely organized on its home page and have a map of the trail with all of the towns having a milepost in the race, would you modify your lesson the next time you teach it?

I would keep the AAA maps. Students learn the geography of one of our states while they apply mathematics to determine the location of unfamiliar places. Both skills are worthwhile.

Do you have any further suggestions for readers?

Require that students submit photocopies of their resources. I forbid originals because I don't want library materials to suddenly and mysteriously have holes in them. Although I did not know it when I created this project, a variety of classroom packets for this race are already available for use in schools. I also highly recommend that teachers show a videotape of the race—it strongly engages student in the spirit and culture of the experience. Finally, dare to be bold. There is no glory in doing something that is easy.

Commentary

Jim's idea to "reveal" (his own word) ratio, proportion and data analysis to students through statistics and data gathering did so in ways to deepen students' understanding of the mathematics and its applications (Focus). His approach is quite different from the traditional method: "Today we are going to solve proportion problems. Turn to page 101." The computations and graphs were all integral to the students' following "their" mushers and the focus on concept, procedural skill and fluency all intertwined in a real-life situation provided opportunities for students to review, enrich and extend their skills (Coherence and Rigor). The real data from the race also presented students with an interesting but challenging situation that is not easily encountered otherwise (MP1: Problem solving). For example, the box-and-whiskers plot, where the median and first quartiles were the same, showed a non-contrived graph of an event that required students to wrestle with making sense of a definition in light of the data: "What do the median and the first quartile represent in this case?" Although students used a calculator to produce the graph, they needed to determine an appropriate range and connect the table of values to the graph in order to make sense of the graph and its related output (MP1: Problem solving, MP2: reason abstractly and quantitatively, MP4: Use of models). Requiring that students provide details about the calculator graphs and to interpret what the intervals on the box and whiskers plot meant in terms of the location of their mushers, pushed students to make sense of the mathematics so that they could think and report clearly about the event (MP5: Construct viable arguments, MP6: Attend to precision, MP8: Repeated reasoning).

Jim's approach to proportional reasoning in conjunction with the calculator also required students to do more than merely push keys. Checking the calculators' results with students' estimations revealed how calculators do not free the mind of the thinking processes necessary to engage in non-routine problems. As an example, to facilitate easy entry into the calculator, Jim chose to show students how to represent rate of speed as: (given miles)/(given number of hours) = × miles/1 hour. This unit-rate approach for solving rate problems "has intuitive appeal because children have made purchases of one and many things and have had the opportunity to calculate unit prices and other unit rates" (Post, Behr and Lesh, 1986, 8).

Jim's use of the internet and the newspaper was a good way for integrating literacy skills and the latest in technology with readily available resources to engage students in a current event outside of their community. Both tools were effective in getting students to see and apply mathematics in making sense of data (MP5: Use tools strategically). In addition, students' sharing of stories about their mushers, or reflecting on the data they collected, provided opportunities for them to engage in communicating and learning about a task that was not only worthwhile but also based in the culture of one of our states. Jim's willingness to wrestle with whatever problems came up as he tried this lesson for the first time is to be commended.

Unit Overview

The Last Great Race
Aim: What are mathematical factors crucial to winning the Iditarod Trail Sled Dog?

Objective: Students will collect information on Alaska's Iditarod Race and deduce factors that helped determine outcomes.

Course: General mathematics, Pre-algebra

Source: Original ·

Grade: 6th

Number of 45-minute periods: 9

CCSSM Content: Ratio and Proportions: 6.RP.(A.1-A.3); Number and Operations: 6.NS.B.3; 6.NS.C.6c; Probability and Statistics: 6.SP.(B.4-B.5);

Mathematical Practices: MP1: Problem solving, MP2: Reasoning, MP3: Arguments, MP4: Modeling, MP6: Precision; MP8: Repeated reasoning

Mathematical Content: Students use a map's scale factor, distance formula, ratio and proportions and compute elapsed time to estimate unknown distances and speed of racers. They plot or interpret circle graphs, line graphs, box-and-whiskers plots

Prerequisites: "Students just need a genuine work ethic. A teacher can attend to skills instructions needed throughout the unit. However, a review of line graph, bar and circle graphs and box-and-whiskers plots is useful."

Materials and Tools: (Note: The race generally begins on the first Saturday in March. Check the Iditarod homepage (www.iditarod.com) for dates. The Iditarod Trail Race Committee also sells classroom kits.)

- ◆ At least one online computer.
- ◆ Graphing calculator with list capability similar to TI-82 (for pairs of students).
- ◆ Iditarod homepage (www.iditarod.com) to download facts and statistics about the running of the race:
  - – list of mushers;
  - – current daily standings of mushers;
  - – data on checkpoints and elevations; and
  - – weather conditions.

- Newspaper covering the race.
- Copy of a map of Alaska for each student.
- Airline map of Alaska.
- Previous periodicals on the Iditarod.
- Overhead projector.

Management Procedures:

- Discuss basic information about the race with students. Interesting trivia information and history are available from the homepage.
- Assign students to find additional information to complete a history of the race.
- Give students a copy of the list of mushers and have them graph rookies vs. veterans, males vs. females.
- Have students:
  - recreate the trail by using a map of Alaska, a copy of the checkpoint distances from Nome, and compasses;
  - draw a line and bar graph of low and high temperatures in Anchorage;
  - draw a line graph of the elevations of the checkpoints;
  - write biographies of two mushers and track them daily; and
  - complete their daily log sheet.

Assessment: Once the race is over, have students submit all entries for a grade and complete an assessment of the project.

10

Ivan Gill: What is a Gill? Meaningful Connections Between Measurement and Graphing

I try to instill in my teachers a sense of confidence to experiment, to use activities, to incorporate math, because these things add richness to the subject and help to build a solid understanding of both science and math. I would like to instill a sense of confidence in subject matter because it helps to have a comfort level in the content to allow you to do interesting things and to teach them accurately. I would like to instill a sense of humor because these subjects are best approached with joy and interest, and they are, ultimately, very human endeavors that we interact with daily.

(Ivan Gill, Ph.D., University of New Orleans, New Orleans, Louisiana)

Ivan Gill has taught in two public schools in New Orleans, one a highly selective magnet high school, the other an open-admission public high school that reformulated itself as a charter after the reconstitution of the public school system in the aftermath of Hurricane Katrina in 2005. I first met him as a Ph.D-level geology professor who enrolled in one of my classes at the University of New Orleans to become a certified science teacher. I was very impressed with his dedication to teaching as well as his insight in making meaningful connections between math and science that would invite students to formulate and test their own hypothesis of important concepts. When an opening for a science education faculty member opened in my department, I was happy that Ivan was accepted. We immediately applied for and received state grants from the Louisiana Systemic Initiative Program (LaSIP) for professional development from a reformed-based perspective of 4th–12th grade mathematics and science teachers. To address activities that would challenge these teachers, we sometimes split them into high school and middle school groups, but at other times we kept them as a whole to illustrate how to present a topic from multiple entry points. This chapter is one of the lessons he taught to eighth grade students and to all of the LaSIP teachers that showcases the LaSIP philosophy of teaching kids or teachers through engaging tasks that stimulate them to learn important mathematics.

The Launch

To launch the investigation, Ivan recounts the following story:

I hold in my hand a brushed stainless-steel cylinder. I found it, you see, in my uncle's house, which was built by my grandfather in the early 1920s. It was on a dresser, along with a hundred other dusty mementos and miscellaneous knickknacks—the footprints of a traveling life, exploring other places, other people. The walls of the house are covered with pictures of ancestors, dating into the 1800s and perhaps earlier. The furniture, likewise, belongs to another place and another time. A photograph on the wall of my grandfather as a young man, posed staring upward into space, perhaps a heroic pose common in the late 1800s. I never knew him. All these things are unsuitable for the climate of a little house built into the walls of a valley in the rainforest, on a little island in the Pacific where they settled. What was this shiny steel cylinder? It is precisely made, with clear grooves the thickness of a fingernail machined into the bottom that appear to be graduations. The lip of the cylinder is smoothly rounded, although the metal thickness is only a millimeter thick. Embossed circumferentially into the underside of the base of the cylinder are the words "Made in England" and "Stainless 18-8." I know the latter to indicate a high-grade stainless steel alloy. Embossed at the top lip of the cylinder are the words "1/3Gill" followed by a tiny stamp of a royal crown and perhaps a maker's-mark and perhaps a date: "77." These last can only be seen clearly, at least with my aging eyes, with a magnifying glass. The entire object gives the impression of care, quality, and precision, and the apparent approval of the Crown of the British Empire. What could this be? What could be its purpose? What is a Gill? I am hoping that you will help me decipher this.

Explore

Unit Measure of the Gill

At this point, the teachers are generating hypotheses, but the predominant one is that the metal cylinder is a measuring device, carefully made, and meant to hold the unit "1/3Gill."

Ivan responds: "A unit of measure? A Gill? What system of measurement? What does it measure and what quantity is it a measure of: Length? Weight? Mass? Volume?"

Georgina: Well, it must be a volume measurement. It is much like a graduated cylinder, but without graduations. The cylinder holds a particular amount of space, three dimensions, and we think the very top of the cylinder must be the measuring point.

Ivan: So, it is an ungraduated cylinder (surely after this number of years it would have graduated)? What, then, does it measure? What is a Gill?"

Henry: "The cylinder is small, larger than a thimble but smaller than a drinking glass. It must be designed to measure a fluid, a volume of a fluid ... so, I think that would make a Gill a unit of liquid volume as opposed to a dry volume?"

Ivan splits the class into groups of three to four teachers in mixed grade-levels and then says, "OK, let's go with that hypothesis. If that's the case, your job is to find out how big a unit a Gill is, to what system of units it belongs, and how it compares to units we know. You have the following materials for your groups and five minutes to come up with some procedures. Ivan directs their attention to a table with the following materials:

◆ One triple-beam balance.
◆ One 10mL-graduated cylinder.
◆ One wash bottle/dropper.
◆ One 600 or 1000mL beaker.
◆ Graph paper.
◆ Ruler (metric and English units).

Groups choose their materials and begin to share ideas on approaches for defining a Gill.

Group 1 decides on direct measurement of the contents of the cylinder.

Georgina: We can measure the amount of water the cylinder holds by using the graduated cylinder to pour a measured amount of water into the 1/3Gill cylinder until the cylinder holds its maximum capacity for water.

John: Agreed. It must be a measure of volume so we will fill it with water and see how much it holds and then . . . we will multiply it by three?

Ivan: By three? Why is three the magic number?

Yves: 'Cause it's only 1/3 of a Gill.

Damian: We can probably measure the volume by using its dimensions too.

Group 2 suggests a variant of Group 1's procedure, but reversed. They wish to fill the 1/3Gill cylinder to its capacity, then decant the water into the graduated cylinder to measure it.

Jou Jou: Where would we stop—all the way to the top?

Serge: Well, it doesn't have any markings on the top, but I guess that is what we should do.

Group 3 plans to use mathematics and a knowledge of geometry to solve the puzzle.

Carlos: We can probably use the volume formula for a cylinder because we can get the dimensions of the 1/3Gill by measuring them.

Julian: We should also fill it up with water to get its actual volume as a comparison.

Group 4 wants to use the balance to measure the weight of the water in the Gill-cylinder. Here Ivan asks some probing questions: "Do you mean *mass* or *weight*? What's the difference? Does it matter?"

Lisa replies: "Well, if we have a volume measurement in a Gill, how do we go from a mass measurement to a volume? We are not sure how this can be done."

"We will explore it further," says Ivan.

While groups are working, Ivan tells the class that there are five minutes left before sharing. The groups collect final thoughts:

Group 1:

Georgina: The 1/3Gill was made in England and if that was about 150 years ago, it was probably measured in British Imperial units. So it would be helpful to figure out the correspondence between the two. Ivan, how long has the 1/3Gill been in your family?

Ivan: I don't know. I was only a couple of months old when my grandfather died. I suspect that it belonged to my uncle, and is therefore perhaps mid-twentieth century or later. That stamp on the surface of the stainless steel might well be a date; but who knows?

Group 2:

Jou Jou: I am thinking the unit Gill has to be related to either alcohol or medicine. What did your grandfather do for a living, Ivan?

Ivan: There are some things one does not reveal [class chuckles].

Jou Jou: You have to answer our questions!

Ivan: OK. I never knew the man. They let him out on weekends occasionally [more chuckles].

Collecting Data

Ivan compliments the groups, has each group share its ideas on an experimental approach, and directs the teachers to the next task: "These are great approaches. Now let's take a closer look at the Gill. We want to find out what it is, what is it used for, how big it is and whether it is a metric or English unit. You will collect data for a table that will be used for graphs that may yield additional information on the Gill. As a whole class, we will decide on which data to collect to make a table. Which data would you prefer: volume of water in each run of the graduated cylinder? Dimensions of the 1/3Gill cylinder to calculate the internal volume? Mass of the water? Any other parameters?"

The class decides to start with the method of calculating volume with a formula after measuring the dimensions, or alternately, that of filling the 1/3Gill cylinder with water and decanting it into the graduated cylinder with which each group is provided. Each member in the group has a role: while one member is pouring, another member is helping by seeing whether or not to add some more water to fill to the top, and a third is preparing the table to input the data. Finding it tricky to get the water precisely to the top, John remarks that it will take several tries because the small 10mL graduated cylinder holds less than the 1/3Gill cylinder. There are also problems because the water level seems to fill well above the lip of the 1/3Gill cylinder. John raises this point with the class, and Ivan says, "Interesting. You are right. The water can actually be 'stacked,' if that is a reasonable word for a liquid, well above the lip of the 1/3Gill cylinder. Should we worry about that?" "Yes." says Claude, "The 'stacked' amount of water seems significant."

Ivan:	"Well, we're going to have to standardize, aren't we? Could we agree to get it as close to the top edge of the lip as possible, but no more than that? What causes the water to rise so high above the lip of the cylinder like that?"
Steven:	"Before we get to that, Ivan, there's another problem: the surface of the water in the graduated cylinder is curved downward—it is not flat. Where do we read the line of the graduated cylinder?"
Ivan:	"Good observation. Can anyone answer that question? Let's use this opportunity to introduce some vocabulary and background information. Well, this is the reverse of the problem we are having with the 1/3Gill cylinder, isn't it? The water stacks upward in a mound past the lip of the Gill cylinder, but curves downward in an arc in the graduated cylinder. In this case, the graduated cylinder is designed and calibrated to read the very bottom of the curved line of water. The curved line of the water in the graduated cylinder is called a *meniscus*, and you need to read the graduated cylinder right where one of the graduations runs across the bottom of the *meniscus*. If the base of the meniscus falls between two lines, you must estimate where between the lines the base of the meniscus falls, and use that for your measurement. What do you think causes the water to produce a curve like that? Is it the same property responsible for the mound of water that forms on the top of the 1/3Gill cylinder?
Damian:	Gravity could be the reason for the meniscus, but I don't know about the mound.
Ivan:	Well, let's read information from a handout I will give you now.

Sara volunteers to read from the handout (Figure 10.1).

Yves comments, "As a kid, I remember doing the experiment of putting a white carnation in red dyed water to show how water is absorbed. I never thought to question *why* gravity allowed the dyed water to rise, nor did that discussion ever come up in class. This is an eye opener!"

With that understanding, the groups continue with volume measurements using the graduated cylinder. Others measure the dimensions of the 1/3Gill cylinder so that they can calculate its theoretical volume. Each group has a small ruler marked with both English and metric (SI) units and they elect to use metric *length* units which will be matched with the metric *volume* units already on the graduated cylinders. Ivan asks the groups for any more questions or solutions.

Figure 10.1 Curving Meniscus and Mounds of Water on a Cylinder

The curving meniscus and the mound of water on the cylinder are caused by the surface tension of the liquid: the strength of the bonds that hold the molecules of liquid together. In the case of water, the molecules are held together by hydrogen bonds, the attraction of the oxygen and hydrogen atoms for each other between, not within, each molecule. Water, with a polar molecular structure, is held together relatively tightly by these hydrogen bonds. They explain the relatively high density of water, its very high boiling point for a liquid of its molecular mass, and its ability to climb up thin tubes, against gravity, by capillary action. This last helps explain how water gets to the top leaves of tall trees from the soil and roots below. Other liquids, alcohol for example, have different degrees of hydrogen bonding, and behave differently than water, or to different degrees. Similarly, water is attracted to different degrees by different materials. If your graduated cylinders are made of glass, which is a traditional material for labware, the water will form a strong meniscus (sharply curved upper water surface) due to the attraction of the water molecules for glass. If however, you use plastic graduated cylinders, the water will form a near-flat surface—essentially no meniscus. Plastic labware has the advantage of being pretty resilient, and therefore relatively safe. It is also often less expensive.

Lisa:	Should we measure the inside or the outside of the cylinder?
Ivan:	Any ideas?
Carlos:	We had the same question and decided to measure the inside of the cylinder since that is where the water will be.
Ivan:	Excellent. In either case, the wall thickness is less than 1mm. It would not affect your measurement by a large amount, and it could be subtracted if you found it easy enough to measure wall thickness.
Serge:	I need some suggestions on how to use the ruler so that I come as close to the real interior diameter as possible. Because there are no straight edges or corners, I am having problems.
Jou Jou:	It's trial and error, I think. I just pivoted the ruler back and forth with one end fixed on a point on the wall of the cylinder until I saw the largest measurement, therefore the diameter, and not something less.
Georgina:	Another problem you will encounter is measuring the inside height of the cylinder directly because the zero mark on our rulers is not at the very end of the rulers.
Serge:	What did you do?
Yves:	To get by that, we stiffened a small piece of paper by creasing it lengthwise, and measured the inside with that. Then we measured the mark on the paper with our rulers. We got 4.4cm to the top of the cylinder, and 3.6cm to the top of the 1/3Gill mark. A diameter

of 3.7cm gives us a radius of 1.85. So using a value of π as 3.14 and substituting in to the formula $V = \pi r^2 h$, we get $V = 3.14 \times 1.85 \times 1.85 \times 4.4$ or 47.3mL.

Ivan: Great. Very good. But I've got two problems: the first is that I don't see any units with your numbers. It is difficult to understand what you are doing, and to check your work, without them. I do like how you were fairly careful with your significant digits.

Yves: OK, you picky bugger. $V = 3.14 \times 1.85cm \times 1.85cm \times 4.4cm$.

Ivan: Thank you, that's better. But my second problem: what are the units for your answer?

Yves: Well, it's cubic centimeters but we don't know or remember how to change that to millimeters.

Ivan: Look at this second table for help. (See Figure 10.2.)

Figure 10.2 Some Useful Measurement Information

Common Metric Units of Volume	
Metric Units of Volume	US Customer Units
mL = 1cm³	2c = 1pt
1000mL = 1L	2pt = 1qt
1000cm³ = 1000mL = 1L	4qt = 1gal
1g water takes up 1ml or 1cm³ of space	32oz = 1qt
Accuracy: the closeness of a measurement value to an accepted value.	1fl.oz = 29.57mL
Precision: the closeness of a set of measurements made in the same way on the same quantity.	
Mass is the amount of substance, material, stuff. The number and size of the atoms making up a material. Weight is the force of gravity acting on the mass; the weight of an object on Earth will be different than the weight of the same object on the Moon, but their masses will be the same. A spring scale will measure the force of gravity, or weight, of an object. But a balance will compare one calibrated mass of material against an unknown object.	
Error in measurement: Some error (or uncertainty) exists in any measurement. The uncertainty (or precision) depends on: the operator, the conditions, the instrument used to measure. Precision is often stated mathematically: 5.23cm +/− 0.01cm	
One of the advantages of using the metric system which is also called the **System Internationale (SI) units,** is that the density of water (at standard temperatures) is 1g/mL. Another is that the unit of mL is defined as being 1/1000th of a Liter, and therefore equal to 1cm³. A common material, such as water and a common measurement which is cubic centimeter, to define the gram make the system easy to use. This is a good time to remind the students of the mathematics of conversion factors, and the math of using them. It is also a good time to deal with the subjects of units, and unit conversions.	

Yves: It has that $1cm^3 = 1mL$. In that case, it is simple to simply change from cm^3 to mL. Now if we multiply the answer for 1/3Gill by three, the Gill is approximately 141.9mL. I wonder how many fluid ounces that is?

Georgina: That is also what we need to know. We got 150mL for our Gill.

Ivan: Take a look at this second handout of units to see how it might help.

Georgina: I see. It has that 1fl.oz. = 29.57mL. We could use a proportion to solve it or take our 150mL and just divide it by 29.57 . . . gives us approximately 5fl.oz.

Ivan: Please come up to the board to show us your thinking.

Georgina: Given that 1fl.oz. = 29.57mL, we could show our kids how to apply proportions here where we let x represent the number of ounces in a Gill.

$$\frac{1\text{fl.oz.}}{29.57\text{mL}} = \frac{x}{150\text{mL}}$$

$$x = \frac{150\text{mL} \times 1\text{fl.oz.}}{29.57\text{mL}} = 5.1\text{fl.oz.}$$

Ivan: Thank you.

Mass Versus Weight, and the Search for Volume if Given Mass

Ivan: The measurements are reasonably close. Good job. Ok, where would you like to go from here?

Damian: Can we use the approach of measuring the size of a Gill using the triple-beam balance to determine the weight of the water? I have never used that balance.

Ivan: Ok, let's do that. Remember to handle the balances carefully. Damian, how are you going to find the weight of the water? Remember that a balance measures mass, not weight. In most cases the concepts are interchangeable, but in some cases the differences are important. Can someone provide an example where they are different?

John: I remember the moon as an example back in my high school days. Since the Moon has less gravity than the Earth, my weight there would be different even though my mass would be the same.

Ivan adds, "Yes, *mass* is the amount of substance, material, stuff: that is, the number and size of the atoms making up a material. *Weight* is the force of gravity acting on the mass. A spring scale will measure the force of gravity, or weight, of an object. But a balance will compare one calibrated mass of material against your unknown object. I use triple-beam balances in this lesson because they are durable and fairly inexpensive. More importantly, the mechanics of the weighing process on a triple-beam balance give a student a more palpable sense of what is happening. There is also a very strong visual sense of the precision of the measurement."

Ivan next directs the groups to make a data table and to apply a procedure for finding the size of a Gill using mass. He allocates five minutes to come up with a procedure, and five minutes to make the data table. While they are working, he reminds them that this is an indirect measurement, unlike the previous ones, and that this has some repercussions on the precision of measurement. The groups decide on filling the 1/3Gill container to a set point, then decanting the contents of cylinder into a pre-weighed container.

As the groups continue to make the table, Ivan sees that Group 4 pre-weighs the 1/3Gill-container first, then carefully fills it to the top with a wash bottle and dropper. At this point he tells the class that the weight of an *empty* container is called the *tare* weight, and the process is called *taring*.

Lisa calls Ivan's attention by asking: "Here is what we did. We weighed the container with water and then subtracted the weight of the 1/3Gill container. We have the weight but we don't have a volume. We aren't sure where to go from here."

Ivan:	Well, what information would you like to have?
Julian:	We want to go from the mass to calculate the volume. What is the relationship between mass and volume for the liquid?
Tyler:	Isn't that a ratio, or proportion?
Ivan:	Yes, excellent, but a ratio between what and what?
Yves:	It has to do with the ratio between mass and volume . . . it's called density?
Ivan:	Density. That's good. What is the relationship in metric units? How is density defined?
Damian:	I know that the formula is $D = M/V$.
Ivan:	OK. But what units are we talking about? That's an equation, sure, but what does it mean?
Tyler:	We are using grams for mass, and milliliters for volume, so it is grams divided by milliliters.
Ivan:	Now we need to use precise language to help you move further. Lisa, you said that you had the weight but no volume. Please be more precise.
Lisa:	Well, we calculated the weight or *mass* of the 1/3Gill which is in grams and how much water or *volume* it can hold using the wash

bottle. But we do not have a measurement for the volume of that water. That is where we are stuck.

Ivan: Well, what you need is a relationship.

Lisa: Don't we all! [Class chuckles.]

Ivan: No, I mean a really good one! Steady, constant. With property. What more could you ask for from a relationship? We will call him density: he will find you volume.

Lisa: So we have a relationship for water? Density = mass/volume?

Edwidge: Well, we could multiply our measured mass of water by the *volume/mass* ratio of water. It would be a conversion. Then you would get volume alone because the multiplication would cause mass to cancel out.

Ivan: Can you explain what you mean by "cancel out?" There is an important mathematical property masked by that term that students often do not see.

Henry: When you multiply mass by the ratio *volume/mass* you get mass over . . . let me show it on the board:

Ivan: Great. Students need to see that cancelling is not a disappearing act but about rearranging or renaming terms to apply the multiplicative property of 1.

Edwidge: OK. So we have the mass of water, in grams, because d = m/v, we can say that v = m/d. That's the same as m times 1/d, which is multiplying by the inverse of density.

Ivan: Really great. That's what you are doing in your table when you say you are dividing Column C by Column D, isn't it? (See Figure 10.3)

Serge: Yes, that makes sense because dividing is the same as multiplying by a reciprocal.

Mary comments that something about her group's data is strange.

Ivan: Please explain what you found, Mary.

Mary: First thing we did was to use the balance for measuring the Gill filled with water. We then measured the 1/3Gill container alone and subtracted its weight to find the net weight of the water. Using the graduated cylinders we measured the volume of water and its actual weight. The weird thing was that our weight for water turned out to equal its volume as well.

For example, for 50mL and 30mL of water, the weights were the same number in grams, and for 20mL it was 19.2mL which is very close to being the same. (See Figure 10.4.)

Figure 10.3 Data and Graphs for Mass Versus Volume (Density) of Water and Sand

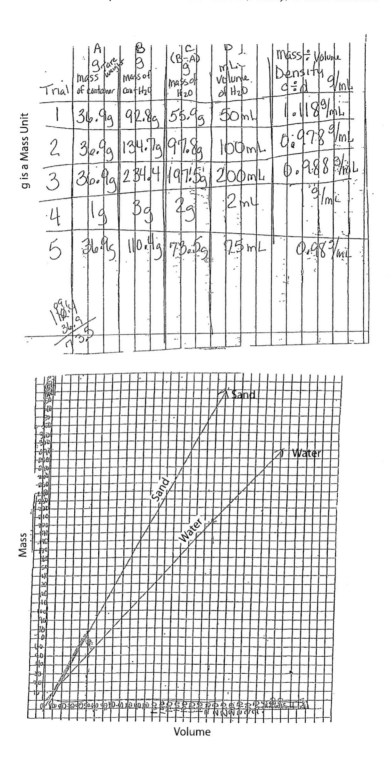

Figure 10.4 Data and Graphs for Volume Versus Mass (1/Density) of Water and Sand

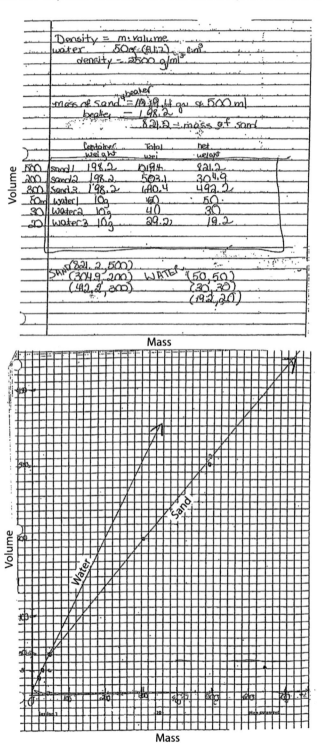

Ivan:	You got the answer that the amount of mass in grams was equal to the amount of volume in mL?
Mary:	Yes and I don't think it's a coincidence.
Ivan:	OK. That is a puzzlement. Could it just be a coincidence? Let's wait for all groups to finish their data table to explore this question. The teachers complete their experiments and fill in their data tables. Measuring the 1/3Gill, they come very close to the number 142cm^3 (or mL). Again, the groups had somewhat of a range of values, with a mean value near the accepted value for a British Imperial Gill. The class discussion suggested that the unit could not be a metric unit, because if a Gill were really a metric unit, it would be a multiple power of 10, like 100 or 1000.

A Dense Discussion

Ivan's next step is to move the group towards revealing the puzzlement in the work of Mary's group which will require an investigation of the density characteristics of water and its relationship to the volume of water. He tells the class: "We now can investigate the question from Group 3 as to why the volume and mass of water measured 1mL and 1g respectively. We've used a ratio called *density*. How do we get that number for density? How could we experiment to find the density of water? You will also determine the density of beach sand to serve as a comparison. Take about 20 minutes to solve it with the tools that you have."

The groups confer and decide to measure the various weights of water in a variety of volumes by using the balances, graduated cylinders and beakers. Ivan circulates to listen to the groups discussions.

Group 1:

Georgina:	Now to make a graph. Hum; we have sand; we could dump it out and measure the mass of beaker with and without water.
John:	300mL water and then what? . . .
Damian:	Measuring it first, the . . .

Group 2: Ivan notes that the group is still trying to determine the density relationship.

Jou Jou:	We're calculating its mass right now, but I can't remember the formula for density.
Sara:	It's how thick something is . . . or . . . is it how compressed the material is? There is a formula for this but I am having a hard time remembering it.

Ivan:	When we concentrate on remembering it as a formula perhaps we don't always remember what the heck it is as a concept.
Henry:	Is it *mass* times *volume*?
Ivan:	I guess what I'm coming back to is, doesn't it help if we think of it as how much "stuff" we have in a space or volume. Stuff means how many molecules, and how big or heavy those molecules are.
Henry:	Isn't that how thick it is?
Ivan:	Well, "thick" as we usually use it in cooking, refers to how rapidly it flows or doesn't flow, and that's best described by the word, viscosity. Remember mercury thermometers: mercury is extraordinarily dense, but really quite fluid. And remember honey: not very dense, but very viscous. There is not necessarily a direct relationship between these properties. So "viscosity" is a better term for "thick" because it's more precise. Neither is really related to density. We wouldn't want to pass on the misconception that these are the same concepts . . .
Sara:	So how about "compact"?
Ivan:	That's a good way of thinking about it. Think about taking a graduated cylinder and filling it full of marshmallows. Then take the graduated cylinder and fill it full of steel ball bearings. The same volume will have a very different weight.

Group 3:

Julian:	We are thinking about water in the beaker . . . remove the water, measure the beaker . . .
Ivan:	So you need that big old beaker then, good . . .
Julian:	Could we fill it with sand?
Ivan:	Sure. If you want, we can attach weights to the balance for weighing heavier materials. How much do you want to weigh?
Claude:	We are thinking that we should measure water and the sand. We want to measure the density of the sand, which includes the spaces in between the grains.
Carlos:	So the density of the sand also depends on the size of the particles?
Julian:	Definitely . . . and also depends on the way they are packed together . . .

Ivan observes that the groups weigh the ½ Gill container then a beaker on the balance before adding any water to the container, which will be the tare (container) weight. They then add a carefully measured volume of water from the graduated cylinder to the container on the balance, being careful not to get water on the balance pan. They record the amount of water added in mL, and the resulting weight gain. For each new volume of water in the beaker on the balance, they calculate the new net weight of the water and enter this onto their tables. One of the columns represents a calculated value for the ratio of mass (g) to volume (mL or cu. cm). Others measure out clean sand, and repeat the experiment. They carefully fill the tared container with measured amounts of sand which has a net mass and a measured volume from the graduated cylinder. They then insert values in the table and plot the points.

Ivan:	As I went around, I noted that you had similar tables but some of your graphs had different labels for the axes. Which variable should we put on which axis? That is, of volume and mass, which is the *dependent* and which the *independent* variable?
Julian:	We poured a measured volume of water from the graduated cylinder into the 1/3Gill to see the effect on the Gill container's contained water mass. So in our case, the mass of the water was dependent on how much measured water volume from the graduated cylinder was added to it. The x-axis, or independent variable, would be *volume*, and *mass* would be on the y-axis, the dependent variable. (See Figure 10.3.)
Henry:	But *we* started with the 1/3Gill full of water, measured its mass in grams, and then poured it into the graduated cylinder to see how much volume the 1/3Gill would contain. So, for us, the volume was dependent on the mass, right, and the volume should be on the y-axis?
Mary:	But when we did our graph, the x axis was the mass and the volume was the y-axis. (See Figure 10.4.)
Jou Jou:	But, you want to find the density, and if you switch the axes, you will have the inverse, which is 1 over the density.
Ivan:	It seems like you are all saying that it is hard to tell because there isn't necessarily a clear dependent vs. independent variable here. Both co-vary because both are necessary in order to describe a property of matter. Let's think further about what Jou Jou said. If you put mass on the y-axis and volume on x-axis, what can you tell us about the slope of the resulting line?
Sara:	Well the slope is really y over x, which translates to mass over volume. That is ... density? The slope will be the density ... neat!
Ivan:	Because of this, let's agree to use the x-axis for volume and the y-axis for mass. Consider the slope of the water line, how can we get it? How would we get the graph?

Claude:	Well, we could put the table in our graphing calculator and have it graph it for us.
Ivan:	OK, since we have very few points, let's probe deeper to understand how the calculator performs its magic. Explain how you would get that calculator line.
Julian:	Since our measurements are not precise, we will have to draw the line of best fit for the data points of water, and a line of best fit for the data points of sand.
Sara:	I have plotted my points and drawn the lines as best as I could. Why do the lines have different slopes?
Ivan:	That's a great question. Any other questions or observations?
Janet:	We've got lines that work well because they go through or close to all of my data points. But our sand line doesn't go through the origin the way the one for water does.
Ivan:	Do we have a problem here? Should the sand line pass through the origin? First, what does it mean for the water line to pass through the origin, that is, the point (0,0)?
Julian:	Well (0,0) means zero volume so there should also be zero mass.
Ivan:	OK. Next, what does it mean if the line for the sand doesn't go through the origin?
Lisa:	It would intersect the y-axis. That would say that there will be something that has zero volume, but at the same time has some mass. That does not make sense.
Claude:	Right. We've made a similar error, and when we corrected it, we found that the slope of the water line is equal to 1g/1mL. The slope of the sand line seems to be a little more than twice that, about 2.5g/mL.
Ivan:	How are you calculating your slope?
John:	We are taking the y-axis value and dividing by the x-axis value.
Ivan:	OK. So that is essentially the rise over the run that you have been teaching your students. It is usually defined as the change in y divided by the change in x, and you have enough data points to do it. What is the equation of the line that goes through those points of yours?
Claude:	Don't know yet . . . got the slope, but how to get the rest of it?
Jou Jou:	Well, look at where the line goes: it must go through the origin where you've drawn it. Where there is no mass, there will be no volume taken up, right? And vice versa. So that tells us the y-intercept is zero.
Claude:	I see. This goes back to what Lisa said.

Damian:	Yes, it is zero so that the equation for both the water and the sand line is $y = mx + 0$.
Ivan:	And if $m = 1$ for water, and about 2.5 for sand, what do the slopes of lines represent?
Susan:	The slope of the line represents the density of the water and the sand, measured in g/mL or g/cm^3.
Mary:	So . . . the slope is 1 for water. The density for water also equals 1. Isn't that amazing?
Ivan:	One other wrinkle we need to re-emphasize here: Who can complete this equation: In the metric system, 1mL H_2O = ___ g H_2O.
Julian:	The answer is 1g H_2O.
Ivan:	Yes. We define 1g of water to be that mass of atoms of water that takes up 1mL of space at 20°C. So 1mL H_2O = 1g H_2O. On the board is another way it connects to what we are doing. Remember: since 1g H_2O corresponds to 1mL H_2O, we can say they equal one another. Thus, 1g H_2O = 1mL H_2O; since they are equal, divide both sides by the right side to get 1g H_2O/1mL H_2O = 1. Since they equal 1, you can use either mass/volume or its reciprocal as a conversion factor, depending on what you are trying to find. Remember that the reciprocal of one is equal to one, so you are multiplying the equation by ONE, which will not change the equation.
Mary:	So . . . we have the answer to my puzzle! This is why our measurement for the volume of the water was the same as its mass!
Ivan:	OK, but be careful: you are now saying 1 = 1. You need to be mindful that the digit has no meaning without its corresponding unit. While 1*mL* is one gram, the density, is 1*gram* per 1mL. The units have different meanings so, what should you be saying?
Mary:	I should say that 1mL of water has a mass of 1 gram.
John:	I like this because the equation of the line has real meaning to real materials.
Karen:	And the slope of the lines has real meaning in that we are dividing the y-value by the x-value and getting the dimensional unit of the axes to be g/mL.
Ivan:	Good. Can we get more information from these graphs?
Sara:	Well, we can use the line to guess at what the value of the mass is given a value for the volume. And vice-versa.
Ivan:	So this mathematical model represents the density of real materials and it can predict the mass of a material given its volume, and the volume of a material given its mass. We need to

continue to show our kids the beauty in these different representations and their power to predict behavior of materials. This is one of the reasons math is so valuable in science: to a certain extent, it allows us to guess how well we understand a situation or material, if we can accurately model behavior.

Claude: But Ivan, how consistent is the number for the sand? What does it mean, since there is a little air space between the sand grains that we measured?

Ivan: What you are measuring is really referred to as the bulk density of the sediment, or sand, which is a number that would be useful to you if you were, say, using the sand for construction and wanted to know how much sand you could carry in your pickup truck, or how much a cubic meter of sand weighed. But look under the microscope, I've got some of the sand there. What do you see?

Claude: Wow, the sand is a bunch of individual grains of clear, milky material that looks a lot like glass. Many of the grains are round and smooth, but a few of them are a little jagged, like little rocks.

Ivan: Yes. This is the sand I got from the construction store to use for sand lots and concrete. This particular sand is common, and the clear material each grain is composed of is a mineral called quartz. The actual density of quartz is a bit higher, 2.7g/mL, than what you are measuring. Like water, the density of quartz is a property of the material. It is constant, and is a function of its chemistry and crystal structure. It can be used to identify the mineral.

Jou Jou: So we got a bit lower bulk density than the actual mineral density. But we could use water to fill the pore space, and calculate the real density, right? We didn't do that because we didn't want to make a big mess for you.

Ivan: I appreciate your courtesy! But this is class—I would have had you clean it up!

OK, so what did we learn? We know a bit about graphing and tabulation of values. We learned about density and conversion factors. We used linear equations and graphically calculated a linear regression. We learned that the slope of a line can represent something real, like a property of a material, in this case density. What else? What did we learn about the unit Gill?

Lisa: It must be English because it has the stamp on it.

Damian: Agreed. In addition, the measurements are messy which is not true for metric units.

Sara:	The Gill is a liquid measure, and is about 140ml or about 5fl. oz.
	The volume of the 1/3Gill turned out to be about 47.48cm^3.
Ivan:	Good. I did a quick search in the dictionary and an online encyclopedia. It turns out as we expected, it has British origins, and is adapted into US Customary units as well. Confusingly, it is 4 US ounces, but is 5 Imperial ounces in England, each of which is 1.2 US ounces. In both places it is ¼ pint (1/4 US pint in America, ¼ imperial pint in Britain). In pubs, it is still commonly used in Britain, where the standard drink in England uses 1/6Gill. Except in Scotland, where they prefer to use 1/5Gill. And except in Ireland, where they use 1/4Gill in their drinks. There is some irony there . . . Confused? Not yet: in southern England, it is also sometimes used for milk and beer, where it is considered a half-pint (American Heritage Dictionary (2000), Encyclopedia Britannica online (2013), Wikipedia online (2013)). When used in this way, it is quite commonly referred to as a Noggin. Except when it is referred to as a Large Noggin, which is two Gills—usually in northern England. Which makes my noggin quite sore, and makes me glad someone invented the metric system and sanity along with it. Finally, can you name some units that were named after famous people?
Class contributes:	*Watt* is a unit of power, *Newton* is a unit of force, *Richter* as a scale for earthquakes, *Hertz* as a unit of frequency.
Ivan:	Yes, named after the giants of science. Well, but my ancestors apparently kept a bar. I guess I can live with that! OK. That's it. Do you have any questions?
Henry:	This was a really good lesson! Thank you!
Mary:	I love everything we do in LaSIP but I have a curriculum to teach and if you can tell me how to find time for these activities in addition to my curriculum, that would be a great help.
Ivan:	Don't think of these activities as *additional* but as engaging activities to guide students' learning of the important content you need to teach. Remember that CCSS does not tell us what sequence to teach but what is important to teach. As an example, let's make a quick list of the mathematics found in this lesson. The teachers' list of content includes, real-life situation requiring ratio and proportions; making tables and graphs; interpreting the meaning of a graph and measurement conversions. They also list at least six mathematical practices. Ivan says,

Thus, you can use this unit to teach any of those content areas by allowing extra time for information and practice on the area you want to place a focus. You can also teach other topics such as fractions if you require that the measurements be done with fractions instead of decimals. Any more comments or questions?.... Thank you, Mary, for that question because it leads us to our reflection and lesson planning activity which is next: For the remaining 45 minutes, please get into grade level groups to reflect on sections of this lesson that are applicable to your students. Begin the writing of a Launch-Explore-Summarize lesson adaptation of this lesson for your students so that you may implement parts or all of it this year. A copy of my lesson is on our LaSIP website.

Discussion Between Colleagues

I liked the launch of your personal story for this unit. What recommendations would you give to teachers without their own "Gill" story, let alone a real Gill?

That is a good question that teachers discuss in their grade-level groups. It doesn't have to be a Gill, but it works for me because I find it to be humorous. But another teacher could make up an imaginary or unknown volume measure of any sort. They could use a section of pipe or cup of arbitrary or unknown size. A good launch can often involve a problem or a project to solve. The students can be engaged in finding a solution; the story simply sets the stage for the exploration of a question.

Having taught this same lesson to eighth graders, please elaborate on some of the difficult concepts for kids and some suggestions for teachers.

Teachers need to be mindful of the timeframe allocated to the different activities. I can always extend the time limit if my teachers are actually working on the problems and need a bit more to reach a useful stage in their discussions—especially since I often allow them the freedom to brainstorm with little direction but the list of available materials. However if middle grade students are given too much time, they may produce nothing of use. Sometimes, with some classes, it can be useful to prime the pump with suggestions on what to try, or in what direction to head. Thus, it is important that teachers know their students well so that they can provide just enough information to guide them through the productive struggle process. Questions for teachers to ponder are: What time limits would work for the students? What is the least amount of direction for using the materials that kids need in order to be motivated to try this activity?

As for the content, the kids usually remember that πr^2 yields the area of a circle, but less commonly remember that the base area, multiplied by the height of the cylinder yields the volume. These relationships can be illustrated wonderfully by the use of cubical models and manipulatives; the cubical model is analogous to a cylinder, but is easier to visualize. In this lesson, the volume of the 1/3Gill turned out to be about 47.48cm^3 but accounting for significant digits, teachers should require the measure to be about 47.5cm^3. The kids should be able to put in their tables that a Gill must have a volume of about 142.4cm^3, since 3(1/3Gill) = 1Gill.

Discussion at this point should raise doubts that a Gill is a metric (SI) unit: there should be some even, round number of cm^3 for a Gill to be a metric unit, as, for example, 1000cm^3 is a Liter. At this point also, units should be discussed because we have gone from linear measure (cm) to volume measure (cm^3), and there is as much difference between these as there is going from feet to gallons. Relatedly, there is a real danger for kids to reason that if there are 100cm in a meter, therefore there must be 100cm^3 in a cubic meter. This sounds plausible except that it is off by 6 orders of magnitude (1,000,000 times), which is no small error. This is not an uncommon mistake for kids to make, and I've made it myself often enough. Again, the use of manipulatives, like volume models, can help build a more intuitive understanding of these calculations among students. This is a good time to remind the students of the mathematics of conversion factors, and the math of using them.

My LaSIP teachers were creative in finding methods to measure the height of a cylinder with a ruler whose zero mark is not at the very end of the ruler. Kids, on the other hand, will often use a ruler without even noting where the zero mark starts so this is an opportunity to review using the ruler as a tool and its limitations. It is also important to note that I worked with a group of math and science teachers so they helped each other in the content areas. Kids will not have that resource so it will be helpful to have the science and math facts that I recounted to the teachers available on a handout, as in Figure 10.2. Finally, this unit would be a nice opportunity for math and science teachers to collaborate at a school to share materials and teach the math and science content at about the same time so that the content for one enriches and supports the other.

Please contrast your use of precision to that used in CCSSM.

The words precision and accuracy have slightly different meanings in science and mathematics than they do in everyday language. In science, the definition of precision is usually: "the closeness of a set of measurements of the same quantity made in the same way." Accuracy is: "the closeness of measurements to the correct or accepted value of the quantity measured." Precision is affected by operator skill, conditions, and the instrument itself and refers to numbers specifically. There is no conflict between the use of the words in science and in the CCSS. I believe that, in addition to getting correct answers, CCSS writers were concerned with language used for expressing an idea with precision, which would include use of proper terminology to avoid ambiguity. The concepts are thus related.

Any other advice for teachers?

Be imaginative, and incorporate a sense of play. There are so many properties worth exploring, and so many great ideas out there for teaching them. It is worth exploring how math is used to help give a sense of how powerful and worthwhile math is; that is certainly not something I had at this age and it would have helped if I had. I'd also like to add a final note: throughout the lesson we have capitalized "Gill," treating it as a unit named after a person, which was my expectation, partly humorous. However, it turns out that most sources I checked do not capitalize it, so it is simply "Gill." I do not know really what the origin of the unit is, although in my heart it must be an ancestral pub owner of modest repute!

Commentary

In research by Garet *et al.* (2001) on what math and science teachers view as effective professional development for improving their practices, teachers reported that the most effective PD experiences were those that used engaging and coherent activities that were also geared towards what they needed to teach their children. Ivan's integrated unit does that for teachers. Teachers also experienced a differentiated approach to learning since the varying grade levels and content knowledge of the teachers are analogous to teaching a typical classroom of students with varying levels of understanding.

According to Hall *et al.* (2011),

Differentiated instruction is a process to teaching and learning for students of differing abilities in the same class. The intent of differentiating instruction is to maximize each student's growth and individual success by meeting each student where he or she is and assisting in the learning process. (p. 3)

Ivan applies the principles of differentiated instruction by creating hetero-geneous groups of teachers engaging in activities that vary by difficulty so that there are challenges at multiple levels. Informal assessment is crucial to differentiating instruction and he ensures that teachers are understanding the process by moving among them to assess progress and to ask probing questions to guide thinking when necessary. His use of science as an entry point to engage all of his teachers in real-life tasks requiring very little science prerequisite knowledge is to be commended. His inclusion of density, mass, volume, metric and English conversions are all important topics in math and science. Indeed, in the *Scientific American*, Moskovitch (2013) reported that the density of plasma around the spacecraft Voyager 1 was the only factor that enabled scientists to determine the date that Voyager 1 left our solar system!

Another aspect necessary to motivate students' participation when differ-entiating instruction is a safe classroom atmosphere. Ivan creates that through classroom humor and appreciation for the confusion and mistakes that natu-rally occur when one has to think outside of the box of formulas. This is exem-plified when one of the teachers laments about having forgotten a formula and Ivan guides him back to the meaning of the concept to help him reinvent the formula. Such thinking and questioning strategies are important for teachers to experience, as students, so that they can in turn help their students develop the concept understanding before applying the formulas. (Note too that Ivan does not give the teachers a copy of his lesson plan until *after* the lesson is over.) Finally, the fact that he is not called "Dr. Gill" is a testimony to the collegiality permeating his class' atmosphere and that he considers teachers as colleagues.

The comment by a teacher about not having enough time to do engaging activities always comes up in workshops I've attended or given. Managing the time so that students get a good balance of skills and concepts while highly engaged in worthwhile activities is no small feat for teachers. Ivan, however, helps his teachers analyze the worthiness of the activities by having them list the CCSSM applied and the mathematical practices that they've experienced. In addition, Ivan's inclusion of a time to reflect supports NCTM's *Professional Standards for Teaching Mathematics* (NCTM, 1991) belief that professional growth occurs when teachers are provided opportunities to "reflect on learning and teaching individually and with colleagues" (p. 168).

Unit Overview

Meaningful Connections Between Measurements, Units, Proportion and Graphing
Aim: What is a Gill?

Objectives: Students use direct and indirect measurement to tabulate and graph data.

Grade Levels: 6–8

Source: Original

Number of 90-minute periods with teachers: 2

Number of 90-minute periods with students: 3–4

CCSSM Content: Ratio (6.RP.A.1, A.3a, A.3d; 7.RP.A.2a-d); Expressions and Equations (6.EE.A.1, A.2; 7.EEA.2, B.3; 8. EE.B.5, C.8c); Geometry (6.G.A.2; 7.G.B.4, G.B.6; 8.G.C.9); Functions (8.FA.1, A.2, B.4, F.B.5)

CCSSM Mathematical Practices: MP1: Problem solving, MP2: Reasoning, MP3: Arguments, MP4: Modeling, MP5: Use of Tools; MP6: Precision; MP8: Repeated reasoning

Mathematical Concepts: Students solve problems with ratio/proportion with connections to linear graphs and the concept of slope. They use various tools to apply concepts of density, mass and volume together with tables and graphs to define the characteristics of an unknown cylinder.

Prerequisites: Although this lesson integrates science, students do not need prerequisite science knowledge. They do need to know how to graph a table of values and the meaning of y = mx+b.

Materials for each group of three to four students:

- ◆ Triple-Beam balance
- ◆ 10mL-graduated cylinder
- ◆ Wash bottle/dropper
- ◆ 600 or 1000mL beaker
- ◆ Graph paper
- ◆ Ruler (metric and English nits)

Management Procedures: Arrange students in groups of 3–4 to explore the following questions:

Part 1:

    A. What's a Gill? What is it used for?
        -length, area, volume, weight, mass?
        -liquid measurement? Solid/dry measurement?
    B. How big is a Gill? How does it compare to the metric units?
        Tabulate your data: place all your data into a neat table.
        What difference does it make if you use a larger or smaller graduated cylinder? Does it change your ability to measure? Does it change the precision or accuracy of your measurement?
    C. How big is a Gill? How does it compare to U.S. Customary (English) units? Tabulate your data: place all your data into the table you made.
    D. How can you solve these problems? What techniques can you use, what methods can you follow? Replicate your measurements.

Part II: So you know "What's a Gill?" What's next?

    A. What is the density of water? Make multiple measurements (replicate your experiment); place your data onto your table.
    B. What is the density of beach sand? How are you going to measure this? Make multiple measurements, place your data onto your data table.
    C. Plot on a graph the results of your two experiments. What do you see? What are the relationships between the variables? What are the variables here? What kind of function is this?
    D. What is the meaning of the slope of the plots? What does it tell you?

Assessment: Assess students informally while circulating. Collect the table and graphs to give feedback.

11

Paterson School 2: Journey Beyond TIMSS

This profile provides documentation for the first implementation of the lesson study process in the United States today. Lesson study continues to be viewed as a valuable form of professional development for teachers. While most of the lead players in the profile are no longer at Paterson 2, I have chosen to keep most of the profile in its original tense but provide an update at the end of the chapter. The information on lesson study as well as the handouts are currently used by lesson study groups in the United States. The content was suitable to fifth graders in 1999 but is now a CCSS seventh grade topic.

In 1991, Paterson Public Schools were taken over by state. All the schools were assessed and our PRE K-8 School was declared one of the four worst in the system. Our population of 720 students is pretty diverse: Ninety-eight percent of our students qualify for free lunch; many come from high stress environments including a hotel for the homeless, a battered women's shelter, and a housing project for children with seriously disabled parents; Ten classes of special education students are bussed to the school from throughout the district, and our rate of transience is 42%.

Collaborative support for applying the Lesson Study process of Japanese teachers in our own classes helped us to create a study group to focus on enhancing the teaching and learning of mathematics. Four main areas guide discussion of the group: curriculum, instruction, professional development, and school culture.

(Middle School Lesson Study Group team members from Paterson School 2, Paterson, New Jersey: Lynn Liptak, Fran Dransfield, Bill Jackson, Isabel Lopez, Magnolia Montilla, Beverly Pikema, Cynthia Sanchez and Nick Timpone)

On April 13, 2000, I (Yvelyne, the author) first learned of the work taking place at Paterson Public School 2 during a national meeting of the Middle School Mathematics Professional Development Network, which is a project of the Eisenhower Regional Consortia and National Clearing House. Having learned of the information above, my very first question to Bill Jackson, who has taught at School 2 for over 16 years and serves as facilitator for mathematics professional development in the school, was: "Why try to import the Japanese way of doing things? We are so different." His response was simple and clear: "What we were doing was not working for our students. Our students were failing miserably so we had nothing to lose. It's the TIMSS videotapes that really grabbed out attention and interests. We saw ourselves teaching in the same way as the American teachers who offered no challenges for students to learn the underlying concepts of mathematics. We wanted to give our students opportunities to enjoy rich mathematics through challenges." Because of my interest in profiling the study group teachers work for this book, Bill invited me to an Association of Mathematics Teachers of New Jersey (AMTNJ, May 2000) conference where I'd see the first large-scale public lesson study open house in the United States.

The conference was held at School 2 and sponsored by: AMTNJ, School 2, the Mid-Atlantic Eisenhower Consortium/Research for Better Schools, Teachers College/Columbia University, and the Greenwich Japanese School. Because of this extensive collaboration and the unique approach to curriculum taken for helping School 2 teachers strive to improve students' learning of mathematics, this profile will stray from the other profiles in this book in that I've included a lot of my own personal comments or reflections as I witnessed this novel, intriguing and powerful form of professional development. Another difference are that the Unit Overview Plan is the actual lesson plan used by the teachers and is placed *before* the Commentary section. Now, the journey beyond TIMSS begins. As I approach the school, I notice that it is nested in the heart of Paterson's downtown-heavily traffic-congested area. Pretty dreary, I think. But when I enter the school, I soon forget about the outside because School 2 beams with a general warm and welcoming atmosphere conveyed by its administrators, teachers and students. Nice bulletin boards, good lighting and a clean space all enhance this atmosphere.

I sit beside Frank Smith, a Columbia University, Teachers College professor who first offered workshops for the principal and teachers when the State Department of Education "took over" the school. "What does it mean for a school to be 'taken over' by the state?" I ask Frank. He explains that because the district of the school is declared low performing and mismanaged, the state disbands the board of education, replaces the superintendent, reassigns or removes the principal and replaces the Central office staff. At School 2, the principal was replaced with Lynn Liptak who, in 1996, became interested in Japanese teaching methods after attending Frank's workshop on the design and results of the TIMSS study (see Chapter 1 for information on TIMSS).

Lynn summarizes what happened next,

> The TIMSS eighth grade videotape study provided a powerful contrast between U.S. and Japanese mathematics instruction. We decided to try it and were encouraged by responses of our students when "Japanese-style" lessons were taught. Groups of School 2 teachers spent the next three summers writing and revising 7th and 8th grade lessons aligned with the New Jersey Core Curriculum and influenced by TIMSS.

In 1999, Lynn decided to try the Japanese approach to professional development through lesson study because, she says, "I don't believe in having teachers work all day and then have to attend professional meetings after school. Such meetings are best conducted as integral parts of the school week." Lynn schedules teachers interested in discussions and creations of innovative curriculum to a study group period once a week.

What is this "Japanese style" and what help did teachers receive to learn and implement it? This question was clearly addressed throughout the conference. Catherine Lewis, an educator from Mills College, Pa., spoke to the question by drawing from both her vast research on Japan's educational system and her actual videotapes of the Japanese process. Excerpts from one of her articles (2000) describing lesson study follows:

> Research lessons or (study lesson) refers to the lessons that teachers jointly plan, observe and discuss . . . Research lessons are actual classroom lessons with students, but typically share five characteristics:
>
> 1. *Research lessons are observed by other teachers.*
>   The observing teachers may include just the faculty within the school, or a wider group; some research lessons are open to teachers from all over Japan.

2. *Research lessons are planned for a long time, usually collaboratively.*
3. *Research lessons are designed to bring to life in a lesson a particular goal or vision of education.*
    The whole faculty chooses a research team or focus.
4. *Research lessons are recorded.*
    Usually teachers record these lessons in multiple ways, including videotape, audiotape, observational notes, and copies of student work.
5. *Research lessons are discussed.*
    A colloquium follows the lesson. Typically, such a gathering begins with presentations by the teachers who taught and co-planned the lesson, followed by free or structured discussions, sometimes an outside educator or researcher also comments on the lesson.

This process is also widespread in China, but how could it work here in the United States? I can list numerous reasons some would agree that it has little or no chance for success in the United States. In his *Los Angeles Times* article on teaching techniques, Richard Cooper (1999) interviews a number of educators for perspectives on differences in the cultures of American and Japanese teachers that have bearings on teaching and learning. I use some of Cooper's sources, as wells as others, to list some reasons why one might argue that lesson study could fail in the United States.

Top Ten Reasons Why Lesson Study Could Fail in the United States

1. Stigler and Hiebert: Systems of teaching are much more than the things a teacher does. They include the physical setting of the classroom; the goals of the teacher; the materials, including textbooks and district or state objectives; the roles played by the students; the way the school day is scheduled; and other factors that influence how teachers teach. Changing any one of these individual features is unlikely to have the intended effect (1999, p. 99).
2–3. Stevenson and Stigler (1992, p. 157):

    – One of the biggest challenges schools will face is that there are few leaders among its teachers for launching this process. Very few teachers have experienced this kind of professional development.

– Americans often act as if good teachers are born, not made. We hear comments implying this from both teachers and parents. They seem to believe that good teaching happens if the teacher has a knack with children and keeps them reasonably attentive and enthusiastic about learning (1992, p. 157).

4. Eugene C. Schaffer of the University of North Carolina: In the culture of American education, you don't come into my classroom and I don't come into yours. That's a long tradition in this country. It's another element of American individualism (Cooper).

5. Cooper: Even when teachers work together in teams, as many do in middle schools and time is budgeted for collaborative planning, the focus is often not on improving specific lessons. One recent survey found that middle school teaching teams often spent most of their meeting time discussing discipline and logistics for things like field trips instead of instruction.

6. Bill Jackson (2010): Whereas in the U.S., student behavior is often seen apart from academics, Japanese teachers see it as part of academics and through their many lesson study experiences, teachers often discuss student behaviors and how to best deal with them . . . The result is that there is a very light feeling to the school and even teachers seem to be genuinely happy in their interactions with students, each other, and administrators. The principal of the school . . . does not have a top down management style but very much sees teacher professional development as a long-term process in which he is intimately involved. [This is a new quote]

7. Catherine Lewis, Mills College: Japanese teachers spend little time . . . in developing or aligning curriculum, or translating national standards into practice. They have a frugal course of study and a number of nationally approved textbooks from which to choose . . . elementary textbooks are written by elementary teachers, based on their actual lessons. Because Japanese teachers start with texts that are teacher-written and lesson-based, they can afford to spend considerable time . . . planning, observing, and discussing actual classroom lessons (2000, p. 16).

8. Marjorie Coyman, Christian Science Monitor: U.S. teachers have developed a thick skin against frequent reforms that encourage wild swings or suggest a lost golden age of learning. They're not helped in their day-to-day efforts by a culture which prizes reading far above math in early grades, and where kids can define "nerd" well before they learn to multiply (2000).

9. Patricia Wang, Research for Better Schools: The limitation in the United States is the lack of support for teachers to grapple together with the teaching of mathematics so it makes sense to the students (Hoff, 2000).
10. Readers—Feel free add your own reason.

Yet, I learned that in 1998, and similarly in 1999, while School 2's eighth grade students' scores increased by 20 percent, their pass rate increased to 77 percent. This is only one year after using a problem-solving approach to engage students. "While we are proud of the results, we warn readers not to assume that Japanese methods were the reasons for the increase. There are too many variables to consider," cautions Lynn. Stigler and Hiebert (1999) write,

> For lesson study to be a viable means of improving teaching nation-wide, . . . two tests must be passed. First, lesson study must meet the needs of teachers . . . Second, lesson study . . . must meet the needs of the U.S. education system. Teachers are under great pressures to perform and the stakes are getting higher. (151)

With so many strong arguments against its success, how could lesson study be active at School 2?

Six Reasons Why Lesson Study Worked at School 2

1. The principal, Lynn Liptak and vice principal, Fran Dransfield both support the process—for Lynn, the combination of experiences provided by lesson study is better than any seminar the teachers attend outside the school. "They're really talking about teaching and learning," she says, "They're talking about what happens in the classroom. That is professional development right where it belongs—in the classroom driven by teachers." In addition to her administration role, Fran is herself one of the study group teachers.
2. The teachers' buy-in to the process has motivated them to change the way they teach in an effort to focus on conceptual understanding.
3. The teachers have teams collaborate to do the work—over the past three summers, teachers have earned stipends to develop the curriculum and write lesson plans to share, discuss and revise with the other teachers. In his role as math facilitator at the K-8 school, Bill runs math meetings period once a week per grade level. Also held

every week is a lesson study period where teachers from all grade levels gather to share their ideas of how they will write or revise lessons that encourage in-depth thinking.

4. The lesson study Research Group (LSRG) which was based at Teacers College, Columbia University, and directed by Drs. Clea Fernadez and Makoto Yoshida, helped the teachers understand the study group process and documents their work. The goal of the LSRG was to provide careful research about lesson study and how it can be adapted to the U.S. context.

5. The Japanese School of Greenwich provides guidance to School 2. Opportunities for both groups to observe each other conduct a lesson study group are part of this unique collaboration.

6. The Regional Eisenhower Consortium for Mathematics and Science Education, a non-profit organization, provides funds for professional development of the teachers as well the assistance of Dr. Patsy Wang-Iverson who is their senior associate for Research for Better Schools.

Specifically, how did teachers apply the lesson study process to make it work for them and their students? What do teachers *actually* do during these meetings? LSRG gave a handout that succinctly defined lesson study and listed four steps summarizing the process used at by the teachers (Figure 11.1). Below each of the four main activities listed, School 2 teachers describe how they applied it.

Figure 11.1 LSRG Handout: What is Lesson Study?

"Lesson study" is a Japanese approach to teacher professional development that involves a group of teachers working on four main activities:

1. Setting a goal they all want to achieve with their students.
In our goal to implement lessons that develop "profound understanding of fundamental mathematics" (Liping Ma, 1999), we have become aware that our students need to take more responsibility for their own learning. Therefore, we strive to provide instruction that emphasizes problem solving, logical thinking, and student autonomy. We also try to provide instruction that actively engages and motivates our students to learn.

2. Planning a lesson study (with a detailed lesson plan), which they will use to examine their chosen goal.
We meet once a week for two hours and plan in groups of four or five to do the work. We spend a lot of time thinking about the development of the lesson because we moved from lesson plans that were hastily written to cover four components: objectives, procedure, material and homework, to lessons requiring thoughts on: What sort of questions should we ask and how might students respond? How should we pace the development? What about individual differences? How should

we pace the development of the ideas? (We learned how to pace by observing our Japanese colleagues because they are constantly aware of time.) How can we tell if students are motivated or have learned the concept? What materials can best help students understand the main ideas? The material section required a good portion of time for making or finding appropriate materials to enhance the ideas of the lesson.

The process also encourages good discussions on the mathematics content and thus helps us to better understand the mathematics in the lesson. Some of us have more experience teaching than others, or a keener understanding of the underlying mathematics. We appreciate the help we receive from each other and the opportunity to share ideas that are later refined and improved upon by the group process.

Once our brainstorming is clarified, deciding who does what just falls into place: those good at typing take notes or create worksheets while others work on making manipulatives.

3. Teaching the lesson study in a real classroom while other group members observe.

At first, it felt strange having five-six other teachers in the classroom but we soon got used it. It's nice having colleagues in the class observing the process because they see things to improve learning that one teacher may not see. The teachers also provide immediate feedback on the progress of the lesson to help guide the lead's teacher next steps. However, we are sometimes guilty of doing too much and must remember to be careful not to interfere with the progress of the lesson. The students wondered about this process but they always rise to the occasion because they like attention and want to feel important.

4. Debriefing to reflect on the instruction witnessed and discuss what it taught them about the goal they set out to explore.

Before this process, we taught a lesson, reflected very little on the outcome of student learning, and than moved on to the next. Now we take the time to check that students are understanding the concept. Knowing that we have to start the discussion with our own reflection on the lesson causes us to be more alert to students' comments and reactions. It also a humbling experience because there is always something that we could have improved. What makes the process so worthwhile, however, is knowing that comments or criticism we receive bring us one step closer to improving our students' understanding of mathematics and our own understanding. Indeed, if it is perfect than we have learned little.

Having shared comments, we next revise the lesson, teach it again to a different group of students, debrief and eventually find ways to disseminate it to other teachers.

A Profile of Japanese-style Teaching at School 2

We are finally at the point of our journey where we visit the classroom. Figure 11.2 has the actual lesson plan created by study group members. My thoughts, as I watched the process, are in Italics throughout the episode. Now readers, as you read the classroom episode, pretend to be an observer whose comments will be solicited later for the *colloquium* portion. As such, you should know that there are guidelines to follow. Figure 11.3 is a conference handout of the guidelines for observation. Keep these in mind as you "observe" the lesson on students discovering the meaning of π.

Figure 11.2

Seventh Grade Mathematics Lesson Study Plan
Teacher: Cynthia Sanchez
Writers: Cynthia Sanchez, Fran Dransfield, Magnolia Montilla, Nick Timpone

1. **Name of the Unit: Circles**
2. **Instruction Plan**: 5 lessons
   - Parts of a Circle
   - Discovering Pi (this lesson)
   - Circumference of a Circle
   - Area of Circles (2 lessons)

   CCSSM Standard: Geometry 7.G. 4
   Mathematical Practices: MP1–MP6, MP8
3. **Instruction of this Lesson**

   Lesson title: "Discovering the meaning of Pi"

   Goal of the lesson: Following a lesson on the parts of a circle, the students will use the parts of the circle to discover the relationship between the circumference and diameter of a circle and the number Pi. Students will work with a variety of circles to establish a pattern that will show that the relationship between circumference and diameter of a circle, and the number Pi are constants for all circles.

   The relationship of the goal of the lesson to the goal of the subject: We would like to have the students gain a solid understanding of what the number Pi stands for and how it is derived. The lesson will require students to interact with one another to develop a method for measuring the circumference of a circle when all that they know is the diameter of the circle. Students will be responsible for using their prior knowledge and the input of their peers to solve problems with little support from the teacher. Class will have to work as a whole group at end of lesson to discover that the relationship between the circumference of a circle and Pi is a constant that works for all circles.

   Materials: Video of teacher riding on a Ferris Wheel, large oak-tag posters representing the Ferris Wheel for each group, individual worksheets with circles and chart for recording information, large chart for black board, large drawing of the Pi symbol, circle and diameter manipulative, basket at each table with string, markers, scissors, tape, and calculators.

Steps	Student Activities	Teacher's Support and things to Remember	Evaluation
Introduction: 5min.	Students will listen actively and recall information from previous lessons	Discuss previous lesson. Elicit responses from student's regarding the parts of a circle. Put terms on the board: circle, radius, diameter, circumference. Link review to today's lesson. Today we will be learning more about the circumference of the circle. Define circumference again and introduce the video.	*Were the students able to recall information from the previous lesson? Were students motivated by the video?*

| Pose the problem and hand out materials: 5 min. | Students will listen actively for instructions and will ask questions about the problem. Students may ask what one complete time around means. | You saw me (teacher) on a Ferris Wheel. I started at one spot and went around and around. Let the Ferris Wheel be a circle and the distance from the bottom of the Ferris Wheel to the top of the Ferris Wheel (100') be the diameter of the circle. Can you figure out how far I traveled when I went once around the circle when all that you know is that the diameter of the circle is 100'. Illustrate the problem with the student worksheet. Tell students to think about how they might solve the problem. Take suggestions and list them on the board. Hand out to each group a large poster board with a drawing of the Ferris Wheel problem. Each group should also have a basket of supplies. Remind students to answer the question: How many times does the diameter go into the circumference? How did you find out? | Are the student's asking questions about the problem? Do they understand what they are being asked to do? Are they offering suggestions for solving the problem? Are they anxious to begin working on the problem? |
| Problem solving: 10 min. | Students will work in their groups to find a number of different ways to solve the problem. Anticipated responses: Students may use string to measure the circumference of the circle. Students may | Teacher will move around the room looking for various and different solutions to be presented after problem solving is completed. | Are the students communicating with each other in their groups? Are they using more than one method to solve the problem? Are they using prior knowledge? |

Steps	Student Activities	Teacher's Support and things to Remember	Evaluation
	redraw the diameter in a few different places and add them to find the circumference. They may use string to measure the circumference and compare it to the diameter.		
Present solutions: 15 min.	One student from 3 or 4 groups will go to the front of the room to display, present, and explain their solution to the problem. Students not presenting will be listening and questioning.	Teacher will call on specific groups to present. Presentations should be varied and presented in order of least correct to most correct. Teacher will encourage students to ask questions of each other and to debate the solutions.	Are the students, who are presenting, speaking in a loud clear voice? Are their explanations clear and understood by the class? Are the students questioning and debating?
Summary: 3 min.	Students will listen actively to teacher's summary.	Summarize student's solutions using presentations on the board. Make connections between different solution methods.	Can the students see that c/d is very similar for all of the circles? Are they able to generalize that c/d is a constant for all circles?

Here's the setting: Lead teacher Cynthia Sanchez is at the front of the room and her team members are standing on the side. Twenty-five fifth graders are sitting in groups of four and, cramped in the back of the room, are 25 strangers like me, eagerly waiting to see action. <<*Yikes!!! Teachers and students, how can you teach or learn among all of this disruption? Good luck Cynthia—you'll need it!*>> Cynthia starts the lesson by asking students questions on the parts of a circle: "What did we learn on Friday? What did we learn about the circumference of a circle? What do you mean by diameter?" As students respond, she notes the responses on the board.

It's interesting to observe that, throughout the lesson, spurts of Spanish dialogues are interspersed between students' and Cynthia's interactions because not all of the students speak English fluently. For example, when she

Figure 11.3 Guidelines for Lesson Observation

Excerpted from the Moderator's Guide, TIMSS Videotape Study:
http://timss.enc.org/TTMSS/timss/teaching/125445/5445_O5.htm)

Following are some suggestions for observing the lesson. Please feel free to move around the room to observe more closely, but please do not interact with the students.

General Suggestions for Viewing the Lesson
– Stay focused on the lesson itself: What do you notice? What do you hear? What inferences do you find yourself making and why?
– Look for patterns that provides clues to how and what the student/teacher was thinking.
– What do you think is the teacher's goal? What does she/he seem to want students to learn? What do you think they are learning?
– What does the teacher do? Are there key moves or moments in the lesson? Are there crucial missed opportunities?
– Why do you see this lesson in this way? What does this tell you about what is important to you? Look for patterns in your thinking.
– What questions about teaching and learning did observing the lesson raise for you?
– Are there things you would like to try in your classroom as a result of viewing the lesson? How would you need to prepare yourself and your students to try these things?

Specific Focus
1. Mathematics instruction
The first, and perhaps most important, focus area may be the teaching methods used and the learning that students experience.

Questions About Mathematics Instruction
– What is the mathematics of the lesson?
– What seems to be the teacher's mathematical goal?
– How does the lesson flow?
– Are there logical connections between the parts of the lesson?
2. Communication between teacher and students
In analyzing the communication, you may find it helpful to look at the roles of the teacher and students with regard to the mathematics discussed in each lesson.
Again, the point is not to focus on what participants might judge as good or bad, but on what can be inferred about student learning from specific evidence in the lesson.

Questions About Communications between Teacher and Students.
– What does the teacher do to orchestrate discussion in the lesson? What are the questions posed to students? When and how are they posed?
– How do the questions elicit mathematical thinking among the students?
– What does the teacher do to use students' ideas in the discussion? Are most students involved? How are students' ideas used?
– What decisions does the teacher appear to make in regard to students' ideas or discussion? Here, you can probe for more detail by asking:
– Do there appear to be ideas that the teacher is pursuing? Are there times when the teacher decides to provide more information, clarify an issue, model a strategy, or let student's struggle? What do you think that says about the teacher's goal?
– What do the students do in the lesson discussion? What do their verbal and nonverbal communication suggest about their mathematical understanding?

asks, "what is meant by diameter?" Raphael responds in Spanish. Cynthia follow up with further questions to him in Spanish, and then proceeds to translate comments and responses to English for the rest of the class. *<<Goodness. This is constant. Yet the lesson flows and students just seem to accept this interaction as quite normal. >>*

Cynthia tells the students that they will learn a bit more about the circumference of circle in today's lesson. She shows a homemade video of her getting on a Ferris wheel. In the video she tells the students:

> Hi, kids. I have a problem I'd like you to help me solve. I am getting on this Ferris wheel and I will travel all round and back again. Can you help me determine two things: First—how far will I have traveled? Second, how many diameters of the wheel can go into the circumference of this wheel? The diameter of the Ferris wheel is 100 feet.

She waves to the students, gets on the wheel, gets off at the end and asks the students for their help again. Students look attentively at the video as they smile and one says "Hey, that's cool Ms. Sanchez!" *<<Neat. That has grabbed students' attention. This is not a textbook picture of the wheel, but teachers who have taken the time to make it real>>*

Cynthia restates the problem and has students brainstorm how they might resolve it while she lists some of their suggestions on the board. The teachers distribute a handout of a large circle with a diameter having a small picture of Cynthia in a box at the bottom of the wheel. Cynthia reminds students that they have a box of materials on their desk to help them with the work. At this point, teachers and guests are invited to move around to listen to students' group processes. Students open their boxes and look at the materials: strings, markers, scissors, tape and calculators. Some students raise their hands for further clarifications. Nick says to one group, "what are we asking you to do? You want to know how far Ms. Sanchez traveled. What do you have in your box that might help?"

Sitting close to where I am are students in group 1. I listen carefully and jot down their comments and then circulate to capture other groups' processes:

Group 1:

Santos: How we gonna do this?

Marie: I don't know. I'm stuck. Maybe we should wrap the string around the circle.

Joe: But what would that give you? I think the answer is 200 because, look: The diameter is 100 and it cuts the circle in two equal parts so that this side is 100 (Joe uses his hand to cover 1/2 of the area of the circle) and this side is 100.

Santos: OK. Let's say 200.

Group 2:

Bonita: Let's split the circle in to four parts with the diameter—like a pizza. Now since each radius is 50, the circumference has to be 50 added up four times . . . or 200.

Angelo: No. Let's split it into eight parts, like a real pizza, and then add them up and get . . . 400.

John: Yeah.

Group 3:

Roberto: Let's wrap the string around the circle.

James: But it doesn't have numbers. It's not a ruler. How is that gonna help?

Roberto: Right. I don't know.

Anna: Let's use the string to measure the diameter. We know that's 100.

Roberto: Yeah. Then we keep up with the 100 and see how many times that goes in the circle.

Group 4:

Kayla: Let's take the string and measure it around the circle.

John: No. Let's see how long the diameter is first, then do that.

Jenny: Mark it off with this red marker. OK. I'll count. Now, that's one, two, three and a little piece left over.

It's time now to call the students together to share results. Cynthia asks a member from Groups 2, 3 and 4 to report. From Group 2, Bonita explains how her group decided to use the diameter to cut the circle into equal parts to get 400 as an answer. "Are there any questions?" asks Cynthia. Raphael asks (in Spanish), "Why did you use only eight? What would happen if you cut it up into more parts? Then your answer keeps changing." Bonita replies, "My group decided to use eight." "How many of you agree with this method?" asks Cynthia. No hands go up. Cynthia calls on Roberto from Group 3 to report: "We figured out that since our string doesn't have numbers like a ruler, we measured the diameter to get 100 and cut the string. We measured around the circle and found that it went in three times so we got 300."

"We did almost the same thing!" says, Jefferson, excitedly, from Group 4. "Come up and explain," Cynthia says. He responds: "We measured the diameter from top to bottom and that was 100 feet. Then we used the string to go around the circle and the answer is 300. But we had a little piece left over that we think might be about 21 so we put 321." Cynthia asks the class: "Well what do you think?" Anna from group 3 says, "There is no piece left over so you get 300." "So you got 300," says Cynthia, "If the diameter is 100 and you divide 300 by 100, what would you get?" Anna says, "three." "Huumm" Cynthia continues, "But is it exactly three or three and just a little bit? Raise your hands if you think it's exactly three." While students ponder on what to think, Cynthia tapes a poster of a huge circle on the board and shows the student a long string of four color ribbons.

Cynthia:	Let's try to answer this question now. First, tell me what you notice about this string of ribbons.
Tania:	It has four colors.
Cynthia:	Ok. What I did was to measure the diameter and used a different color to represent its length each time. So, this yellow ribbon is as long as the diameter and so is this red, blue and green. Now we will see how many times I can wrap the string around the circumference of the circle. As I go around, I will tape it so that it stays in place, and then count the different colored ribbons. Amy, count for us, please.
Amy:	OK, that's one . . . two . . . three . . . and . . . there IS some left over!
Cynthia:	Yes. Can you all see that I had to use a little bit of the green ribbon to keep going? So . . . whenever you divide the circumference by the diameter, you get three diameters and a little bit left over. Remember that Ferris wheel from the video? would this be true for it too? Do you think this relationship is true for ALL circles? Let's try to find out.

<<What are members of Group 1 thinking? Do they now see where they were wrong? I don't think so. While the activity and demonstration were excellent for developing the concept, I can see from their dazed facial expressions that all of this important discussion is probably having little impact on their understanding. I wish they had been asked to report too. That might have caused them to reflect further or to pay closer attention or maybe to ask a clarification question>>

For the next activity, the teachers give each group of students a set of four circles with different diameters labeled and Cynthia says: "You are to compute C divided by D for each circle and note your results on the worksheet with the four columns named diameter, circumference, and C/D. As you can see, the diameters range from 2 to 25 inches." <<Group 1 is definitely in trouble >>

I look at group 1 students. Not much activity going on. They've got circles labeled with diameters of 2, 6, 12 and 15 inches. One student takes a ruler to measure the diameter of a circle that is already given as 12 inches. Another takes a string to measure the diameter of a circle already given as 2 inches. They measure, then look bewildered, and finally, stop work. The other two members look on. <<*They really lack basic understanding of the definitions and concepts but if I can get them to review what Cynthia did with the ribbons, maybe that might give them a clue about this activity. Let me give it a shot*>>. As the audience and teachers circulate to observe the groups, I approach Marie and whisper, "Marie, remember how Ms. Cynthia measured the distance around the circumference of that big circle on the board? What . . ." Before I could pursue my line of questioning, Patsy Wang-Iverson pulls me over and reminds me not to interfere with the group's process. <<*"Oh No!" the child in me wails, "I've been caught violating the cardinal rule! This is no joke, Readers, I really felt like a kid caught with hand in the cookie jar*>> "Patsy," I say in a whisper, trying to redeem myself, " I was just going to ask some probing questions on the first problem to get them moving. They don't understand the first problem so they are now stuck on the second." "No. Don't do that," she whispers, "They may be overwhelmed from all the activity today, but let them try to work it out together. Go over to Group 2 and look at how the students there are working." This is the group that had used a similar parts-of-a-pizza approach on the first activity. Members seem to now understand the process and are actively working and enjoying each other's help. Rather than each student working independently on one circle, they work jointly on one circle at a time: One student measures, another helps tape the string around the circumference, and the third records the solution and uses a calculator for the computation—really nice. I refrain from making any complimentary comments to Group 3 and sit quietly to observe Group 1 again. Patsy poses a few questions and tells the students to work together on the problem. I am hoping to see something happen to make that happen, but to no avail. They just give up. <<*I'll need thicker skin for this observer role next time. How can I see this happen and not try to make a difference? I should have called one of the teachers and made them more aware of the problem . . . but no . . . no . . . my role here is to just observe*>> The words, "Ok Class," said by Cynthia, takes me out of the reflective mode and back into the classroom. She continues, "Let's record your data and then pay particular attention to the C/D column. One person from each group will call out the measures." As students do so, Cynthia records them on the board. Because another group also has Group 1's diameters and reports the results, Group 1 does not have to do so. The dialogue below shows how worthwhile tasks together with skillful questioning techniques can guide students to important discoveries:

Cynthia:	Look at the C divided by D column. What do you notice about all the numbers in the column?"
Eve:	Every number has a decimal point and every numbers has three in it.
Cynthia:	Good. What does the three mean?
Joe:	There are 3 diameters in the circumference.
Cynthia:	What about the decimal part? What does that tell us?
Anthony:	It doesn't go in evenly. There is some left over.
Cynthia:	Great! We discovered that, in the Ferris Wheel circle, the circumference was about three times bigger than the diameter or, that about three diameters go into the circumference. Do you think that is true for all circles?
James:	That seems to be true.
Cynthia:	The Egyptians discovered this and used it a long time ago. It tells us that C DIVIDED BY D is always the same number. That little piece left over is approximately point 14 or 14 hundredth. What you have all discovered is an important relationship between the diameter of circle and its circumference. This number is actually close to 3.14. Does any one know what we call this number?
Roberto:	Pi.
Cynthia:	Yes, Pi. Now, who can tell me what we learned today?
Amanda:	We learned how to compute C over D.
Anna:	We learned how to measure without a ruler.
Cynthia:	Having gone through the chart of circles with different diameters, do you think you can calculate C DIVIDED BY D for a circle of diameter 25 inches? Here is a homework sheet to complete.

The bell rings, students leave, and guests proceed to the lunchroom for the colloquium portion. <<*Why did I have such hard time being a passive observer? Do I tend to help students too quickly and thereby cheat them of the important experience of having to struggle to solve some problems? I'll be mindful of that next time . . . No . . . better yet, I'll get a colleague to work with me!*>>

Colloquium

As we move chairs to form a large circle, I notice that some Japanese teachers and Mr. Tanaka, who is the principal of the Japanese School, are present. As is customary in a lesson study colloquium, the lead teacher reflects first and then the other team members offer their comments. Questions and comments from guests follow next, and then a final commentary of the lesson by a designated person, in this case, Mr. Tanaka.

Cynthia's reflection on the lesson:

> I think I was very nervous for the first part of the lesson. That is why I spoke very fast—too fast sometimes. But I was very happy to see that students finally got the idea of the circumference being three times the diameter and a little bit. I also thought it was very nice how students worked together to come to an answer as a team. I was pleased when a student said that he learned how to measure without a ruler. In the future, I do think that they will remember what 3.14 is and where it came from. The manipulatives were very useful.

Nick, Team Member:	Cynthia did a wonderful job! I know how hard it is to teach in front of so many people. I think she really used the manipulatives well and stressed the important concepts. This is the final teaching of this lesson for us. We first tried it using a carousel to pose the first activity but it didn't work well because students couldn't see the entire circumference. The Ferris Wheel is a good improvement. I find this process of collaboration so worthwhile and enriching to me professionally. I teach seventh grade and one of the things that I had to learn was how to talk so a fifth grader could understand. I also learned how important it was to give groups of students one big worksheet or material rather than smaller individual ones. This forces students to work together because they have to help each other.
Fran, Team Member and Vice Principal:	I taught this lesson the very first time and find Cynthia's version different in so many positive ways. It was good to make our own videos serve as motivating factors for the students. It really worked well. This collaboration is a phenomenal experience! We all teach the students and they see us working hard to improve our lessons for them. This suggests to them that they too have to work hard. I strongly recommend that you try this approach in your school and if so, to practice it across grade levels.
Magnolia, Team Member:	What this process does for us is to take us out of our egocentric world to take a close look at what students are learning. As team observers, we also look closely at the teaching to give advice while it is in progress. We gave

advice to Cynthia on which students to call and in what order, so that a variety of approaches could be seen or discussed.

Nick: As writers, we would now like to invite your comments or questions on the lesson. We welcome comments on any aspects of the lesson: the use of the manipulatives; wording, theme, sequencing, or any questions you might have that may help us improve on it.

Yvelyne: I have seen the use of circles with different diameters to help students discover Pi, but this lesson's use of the ribbons was an excellent visual. I was also impressed with Cynthia's persistence in asking students questions to elicit the main ideas of the lesson. She did a really nice job.

Observer: The Ferris Wheel video was a great idea. I also liked the model using the cardboard circles and the ribbon.

Yvelyne: I do have a question about timing. I see that each segment of the lesson has a time limit. Is this the reason why every group did not get an invitation to report on the results of the first activity?

Nick: Yes. The first time we did the lesson, we called on every group and found that it took too much time. This time we looked at each group's work and chose one group that had a really wrong answer—Group 2, one not so wrong—Group 3—and the last one right—Group 4.

Yvelyne: But, as a result, students in one of the group's not reporting were not challenged to think through their work and later had no idea on how to complete the next problem.

Cynthia: We don't expect every student to get every lesson, every time. As I teach, I try to get a feel for how the lesson is going to decide on whether I should move on the next day.

Nick: I know which group you are talking about, Yvelyne. You are talking about Marie's group. We anticipated their approach, which was the same as Group 3's. We hoped that reviewing Group 3's work with 8 diameters would help Group 1 see why working with one diameter was also wrong. But don't worry. Students will get to see the concepts presented again in other lesson so that they will get opportunities to think about them again.

Observer: Does a timed sequence determine whether or not you follow-up on those teachable moments? For example, when Raphael asks students in Group 3 why they didn't

	use more diameters in their argument, there was no further discussion on it.
Nick:	Yes. I know what you mean. We could have pursued it and talked about what an increasing number of diameters would look like on the resulting inscribed polygon and then maybe get to the point of showing a circle as a polygon with an infinite number of sides. But that would have taken us off the major goal and we might not have had the time to finish the lesson.
Magnolia:	We have to be careful sometimes because so many different lines of interesting questions can come up but we have to focus on our major objective —getting students to learn the concepts in the lesson at hand.
Yvelyne:	I was aware of how little you had to "manage" the students. They knew the procedures, what was expected, and pretty much stayed focused on the task. You merely managed who did what next. This was nice flow of work that revealed lots of good preplanning and thought. You also always had a question ready for students to consider supporting or refuting. But tell me about Raphael and the Spanish dialogues you have with him and other Spanish-speaking students in the class.
Cynthia:	With so many Spanish-speaking kids here, one of my major goal is to make sure that they are not afraid to ask questions. I just automatically flow from one language to the other in a casual way so that it doesn't call attention to itself. Thus we have rich dialogues in both languages.
Observer:	At the end of the first activity, Cynthia quickly told students that C divided by D would always give three plus a bit rather than get students to think it through. I don't think some students had time to process this most important result.
Cynthia:	Yes. You are right. I was so nervous that I did rush through some things. I think that the next time we do this lesson, we will consider spending more time to give students a firm understanding of the first activity's concepts. Maybe the first activity should be the entire lesson?
Observer:	Or you might consider reducing the number of circles in the second activity from 12 to 6, thus allowing more time for the first part.

Fran:	But with fewer entries in the chart, students' measurement mistakes will likely make it difficult to see the pattern.
Observer:	In the lesson, you asked students the key question: Will C DIVIDED BY D be the same constant for all circles? I wonder how we could structure this lesson so that this question comes from students. Thus they do the investigations to answer their own question rather than the teacher's. Maybe if they do the chart first and see the pattern, this might motivate that question. But then we'd have to think of a motivating reason to do the chart too.
Observer:	How many lessons have you written after three years of work?
Magnolia:	We have completed curricula for grades seven and eight. By next year we hope to finish a new sixth grade curriculum.
Nick:	Colleagues, we will certainly give your comments and ideas a lot more thought. At this point, I would like to thank everyone for sharing observations and ideas with us. We have made note of them for further reflection later. It is now time to have a summary of the lesson from Mr. Koichi Tanaka, Principal of the Japanese School in Connecticut. Dr. Makoto Yoshida will translate Koichi's comment.
Koichi:	The video was very good and served its purpose in motivating students. Giving students the big circular board for the first activity was good but caused difficulty for some students to easily put strings around the circumference. I think 3-D objects would have been better because they would have been easier for students to handle. You may want to consider the approach of first giving the students the 3.14 as the answer to the problem and then require that students determine how to get it. I understand that the teacher was nervous, but still, the lesson was much too rushed and the speed was too fast. There also needs to be a better summary after the first activity. I don't think students got the major point of that activity. The summary at the end of the lesson, however, was very good and likely to help students gain a deeper understanding of succeeding lesson. I noticed that classroom management was excellent and that students were attentive and interested. This was a good lesson

Discussion Between Colleagues

Lynn, could you outline the general agendas for teacher meetings and how you allocate time to have them happen?

We have regular grade level meetings to discuss business or other routine concerns. Sometimes curriculum issues also emerge but most of those issues are addressed during study group meetings or math meetings. Study group meetings are facilitated by anyone of the 16 teacher-volunteers. The meetings are scheduled for two hours per week and may center about any issues or lessons teachers want to discuss. Sometimes we may have a guest speaker from the community, or discuss a book or articles that all the teachers read. The grade level math meetings, which Bill facilitates, are one day per week and last 80 minutes for grades K-4 and 40 minutes for grades 5–8. The focus is on helping all the teachers to develop and implement effective lessons. When a teacher needs help getting an idea through to the kids, the teachers asks Bill to co-teach or to observe the lesson and provide feedback.

Now, how do I make this happen? Not with substitutes because we all want to maintain the continuity and foci of our work with the students. Our school has additional teachers from special programs like English as a Second Language, Special Education, Clinton's program to downsize classes, and teacher assistants for the lower grades. We also get students teachers from William Patterson University to work closely with our students. I partner each of my regular teachers with one of these special program teachers. Partner teachers work closely together so that the students perceive both as regular teachers. Thus, on meeting days, regular teachers leave their students with the special program's teacher who continues with the lesson. There are times when I may have to call on a guidance counselor or the vice principal to help but this system generally works fine.

Do you envision the entire school using a study group process if it continues to help students?

This would be a marvelous goal to attain. However, we know that there are many cultural barriers to overcome such as teachers' tendency to work in isolation, or high-stakes testing's tendency to motivate teachers to cover, rather than uncover, important concepts.

Do the teachers meet regularly with the other collaborators?

No, but we do see Patsy about once a week. She just pops into a class to observe a lesson or a lesson study. She then follows with immediate feedback through emails.

Who provides funding for the teachers to participate in professional development?

Patsy, through the Research for Better Schools funds the summer. LSRG helps with substitutes. We also tap our district's funds. We truly appreciate the funding opportunities because they served as catalysts for our process and still enhance what we do. However, it is the teachers' energy and motivation to improving teaching and learning that drive our process. We don't depend on the funding as much because of our modified schedules for working during regular school hours.

Please summarize the data on School 2's state pass rate and comment on the effects of high-stakes testing on your programs.

In the course of the past four years, we used at least three different tests; students have changed, teachers have changed and teaching methods have changed. Thus, I must state that there are too many variables at play here to make any statement about causality. Using the same type of test, our pass rate was 57 percent in 97, and 77 percent in 98. Using a harder test, it fell (as was true for other districts and the state) to 46 percent in 1999 and 40 percent in 2000. We are still below the state pass rate but we are scoring at or above the district's rate.

I must stress that we are not letting the pressure to raise test scores adversely affect what is best for our students. Our major goal is not to improve test scores but to improve the learning of our students. We hope and trust that ultimately what we are doing will positively effect scores, however we know and accept the fact that this is not necessarily an immediate outcome. We believe that real lasting change requires time for teachers to reflect deeply on how students learn, as well as on the curriculum and how it is to be taught. Ours is thus a long-term process of improvement and definitely not a quick fix.

Teachers: Are more students doing homework?

Nick: Yes, but a major reason for this is that we don't assign as much homework as we used to—just a few for practice on major ideas. Students are thus enticed to give it a try.

Has the study group process impacted your math content knowledge?

Nick: Definitely. None of us has a certification in mathematics even though some of us have enough content knowledge to do so. Those of us who would qualify, forgo that process because automatic placement in high schools where math teachers are in dire need, is almost a given. We thus have a good mix of colleagues willing and eager to help others whose content knowledge maybe weaker.

Where does the work grow from here?

Bill: Well we will continue to improve our seventh and eight grade lessons through lesson study, and we will try to maintain our partnerships. Extending Japanese lessons to the lower grades may not be as daunting because Singapore uses the lesson study process and their texts for grades one to eight are in English. We have begun to use these texts in the lower grades and are having positive experiences.

Any further comments?

Lynn: Professional development is a must for improving education of our students. Yet we seem to change everything except for the core. Lesson study focuses on that core.

Patsy: In a 1998 focus group of students, which I conducted, a student said, "Before the book did the thinking. Now we do the thinking."

Frank: Yvelyne, you should know that you are not the only American observer that had a difficult time just observing the lesson. I noticed the same thing among most of the other American observers during the conference. They wanted to serve as tutors, while the Japanese teachers made notes about the lesson. I think that is the key difference in the training for the lesson study. Even though they were given guidelines, the American teachers did not know what to do as a lesson observer, as they seldom do such, while the Japanese teachers were in fact trained to be observers.

Yvelyne: My jaw dropped when I heard your comments, Frank. Trained to be observers? Who would think to do that? Is it part of our cultural script that we think we KNOW we can do that easily? I don't think that I would have thought training was necessary had I not experienced the pangs of passive observation. I can see how right you are. Thanks—I now better understand my reaction.

Commentary

Given that Public School 2 teachers said the Japanese method of teaching was new to them, I think the method has possibilities for reforming teaching in the United States. Stigler and Hiebert (1999) write, "In our view, lesson study is not the kind of process in which teachers must first develop a list of capabilities and then begin to design improved lessons. Lesson study is, in fact, the ideal context in which teachers develop deeper and broader capabilities" (152).

As I reflect on Cynthia's lesson, I ask the question: How different is her lesson from the lesson overviews profiled in this book? A look at both plans shows definite differences in the depth of detail provided. Different elements in the lesson study plan include minutes allocated to each section, students' anticipated responses, and an evaluation column. The insertion of evaluative, focused questions valuing both process and affective results in the assessment of students' learning, while providing acute reminders to keep a focus on students' learning, also serve to guide the teachers' later reflections and comments about the lesson. For example: "Are students using their prior knowledge to solve problems? Are they anxious to begin working on the problem?" Unlike the plans in this book, which I now see as static, the lesson study plan has a dynamic quality which is projected by its details for monitoring teacher and student interactions throughout the development of the lesson. The examples of students' anticipated responses are prime examples of how this plan "moves" towards keeping students at the center of the lesson. What strikes me too, is the effective use of columns to organize the major pieces so that a glance quickly shows what teacher and students are doing at any given segment, as well as whether students are behaving in a way that hints at an understanding of that segment. Thus, the lesson study plan also *visually* seamlessly integrates teaching, student learning and assessment, while it prepares to provide answers to elements that may hinder or enhance learning. Wow! What caring teacher's teaching would not show some noticeable improvement from carrying out such a plan? What caring teacher's teaching would not show *remarkable* improvement from participation in the development *and* implementation of such a plan?

As I focus on the classroom environment, however, I surmise that there is little or no difference in the *learner desired outcome* or *the actual classroom teaching* of the Japanese method when compared to those guided by the NCTM Process Standards/Mathematical Practices. Indeed, in his examination of five classroom situations in Japanese elementary schools, Sawada (1997) concluded that the situations demonstrated that Japanese teachers' knew of and followed guidelines from NCTM *Standards* documents. What School 2 teachers show is that with appropriate support and collaboration, American teachers can move closer to applying the CCSSM practices and can make a positive difference in students' learning and attitude towards mathematics. The *Principles and Standards* (2000) make explicit reference to the value of such collaboration:

> Reflection and analysis are often individual activities, but they can be greatly enhanced by teaming with an experienced and respected colleague, a new teacher, or a community of teachers. Collaborating

with colleagues regularly to observe, analyze, and discuss teaching and students' thinking or to do "lesson study" is a powerful, yet neglected form of professional development in American schools (Stigler and Hiebert, 1999). The work and time of teachers must be structured to allow and support professional development that will benefit them and their students. (19)

In answer to her question, "Does Lesson Study have a future in the U.S.?" Catherine Lewis (2000) writes,

My question of whether lesson study has a role to play in the U.S. is an emphatic "yes," though I think we will need to find the most effective ways to adapt it to our cultural settings. The graveyards of educational reforms are littered with once-promising innovations that were poorly understood, superficially implemented, and consequently pronounced ineffective. If lesson study is to be any different, it will require a deep understanding of what it is and why it has been useful to Japanese teachers, and how it can be adapted to our very different settings. (19)

Update on Lesson Study at P.S.2

Lesson study is discontinued at P.S.2 because its top six reasons for success are no longer present. Few of the teachers are still teaching there and its lead supporters have either retired or moved to different positions not associated with the school. However, the effort of P.S.2's lesson study group served as a catalyst for other U.S. lesson study implementations: Since my participation at the open house, I have co-directed Louisiana professional development state grants for implementing lesson study with grades K-12 teachers; as of 2004, at least 32 states, 150 lesson study clusters/ groups, 335 schools, 125 school districts, listserv with 900+ members, and 2,300 teachers are involved in lesson study.

For more information on lesson study and opportunities to attend open houses, visit:

- ◆ Global Education Resources founded by Makoto Yoshida (www.globaledresources.com/team.html)
- ◆ The Chicago Lesson Study Group under the guidance of Akihiko Takahashi (www.lessonstudygroup.net/06about_us.html).
- ◆ The Lesson Study Group at Mills College directed by Catherine Lewis (www.lessonresearch.net/).

References

Ball, D. (1998). *The Subject Matter Preparation of Prospective Teachers: Challenging the Myth*. National Council for Research in Teacher Education, East Lansing, MI.

———. (1997). Developing Mathematics Reform: What Don't We Know about Teacher Learning–but Would Make Good Working Hypotheses. In *Reflecting on Our Work: NSF Teacher Enhancement in K–6 Mathematics*, edited by Susan N. Friel and George W. Bright. Lanham, MD.: University Press of America.

Board on Science Education. (2012). A Framework for K–12 Science Education: Practices, Crosscutting Concepts, and Core Ideas.

Borko, H., Eisenhart, M., Brown, C. A., Underhill, R. G., Jones, D., and Agard, P. C. (1992). Learning to teach hard mathematics: Do novice teachers and their instructors give up too easily? *Journal for Research in Mathematics Education*, 23(3): 194–222.

Burrill, G. (1998). Conversations with Author. NCTM Annual Conference, April, Washington, DC.

———. (1997). Choices and Challenges. *Teaching Children Mathematics*, 4(1): 58–63.

———. (1996). President's Message Column. National Council of Teachers of Mathematics News Bulletin (July/August): 3.

Caine, R. N., and Caine, G. (1997). *Education: On the Edge of Possibility*. Alexandria, VA: Association for Supervision and Curriculum Development.

Chapin, S. (1997). Introduction. In *The Partners in Change Handbook: A Professional Development Curriculum in Mathematics*. Boston, MA: Boston University Press.

Chval, K. B., and Khisty, L. L. (2009). Latino students, writing, and mathematics: A case study of successful teaching and learning. In *Multilingualism in Mathematics Classrooms: Global Perspectives*, edited by R. Barwell, Multilingual Matters: Bristol, p. 128.

Cobb, P., Wood, T., and Yackel, E. (1990). *Classrooms as Learning Environments for Teachers and Researchers. Constructivist Views on the Teaching and Learning of Mathematics*, edited by R. B. Davis, C. A. Maher, and N. Noddings. Reston, VA: National Council of Teachers of Mathematics: 125–46.

Confrey, J. (1990). What Constructivism Implies for Teaching. *Constructivist Views on the Teaching and Learning of Mathematics*, edited by R. B. Davis,

C. A. Maher, and N. Noddings. Reston, VA: National Council of Teachers of Mathematics: 107–22.

Cordel, B., and Mason, R. (2000). *Proportional Reasoning*. (Algebraic thinking series). Fresno, CA: Aims Education Foundation.

Cooper, R. (1999). A Call to Focus on Techniques of Teaching. *Los Angeles Times*, September 22. Retrieved October 20, 2013 from http://articles.latimes.com/1999/sep/22/local/me-12956

Coyman (2000). U.S. School, Japanese Methods. *Christian Science Monitor*, May 23, 2000.

Crowley, A. (2013). Teaching the Common Standards in Math: Getting Rid of the GPS. *Education Week*, March 13, 2013. Retrieved October 20, 2013 from www.edweek.org/tm/articles/2013/03/13/ccio_crowley_math.html

Cuevas, G. (1991). Developing Communication Skills in Mathematics for Students with Limited English Proficiency. *The Mathematics Teacher*, 84(3): 186–90.

Dewey, J. (1929). *The Quest for Certainty*. New York: Minton, Balch and Company.

Fair, J. (1997). *Algebra 1*. Prentice Hall.

Fensham, P., Gunstone, R. and White, R. (1994). *The Content of Science: A Constructivist Approach to its Teaching and Learning*. Washington DC: Falmer Press.

Fullan, M. (2013). The Power of Professional Capital. *Journal of Staff Development*, 34(3): 37.

Garet, M. S., Porter, A. C., Desimone, L., Birman, B. F., and Yoon, K. S. (2001). What makes professional development effective? Results from a national sample of teachers. *American Educational Research Journal*, 38: 915–45.

Gojak, L. (2013). Common Core State Standards for Mathematics: An Uncommon Opportunity. Summing Up, April 4, 2013 (2012–2014) National Council of Teachers of Mathematics. Retrieved October 20, 2013 from www.nctm.org/about/content.aspx?id=35990

Goleman, D. (1995). *Emotional Intelligence*. New York, NY: Bantam Books.

Hall, T., Strangman, N., and Meyer, A. (2011). Differentiated Instruction and Implications for UDL Implementation. Retrieved October 14, 2013 from http://aim.cast.org/learn/historyarchive/backgroundpapers/differentiated_instruction_udl#.UkCpf

Hiebert, J., Carpenter, T. P., Fennema, E., Fuson, K., Human, P., Murray, H., Olivier, A. and Wearne, D. (1996). Problem Solving as a Basis for Reform in Curriculum and Instruction: The Case of Mathematics. *Educational Researcher*, 25(4), 12–21.

Hiebert, J., Gallimore, R., Garnier, H., Givvin, K. B., Hollingsworth, H., Jacobs, J., Chui, A. M. Y., Wearne, D., Smith, M., Kersting, N., Manaster,

A., Tseng, E., Etterbeek, W., Manaster, C., Gonzales, P., and Stigler, J. (2003). Teaching Mathematics in Seven Countries: Results from the TIMSS 1999 video study. (NCES 2003–2013). Washington, DC: U.S. Department of Education, National Center for Education Statistics. Retrieved March 4, 2012 from http://nces.ed.gov/pubsearch/pubsinfor.asp?pubid=200313.

Hoff, D. (2000). A Teaching Style That Adds Up. *Education Week*, 19(24): 32–7.

Jackson, W. (2012). A More Global Perspective On Teacher Development. Retrieved December 2013 from www.thedailyriff.com/2010/06/would-us-teachers-be-open-to-a-japanese-critique-professional-development.php

Kaput, J. J. (1993). Technology and Mathematics Education. *Handbook of Research on Mathematics Teaching and Learning*, edited by D. A. Grouws. New York: Macmillan Publishing Company: 515–55.

Khisty, L. L. (1997). Making Mathematics Accessible to Latino Students. NCTM 1997 Yearbook, *Multicultural and Gender Equity in the Mathematics Classroom: The Gift of Diversity*, Reston, VA: National Council of Teachers of Mathematics: 92–101.

Lampert, M., and Ball, D. (1998). *Teaching, Multimedia, and Mathematics: Investigations of Real Practice*. New York: Teachers College Press.

Langrall, C., and Swafford, J. (2000). Three balloons for two dollars: Developing proportional reasoning. *Mathematics Teaching in the Middle School*, 6, 254–61.

Lappan, G. (1998). President's Message Column. National Council of Teachers of Mathematics News Bulletin (May/June): 3.

Lewis, C. (2000). Lesson Study: The Core of Japanese Development. Paper presented at to the Special group on Research in Mathematics Education, American Educational Research Association Meetings, New Orleans, April 2000, session 47.09.

Linton Professional Development Corporation. (2000). Teaching Mathematics to Increase Student Achievement. *The Video Journal of Education*, 9(5).

Lobato, J., Hohensee, C., and Rhodehamel, B. (2013). Students' Mathematical Noticing. *Journal for Research in Mathematics Education*, 44(5): 809–50.

Ma, L. (1999). *Knowing and Teaching Elementary Mathematics: Teachers' Understanding of Fundamental Mathematics in China and the U.S.* New Jersey: Lawrence Erlbaum.

May, T. (2012). Why the Word 'Career' Has Become Obsolete. *Computer world USA*. Retrieved October 2, 2013 from www.computerworld.com/s/article/9234728/Thornton_A._May_Why_the_word_career_has_become_obsolete.

Molina, C. (2012). *The Problem with Math Is English: A Language-Focused Approach to Helping All Students Develop a Deeper Understanding of Mathematics.* Cailfornia: Bassey Bass.

Moskowitz, C. (2013). Voyager 1 Leaves the Solar System—for Real This Time *Scientific American*, Thursday, September 12, 2013. Retrieved October 20, 2013 from www.scientificamerican.com/article.cfm?id=voyager–1-leaves-solar-system&WT.mc_id=SA_WR_20130920

National Council of Teachers of Mathematics. (2014). *Principles to Actions: An Urgent Agenda for School Mathematics.* Reston, VA: National Council of Teachers of Mathematics.

——. (2000). *The Principles and Standards for School Mathematics.* Reston, VA: National Council of Teachers of Mathematics.

——. (1995). *Assessment Standard for School Mathematics.* Reston, VA: National Council of Teachers of Mathematics.

——. (1991). *Professional Standards for Teaching Mathematics.* Reston, VA: National Council of Teachers of Mathematics.

——. (1989). *Curriculum and Evaluation Standards for Learning Mathematics.* Reston, VA: National Council of Teachers of Mathematics.

National Governors Association Center for Best Practices & Council of Chief State School Officers. (2010). Common core state standards for mathematics. Washington, DC: NGA Center for Best Practices and CCSSO. Retrieved October 20, 2013 from www.corestandards.org

National Research Council. (2001). *Adding It Up: Helping Children Learn Mathematics.* J Kilpatrick, J. Swafford, and B. Findell (Eds.). Mathematics Learning Study Committee, Center for Education, Division of Behavioral and Social Sciences and Education. Washington, DC: National Academy Press.

New York State Department of Education. (2013). *Keeping Quality Teachers: The Art of Retaining General and Special Education Teachers-Making the Case for Teacher Retention.* Retrieved October 20 from www.p12.nysed.gov/specialed/publications/persprep/qualityteachers/retention.htm

Phillip, R., and P. Schappelle. (1999). Algebra as Generalized Arithmetic: Starting with the Known for a Change. *Mathematics Teacher*, 92(4): 310–15.

Piaget, J. (1973). *To Understand is to Invent.* New York: Grossman.

Post, T., Behr, M., and Lesh, R. (1986). Research-based Observations About Children's Learning of Rational Number Concepts. *Focus on Learning Problems in Mathematics*, 8(1).

Reardon, S. (2013). No Rich Child Left Behind. *New York Times*. Retrieved October 20 from http://opinionator.blogs.nytimes.com/2013/04/27/no-rich-child-left-behind/

Reeves, C. (2000). The Chicken Problem. *Mathematics Teaching in the Middle Schools*, 5(6): 398–402.

Robelen, E. (2012). Achievement Gap in Math And Science Still Plagues United States. Retrieved October 20, 2013 from www.howtolearn.com/2012/12/achievement-gap-in-math-and-science-still-plagues-united-states/

Sawada, D. (1997). NCTM's Standards in Japanese Elementary Schools. *Teaching Children Mathematics*, 4(1): 20–23.

Shapiro, L. A. (1992). *We're Number One*. Vintage Books, N.Y.

Schappelle, B., and R. Phillip. (1999). Algebra as Generalized Arithmetic: Starting from the Known for a Change. *The Mathematics Teacher*, 92(4): 310–16.

Shriner, J., Ysseldyke, T., and Honetschalger, M. (1994). "All" means "All" – Including Students with Disabilities. *Educational Leadership*, March 1994: 38–42.

Silva, E., and White, T. (2013). Using Psychological Strategies to Help College Students Master Developmental math. Carnegie Foundation for the Advancement of Teaching. Retrieved October 20, 2013 from www.carnegiefoundation.org/sites/default/files/pathways_to_improvement.pdf

Simon, M. A. (1995). Reconstructing Mathematics Pedagogy from a Constructivist Perspective. *Journal for Research in Mathematics Education*, 26(2): 114–45.

Slavin, R. E. (1990). *Cooperative Learning: Theory, Research, and Practice*. Englewood Cliffs, NJ: Prentice Hall.

Smith, M. S., and Stein, M. K. (2011). *5 Practices for Orchestrating Productive Mathematics Discussions*. Reston, VA: National Council of Teachers of Mathematics.

Stevenson, H., and Stigler, J. (1992). *The Learning Gap: What our Schools are Failing and What We Can Learn from Japanese and Chinese Education*. Paperback reprint edition, Touchstone Books.

Stiff, L.V. (2000a). President's Message Column. National Council of Teachers of Mathematics News Bulletin. May/June 2000, 36: 10.

——. (2000b). President's Message Column. National Council of Teachers of Mathematics News Bulletin. November 2000, 37: 4.

——. (1993). *Reaching All Students*: A Vision of Learning Mathematics. Cuevas, G. and Driscoll, M. (Ed), Reaching All Students With Mathematics, Reston, VA: National Council of Teachers of Mathematics: 3–6.

Stigler, J., and Hiebert, J. (1999). Understanding and Improving Mathematics Instruction: An Overview of the TIMSS Video Study. *Phi Delta Kappan*, 79(1): 14–21.

——. (1999). *The Teaching Gap*. New York: Free Press.

Stipek, D., Salmon, M. J., Givvin, B. K., Kazemi, E. Saxe, G. and MacGyvers, L. V. (1998). The Value (and Convergence) of Practices Suggested by Motivation Research and Promoted by Mathematics Education References. *The Journal for Research in Mathematics Education*, 29(4): 465–88.

Van de Walle, J. A., Karp, K. S., and Bay-Williams, J. M. (2013). *Elementary and Middle School Mathematics: Teaching Developmentally (8th edn)*. New York, NY: Pearson Education.

Vygotsky, L. S. (1978). *Mind in Society: The Development of Higher Psychological Processes*. Cambridge, MA: Harvard University Press.

Wheatley, G. H. (1991). Constructivist Perspectives on Science and Mathematics Learning. *Science Education*, 75(1): 9–21.

Yetkin, E., and Capraro, M. M. (2009). Research Summary: Teaching fractions in middle grades mathematics. Retrieved April 30, 2012, from www.nmsa.org/Research/ResearchSummaries/TeachingFractions/tabid/1866/Default.as

Yoshida, M. (1999a). Lesson Study: An Ethnographic Investigation of School-based Teacher Development in Japan. Doctoral dissertation, University of Chicago.

Yoshida, M. (1999b). Lesson Study in Elementary School Mathematics in Japan: A Case Study. Paper presented at the American Educational Research Association Annual Meeting, Montreal, Canada.

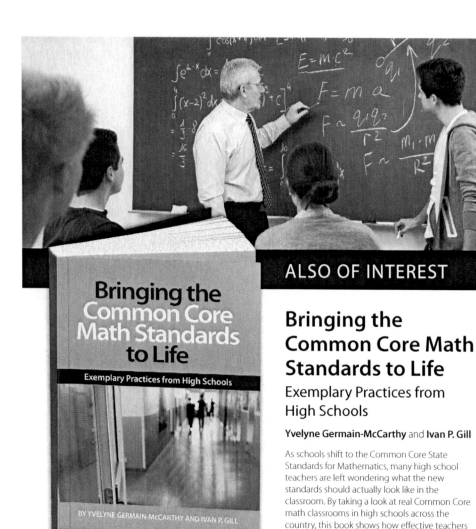

ALSO OF INTEREST

Bringing the Common Core Math Standards to Life

Exemplary Practices from High Schools

Yvelyne Germain-McCarthy and **Ivan P. Gill**

As schools shift to the Common Core State Standards for Mathematics, many high school teachers are left wondering what the new standards should actually look like in the classroom. By taking a look at real Common Core math classrooms in high schools across the country, this book shows how effective teachers are meeting the new requirements and covering topics such as proportional reasoning, problem solving, and geometry.

Pb: 978-0-415-73342-7 • 208 pages

SPECIAL FEATURES:

- Real examples of how teachers are meeting the CCSS in engaging ways
- Commentary sections to show how you can implement the exemplary sample lessons in your own classroom
- Practical, ready-to-use tools, including unit plans and classroom handouts